Sounding Like a No-No

Sounding Like a No-No

Queer Sounds and Eccentric Acts in the Post-Soul Era

Francesca T. Royster

The University of Michigan Press

Ann Arbor

Published in the United States of America by
The University of Michigan Press
Manufactured in the United States of America
♾ Printed on acid-free paper

2016   2015   2014   2013   4   3   2   1

A CIP catalog record for this book is available from the British Library.

Library of Congress Cataloging-in-Publication Data

Royster, Francesca T.
    Sounding like a no-no : queer sounds and eccentric acts in the
post-soul era / Francesca T. Royster.
       p.   cm.
    Includes bibliographical references and index.
    ISBN 978-0-472-07179-1 (cloth : alk. paper)—
    ISBN 978-0-472-05179-3 (pbk. : alk. paper)—
    ISBN 978-0-472-02891-7 (e-book)
    1. Popular music—Social aspects.   2. Soul music.   I. Title.
ML3918.P67R69   2013
781.640973—dc23   2012033639

To Annie and Cecelia
and the future

Acknowledgments

In the process of writing this book, past, present, and future have come together, sometimes with unexpected moments of synchronicity.

First, I'd like to thank the artists, living and dead, who inspired this book, including George Clinton, Michael Jackson, Grace Jones, Eartha Kitt, Janelle Monae, Meshell Ndgeocello, Janelle Monae, Prince, Sylvester, and Stevie Wonder.

I'd like to thank my editor at the University of Michigan Press, LeAnn Fields, for her ongoing support for this project, great stories (including her experience of being in the audience for Stevie's "Fingertips"), and her sharp eye. I'm so appreciative to the readers of the manuscript, and to Alexa Ducsay, Marcia LaBrenz, and the production staff of the University of Michigan Press.

I'd like to thank my students and colleagues at DePaul University, who've listened to me spin my theories, and who've shared their time and insights. I'd especially like to thank Tina Chanter, Laila Farah, Camilla Fojas, Amor Kohli, Julie Moody-Freeman, Michele Morano, Ann Russo, and Lourdes Torres, who read and gave thoughtful feedback at many different points of this book's evolution. Thanks to my three great chairs, Lucy Rinehart, Bill Fahrenbach, and Helen Marlborough, and to the College of Liberal Arts and Social Sciences, the University Research Council, and the College of Academic Affairs for financial support for this project.

I'm very grateful for the rich community of scholar-friends with their smart brains, good cooking, conversation, and tricks to get the writing done: Myron Beasley, Natalie Bennett, Sharon Bridgforth, Jennifer Brody, Daphne Brooks, Gary Cestaro, Salome Chasnoff, Amina Chaudhri, Cathy Clark, Kristal Moore Clemons, Justin Cooper, Maxine Craig, Jennifer Curley, Farrad DeBerry, Misty DeBerry, Jerry Dees, Asher Diaz, Monica Dolan, Richard Doyle, David Dulceany, Cor Ece, Michelle Emery, Peter Erickson, Johnathan Fields, Cynthia Franklin, Laurie Fuller, Dustin Goltz, Bill Johnson Gonzalez, Amy Greenberg, Jonathan Gross, Kim F. Hall, Don Hedrick, Devorah Heitner, Mark Hoffman, Sharon Holland, Sandra Jackson, Margo Jefferson, E. Patrick

Johnson, Omi Osun Joni L. Jones, Richard Jones, Cricket Keating, Jason King, Joyce Green MacDonald, Peter Majda, Sheena Malholtra, Jeffrey McCune, Erica Meiners, Koritha Mitchell, Darrell Moore, Madison Alexander Moore, Fred Moten, Sanjukta Muhkerjee, José Estaban Muñoz, Jacqueline Shea Murphy, James Murphy, Seana Murphy, Deborah Murray, Mark Anthony Neal, Jeffrey Nealon, Paige Nichols, Tavia N'yongo, Kimberlee Perez, Marc Piane, Lori Pierce, Brian Ragsdale, Beth Richie, Ramón Rivera-Servera, Chris Rivers, Aimee Carrillo Rowe, Ricky Rodriguez, Elsa Saeta, Lance Schwultz, April Scissors, Shaija Sharma, Eileen Sieffert, Andrea Solomon, Kathryn Sorrells, James Spooner, Kaila Story, Chuck Suchar, Andrew Suozzo, Willa Taylor, Ayanna Thompson, Erin Tinnon, Irene Tucker and the staff at *Tri-Pish Quarterly*, Adaku Utah, Anna Clissold Vaughan, Shane Vogel, Choua Vue, Catherine Weidner, Cheryl West, Elizabeth Wheeler, and Daisy Zamora.

I'd like to thank my sister Becky, who has always been my partner in crime, memorizing songs on the radio and making up our own words with me from the very beginning. Thanks to my wonderful nieces Allie and Demitria, whom I admire greatly, and who don't mind informing me about what "the young people" are listening to these days. I'd like to thank my sisters Tara, Barbara, and Dericka, my niece Abbie and nephew Randy, and the rest of my family: the Roysters, Harveys, Russos, and Castenedas, who embrace me in all of my eccentricity while modeling new ways of being. I am so lucky to have two beautiful parents who model love, grace, and connection, Philip and Phyllis. And I would also like to thank those who have passed on, but who are always still with me, especially my mother, Sandra, my grandmother, Gwen, and my great-grandmother, Lucille.

Finally, I want to thank my partner, Annie, for bringing love, light, and joy to my life every single day. And to our sweet CeCe, who has changed my life forever for the good. This book is for both of you.

Earlier versions of some of the materials in chapters 3, 4, and 5 were published in Poroi, *American Sexuality and Women and Performance: a Journal of Feminist Theory*.

Contents

Introduction

Eccentric Performance and Embodied Music in the Post-Soul Moment

Eccentric: a. Of actions, movements, and things in general: irregular, anomalous, proceeding by no known method, capricious. b. Of persons or personal attributes: Deviating from usual methods, odd, whimsical. *fig.* Regulated by no central control . . .
　　　　　　　　　　　　　—*Oxford English Dictionary,* 2nd ed.

When Prince arrived in our bedroom via the cover of *Right On!* magazine some time in 1980, shirtless in suspenders and loose red jogging shorts, a horizon of endless space and stars twinkling behind him, my sister Becky and I hastily replaced our pinup posters of Shaun Cassidy and Foster Sylvers with those of him. Prince *seemed* innocent, at first: he had the pout and big brown-eyed, long-lashed androgyny of Shaun Cassidy, and the softly picked 'fro and shy gaze of Foster. Prince's voice *seemed* gentle, like Michael Jackson's did, almost even the same pitch as our own, and in most of his songs he seemed to be pleading for our attention. And besides, Prince was a music nerd—he wrote and produced his own albums and played all of his own instruments. But we soon learned to turn the volume down low, singing along to those images of sex as melting sugarcane and trembling butterflies, panting along with the unnamed "Sexy Dancer" when we were sure my mother wasn't home. Prince's appeal was tauntingly open-ended, whatever we wanted to dream up, it seemed. In "I Wanna Be Your Lover," Prince adds that he wants to be "your mother and your sister, too." And he takes this ability to mack by both performing and desiring femininity even further in his song "If I Was Your Girlfriend," also covered by the band TLC, where he seduces the listener with the promise to wash her hair, make her breakfast, and take her to a movie—presumably a "chick film" where they can cry together.

　　As Prince grew as a phenomenon and took a more explicitly controversial stance in his music and iconography, everyone seemed to have an opinion about him. Alvin Poissant, MD, renowned psychiatrist and frequent contributor to *Ebony* magazine on matters of the black psyche, wrote with alarm about him:

> Like Boy George and Michael Jackson, Prince has an androgy-nist quality—a male-female aura, expressed with defiant flamboy-ance. . . . He emotes the wild, primitive dreamlike abandon of the unconscious mind. . . . His cartoonlike charisma is heightened by his ostentatious wardrobe, especially his cape, which gives him a mysterious, satanic, messianic quality. . . . He appears to have become the Pied Piper for a sexually obsessed, sentimental and perhaps classic generation of young Americans who can relate to the beat of his histrionic musical configurations.[1]

Maybe Dr. Poissant was right. There was something in Prince's coos that were edged with a growl, something slippery in his damsel-in-distress sighs that worked its way into my impressionable teen mind like a funky worm. Prince even got the goat of my grandmother, who called him, despite his prettiness, "That Ugly Little Man." But I suspect that there was something complicated in the way she'd drop what she was doing to watch him, shaking her head but giving him the attention that her favorites, Phil Donahue and the Reverend Jesse Jackson Jr., didn't always get. And who could blame her? Prince appeared on stage in bikinis and open trench coat. He sang about having sex with his sister. He refused to an-swer the question of his race. He wore eyeliner and feathers and leather and ruffles, and later cutouts that showed the curve of his hip bones. He wore high-heeled boots and spoke of himself in the third person.

Prince is in many ways the consummate eccentric: creative, elusive, rocking racial, gender, and sexual lines. His performances reveal an erot-icism attached to multiple objects: lovers, specifically and enthusiasti-cally women, but also God, his guitar, James Brown, and himself. Prince forms "strange relationships" with his listeners, with his instruments, and with his own performing body, which he struts, caresses, adorns and then pushes to create a wild range of sounds: whispers, squeals, pants, falsettos, and deep, sometimes electronically produced commands and pleas. His gender and sexual fluidity might also be linked to his musical style—a repertoire of mastery over a range of styles and past performers. A little Joni Mitchell here, some Marvin Gaye there, Bowie and Iggy, Jimi Hendrix, Bootsy, Little Richard, and a whole lot of James Brown. He is, as music critic and journalist Nelson George suggests, "a great musical historian,"[2] able to take the strengths from past influences of rhythm and blues, soul, blues, and rock and put them in his own fresh and quirky world of sound. And as Mark Anthony Neal, a black feminist theorist, points out, at a time when black culture saw the emergence of strict codes of masculinity as tough and hard with the emergence of hip-hop, Prince countered with his own and very fluid ideas of black masculinity.[3] From early on, on the cover of his eponymous album *Prince,* with his relaxed hair tossed into a Farrah Fawcett flip and the direct sexual gaze of his Bambi eyes, Prince insists on the pleasures of gender play. Is he woman or man? Gay or straight? he asks us. He doesn't answer directly, but offers us instead a sexual dream space. On his album covers and videos, he appears flying naked on a white Pegasus or soaking in a violet-strewn bathtub or dreamily writhing on a four-poster bed, his sex always tantalizingly out of sight.

Even when flavored with hard urban funk, his songs seek to take us somewhere else: "a courtyard with oceans of violets in bloom"; the psychedelicized, purpled Minneapolis reimagined as Paisley Park; or a changed experience of our own bodies, as "sugar walls" or "a little box with a mirror and a tongue inside." Some of this power to evoke an elsewhere is fueled by his merging of the sacred and the profane in his lyrics. In songs like "When Doves Cry" and "Let's Pretend We're Married," he presents sex, even and especially hot and not necessarily reproductive sex, as sacred ritual and worship, a John Donne for the late twentieth century.

Prince raises key questions that will continue to be important to this book. How might such surprising and edgy performances of blackness, sexuality, and gender reflect the social condition of the Post-Soul United States—with its gains and limits of black political and economic freedom—and at the same time provide a space in which to think about an elsewhere, a space not yet invented? How might these performers speak not only to our own emerging political selves but also to our imaginations and desires? How might musical performance be the consummate form in which performers can negotiate the past as well as create new futures? This book explores a group of maverick performers who push the norms of blackness as they get entangled with sexuality and gender through the powerful platform of popular music. But because there are so many compelling examples to choose from, it's not meant to be an exhaustive study. It intends to provide a theoretical lens through which to explore other black performances eccentrically rather than capture a finite set of eccentric performances.

Born in the midst of key civil rights decisions—thirteen years after *Brown v. Board of Education*, one year before *Loving v. Virginia*, on the cusp of the Summer of Love, and two years before Stonewall, I claim the term *Post-Soul eccentric* for myself. My parents were shapers of and shaped by these forces, each charting new paths from family and neighborhood. Both were the first to go to college in their families, and the first in a few generations to move away from Chicago and the rest of the family. They met while performing in an African dance troupe, my mother a dancer, my father a drummer, at the University of Illinois' now defunct Navy Pier campus, an institution that served first-generation college students, the working poor, and students of color, or, like them, students who were all three. The choices that my parents made in their lives (completing college, pursuing graduate degrees, establishing careers in the arts) were very different from those of their parents, and the options that their lives gave me made my own choices for a life as an academic and writer very different from theirs. Much of their decadelong marriage was spent working together as activists and poets, publishing with Third World Press, being involved in the rich political and artistic life at Fisk University in the early 1970s. My first adult friends were part of these circles: Cookie, John Hershey (Bar), Brenda and Baba Tu, students who would take my sister and me to rallies and football games and poetry happenings on Fisk's campus. The influx of cultural capital (if not always plain old economic capital) that came then and later gave my sister and me a kind of cultural and aesthetic mobility that was for my parents hard won, and that we sometimes took for granted. Moving between cities and neighborhoods, and sometimes the deeper structures of race and class, we became fluid in our tastes and styles in fashion, and in music too. My mother encouraged my first Afro, although I was the only girl in my neighborhood in those post–Angela Davis days to wear one. By high school I'd shaved one-half, leaving the other to fall over my eye in a puffy version of a flock of seagulls flip.

I am convinced that the freedom to be "strange" that I was allowed reflects both the open ethos of my parents as individuals and a changing sense of community rules and possibilities of the time. In our shared room, my sister Becky and I listened to our 45s, LPs, and eight-track tapes, which looked both to the past and to the future: the Beatles' *Magical Mystery Tour* and Stravinsky's *Firebird*, *ABC* by the Jackson 5 and the soundtrack to *Black Orpheus*. Later we grew into Parliament's *Theme from the Black Hole* and Prince's *Controversy*. On television we caught flashes of utopian multiracial futures on *Sesame Street, Soul Train,* and occasionally *Star Trek,* as well as dystopian countercritique (in the guise of urban situation comedy) on *Good Times, Welcome Back Kotter,* and *Chico and the Man.* One of the songs that helped me move from wall-flower to dancer was "Funkytown," by Lipps, Inc. That 1979 disco hit spoke to an availability of choice and movement that catalyzed my desires as I came of age: "Got to make a move to a town that's right for me." Part nerd, part queer, part leftover Angela Davis wannabe, I always had the feeling that my own personal "Funkytown" was out there, and that some-day I was going to find it. This yearning is also felt by the protagonists of Post-Soul novels by Zadie Smith (*White Teeth*), Junot Díaz (*The Brief Wondrous Life of Oscar Wao*), Paul Beatty (*The White Boy Shuffle*), and Danzy Senna (*Caucasia*). These novels explore coming of age in a global Post-Soul landscape of shifting racial, gender, and sexual identity. In each of these novels, recently integrated schools and blurring neighborhood color and class lines, as well as the ghostly return of histories of racial violence, become the backdrop for the production of nerdy, eccentric, or "strange" selves, forged between the cracks of family and community. We can also hear this new sensibility in the hypnotic autobiographical voice of Daphne A. Brooks's music writing, as she wanders the Southern California landscape in her Honda ("post-earthquake, post-mud-slide, post-riot, and right smack in the middle of the O.J. era of malcontent" [*Grace* 1]), singing along to Jeff Buckley's iconic album *Grace,* or to the blue-eyed soul of Journey's "Lights," reflecting on the pleasures and con-straints of interracial cultural identification. Or in cultural critic Michael C. Ladd's forging of a global black "quadruple consciousness" while in boarding school in the Himalayas, via Parliament and Funkadelic.[4] The blogs *Afro Nerd* and *Black Nerd Network* also give testimony to a grow-ing space for discussion of nonnormative blackness that might fit into the realm of the Post-Soul eccentric, as do musical meeting spaces like the Afropunk Festival and the Black Rock Coalition.[5] These works reflect what I suggest are an emerging discourse of Post-Soul eccentricity that is both individual and, to some extent, shared, grounded in the history and cultures of the African diaspora. This contrary lens of eccentricity is a tool used to bring to light understudied aspects of the Post-Soul era.

The term *Post-Soul* describes both a period—one that is still with us—and an aesthetic. The Post-Soul took shape in the wake of profound changes in black diasporic political and cultural life, including racial in-tegration's sometimes violent shifts in living patterns, relationships, and ways of racial knowing, affecting neighborhoods, schools, businesses, urban spaces, and eventually airwaves. These social changes brought, on the one hand, increased access for the black middle class and, on the other, the solidification of poor urban spaces. Legislated social changes like the Civil Rights Act of 1964 and the Voting Rights Act of 1965 meant greater political representation and access to institutions for this next generation. Desegregation of schools and the rise of a black middle class meant greater everyday contact between different races, classes, ethnicities, and cultures. Yet these changes have not meant the erasure of tensions and bias around race and class; rather they present a new context for them.

Global nationalism, and the increasingly profitable traffic in US black culture as representative of US culture, also shapes Post-Soul culture, as does the continued influx and intermingling of multiple international influences in what we think of as black sound, produced out of what theorist Stuart Hall calls the "global postmodern."[6] With this transnational black cultural traffic has come postmodernism's promise of identity fluidity, on the one hand, and the threat of historical and cultural forgetting on the other. And of course there remains a lingering hunger for blackness as the marker of the authentic, primitive, and "real."

As an aesthetic, "Post-Soul" features an intensified exploration of blackness—what theorist Bertram Ashe calls "blaxploration,"[7] arguably distanced from the nitty-gritty of everyday political struggle; the examination of, wrestling with, and sometimes abandonment of past black cultural norms of racial purity and the embrace of the "cultural mulatto," a term first coined by cultural theorist Trey Ellis in 1989 in his essay "The New Black Aesthetic";[8] and with it the artistic use of a wide range of cultural influences, associations, and markers within and outside of black culture. The aesthetic also reflects changes, tensions, and fissures in black life, including deindustrialization, globalization, the rise of the prison complex, and increasing commodification of black cultural work in its critical and sometimes satiric mood.[9]

While some cultural critics see Post-Soul as an aesthetic reflecting a loss of political ground, cultural authenticity, and overall discombobulation, my book instead sees powerful possibility in the very experience of racial unmooring, particularly as it opens up gender and sexuality. Recent work on Post-Soul music has characterized the Post-Soul as a period of loss. In *Footsteps in the Dark,* historian George Lipsitz suggests that for many Americans the period of the 1980s and 1990s was accompanied by the experience of an "exhausted and obsolete culture" in which "faith in the future is hard to sustain" and, even given a highly mediated world of magazines, newspapers, and television, answers can be hard to find.[10] Lipsitz documents the ways in which black audiences have wrestled with the immediate economic and political negative forces of the post-civil-rights moment, including the white backlash against affirmative action, economic loss, deindustrialization, the growth of the prison industrial complex, and most profoundly, the growth of the AIDS epidemic. In the face of this shaken faith, Lipsitz argues, we can hear in the black music most embraced a longing for better and more meaningful lives, a longing for connection to others.[11] This sense of a lost political and aesthetic ground is voiced even more sharply (if not without a sense of humor) by Nelson George in his *Post-Soul Nation: The Explosive, Contradictory, Triumphant, and Tragic 1980's as Experienced by African Americans {Previously Known as Blacks and Before That Negroes}*. As we consider the musical performances that sprang out of the Post-Soul period, as well as the reception of the audiences that love them, we must take seriously the discombobulation, loss, and yearning described by George Lipsitz and others. But what these studies miss is the sense of possibility also offered by the Post-Soul moment—and in particular, the quest for an embodied and liberatory blackness.

As a departure from previous studies of the Post-Soul era, this study is particularly interested in Post-Soul musical departures from sexual and gender respectability so central to discourses of black uplift and national unity. We hear and see these possibilities of "strange" black embodiment on dance floors, in concert halls, on street corners, between headphones, and on celluloid, and, eventually, in the world of the Internet, including MySpace and YouTube, where the commercial and homemade intermingle.

The Post-Soul era has seen the birth of funk, disco, and hip-hop, and significant shifts and developments in soul and rhythm and blues. But this era is also responsible for a group of cultural mavericks, genre crossers whose music is less easy to categorize and who sometimes make their audiences uncomfortable. *Sounding Like a No-No: Queer Sounds and Eccentric Acts in the Post-Soul Era* centers on performers of the Post-Soul period who are both familiar and "strange" or eccentric (including Eartha Kitt, whose career spans the near beginning to the Post-Soul end of the twentieth century, as well as Michael Jackson, Grace Jones, George Clinton, Stevie Wonder, Meshell Ndegeocello and Janelle Monáe)—

those who in their embodied voices, movements and gestures, iconography, appropriation of multiple styles, choice of cover songs, and other artistic projects blur categories of music genre, as well as race, gender, sexuality, and other aspects of identity. These reinventions of popular forms become more possible with the rise of appropriation, pastiche, sampling, and irony in postmodern aesthetics.[12] I've chosen this roster of performers in particular for their distinct sexual and gender theatricality, conveyed both musically and visually, and because of the often understudied elements of critique and contrariety in their music. Despite their contrariness, these figures are highly visible, notorious even—something like Cameo's object of desire in its 1984 song "She's Strange," renowned, distinct, and yet hard to categorize: "She's my Twilight Zone, my Al Capone / She's my Rolling Stones and my Eva Perón."

These performers often wear several hats, producing music, starring in films, and collaborating with other artists, often across racial and gender lines. Many are famous for being themselves—as "personalities," as well as artists. Their theatricality—the self-referential, sometimes outsized performance of their own personae or selves, as well as invented characters, is a significant aspect of their eccentricity or strangeness, and provides a space for lampooning and critiquing past and present versions of blackness.

By "eccentric," I mean not only out of the ordinary or unconventional performances but also those that are ambiguous, uncanny, or difficult to read. These eccentrics of the Post-Soul generation have created a controversial and deeply historically informed response to the dehumanized black subject and stretched the boundaries of popular forms of music, ultimately shaping a new public dialogue.

Through acts of spectacular creativity, the eccentric joins forces with the "queer," "freak," and "pervert" to see around corners, push the edges of the present to create a language not yet recognized: new sounds, new dances, new configurations of self—the makings of a black utopia. Here I turn to the home girls who have chosen to become exiles, brothers from another planet, the tribe of the Black Bohemian, nerds, queers, Trekkies and Funkateers. In my appropriation of *eccentric,* a term that, unlike *queer, pervert,* or even *freak,* has been depoliticized in most popular discourse, I explore a particular and underreported aspect of black experience in the late twentieth and early twenty-first centuries. I want to highlight here how these eccentrics create the space for creative and intellectual production, which, while maintaining ties to the familiar—to home, to the black community, and to corporate forces—also manages to open up new imaginative worlds with their own sense of logic and beauty. Eccentric performances are fueled by contradictory desires for recognition and freedom.

Soul versus Post-Soul Eccentricity: More Than a Feeling

How has Post-Soul eccentricity been forged from the fires of Soul? Soul is seen as the aesthetic and philosophical embodiment of Black Power—an ideal of a unified blackness and beauty. Soul feels like a recovery project that centers heretofore suppressed black physicality and sexuality: Isaac Hayes's gold chains and bare chest, James Brown's hard-earned sweat, Angela Davis's Afro, the righteously bold stance of Pam Grier bearing a machine gun. Soul feels like the crooning seductions of Teddy Pendergrass, Roberta's warmth and Aretha's gospel shout. Soul claims its roots in the shared cultural memory of black history. In Monique Guillory and Richard C. Green's critical exploration of Soul, they say that "Soul is the stuff of our dreams and marks that magical domain of powerful nothingness where fantasies and ancestors live."[13]

Soul is a reembrace of the black body beautiful: black sensuality, black sexuality and heart. It is invested in claiming a black self in response and contrapuntal to the earlier freedom projects of the civil rights generation—the Malcolm to its Martin—*and* to whiteness and the myth of objectivity. It is the voice of a younger generation invested in black nation time that has a widely recognizable beat—the beat of heart and cock. Soul is often male centered. Soul is informed by the revolutions around it, but it seeks a kind of consistency. Soul is driven by style, deeply invested in its own coolness, and for that reason, it sometimes ignores the lessons of its deepest reaching, when the spirit, the rhythm shakes us, or leaves us confused. Soul privileges the natural over the artificial, the pure over the mixed. As an ideal, it privileges and polices heterosexuality and masculinity, and it reflects a Christian influence at its base (i.e., Soul's link to gospel), along with the embrace of a both sensual and procreative sexuality.

Post-Soul eccentricity, on the other hand, asks, what happens after the basic needs of family and community are met? What if the clothing of unity is too tight? What if the rhythms of the black body are less distinctly steady or comfortable? Post-Soul eccentricity draws on the contemporaneous development of the aesthetic of punk, which takes castaways and garbage and refashions them in all of their dirt. Punk movement and dance reembrace the awkward, hunched shoulders and stiff movements of the wallflower, and fire them up with the spirit of rebellion.

Post-Soul eccentrics ask, where might blackness not only uplift us, or feed our souls, but sometimes also fail us, erasing our desires or constraining the ways we move in the world as sexual and sensual beings? If black is beautiful, do we squelch the fact that we feel awkward in these bodies, even among each other? What if we take that awkwardness, make it into sound, make it into dance, claim it, too, as black sound, as well as something else, something strange? This is a question that haunts the scratchy sounds of Eartha Kitt; the awkward, Mickey Mouse, knock-kneed stance of Michael Jackson in the "Billie Jean" video; the gruffness of Grace Jones; and the boyish slouch of Meshell Ndegeocello. Black as it is *not* necessarily beautiful is another truth of our lives that we need to tell, how it feels to dwell in the spaces outside of the known, beautiful, and loved, where the air gets thinner, giddier, stranger. This is a space of evolution, shifting, becoming. This space of excess turns out to be not one of lack, but an embarrassment of riches. It can even be entertaining, this body not just beautiful but beat, ashy, stinky, too big, too femme or butch, otherwise found wanting.

I am compelled by cultural theorist Ann Cvetkovich's book *An Archive of Feelings* in its formulation of music's power to open up traumatic responses (for her sexual violence, for me the violence of racism and also internalized racial surveillance), especially as it takes the form of musical performance. These performances recenter the effects of racism and gender surveillance back to the body, yet a return to the body with a difference. One of the difficult messages that some of these performances voice is the yearning to become white, to surround oneself with whiteness, or to neutralize race—to say, at least at first, that race doesn't matter. Rather than glide over these moments, this book explores them: Eartha Kitt erasing her black southern voice in her biography (and claiming that she always spoke like a continental queen); and Jackson's manipulation of technology to support his idealized notion that "It don't matter if you're black or white," living for the moment the dream of racial, as well as gender and national, fluidity. When that "desire to be white" is stated up front, it has the power of a bomb. These moments in black performance are dangerous—confirming the worst fears of the critics—but they are not static. This is a moment, a phase, a response to trauma, and then we see a return, through music, through bodily transformation—toward healing, toward reconnection. Music becomes a site of healing and also a site of root working, political activism, revenge. Cvetkovich's description of music's function in the experience of lesbians' sexual trauma captures the place of music in this troubled "return" of the Post-Soul eccentrics: "The music helps us return the listener to the pleasures of sensory embodiment that trauma destroys: 'cuz those are your arms, that is your heart, and no no they can't tear you apart.'"[14]

Post-Soul eccentricity is a layered rather than separate time, living on the hyphen of past and present, daring itself to look behind. In my analysis of the eccentric performances that follow, we see the remnants of cultural shame: minstrelsy, the outsized naughtiness and down-home funk of the blues women, the cultural memories of miscegenation, bad ethnic jokes, and also the queerness, softness of the captured slave—in other words, all that has been left behind or found in excess of the Soul project. This is how the eccentric complicates the "post " in Post-Soul, because Post-Soul eccentrics do not just wipe the slate clean. They are both forward and backward moving, navigating a set of reference points that include the past as well as the future, that "something new."

In Post-Soul eccentricity, transformation and alteration become a way of reclaiming bodies that are the sites of racial and sexual conflict and violence by changing them physically and sometimes permanently, through technological manipulation, for example, Grace Jones in the *One Man Show* or on the cover of her most recent, *Hurricane* (2008), where she is figured as a factory-made chocolate confection, broken on the assembly line, made to be hollow; Michael Jackson's infamous bodily transformations over the course of his life, as well as on video (from Macaulay Culkin to Dancing Black Man to leopard; from little brown gingersnap boy to svelte, light-skinned, elfin man; from heartthrob to corpse in *Thriller;* and in terms of the extrafilmic and performative self, from troubled celebrity to hero, postdeath); Janelle Monáe's reinvention as Cindi Mayweather, in which her android-muse must die and be re-animated, returning with each new song to groove us. In these examples, bodily transformations in performance are not just unconscious by-products of this haunted return to the site of black trauma: they are creative triumphs, attempted blueprints for new ways to live.

Post-Soul eccentrics also ask, how might past ideas of black nation time limit or constrain the ways we imagine our flights to the future—

and who gets to join us on those flights as our lovers and children? The sense of restlessness and the desire for an elsewhere bridges Eartha Kitt's resistant spirit of rejuvenation and reinvention with the futurist impulses of Post-Soul artists: Stevie Wonder's plants, Meshell Ndegeocello's Soul spaceship, George Clinton's space pods, Janelle Monáe's escape from the Palace of the Dogs in her song "Tightrope." Each trades allegiances, shifts genders, and instruments, always also seeking collaboration, between other races, peoples, nations, planets, sound-making machines.

I place these popular performances in the context of critical and artistic conversations—conversations that sometimes blur the line between theoretical and artistic—about the black fugitive imagination. These conversations have primarily centered around poetic and musical performance, especially jazz performance, but may also arguably include Post-Soul pop performances.[15] The fugitive describes the artistic impulse to escape the constraints of the objectification and social death of slavery—but also to never fully escape its embodied lessons. These informed "dark songs" of pain and struggle embody what poet and critic Nathaniel Mackey, after Federico García Lorca, characterizes as *duende,* the darkening of sound, the tearing up of meaning, restlessness, versioning, the slide away from tradition and the familiar (Mackey);[16] shrouding or "afro alienation acts," as Daphne A. Brooks calls them;[17] the desire for misrecognition (in the words of Fred Moten);[18] hovering always at "the rim of the wound";[19] the space of the break.[20] This is purposeful and artful disorientation hidden in the plain sight of commercial radio, MTV, and *Soul Train,* it's purpose: to "Let loose from the noose that's kept me hanging around" (in the words of AC/DC's Angus and Malcolm Young, but as reconstructed and recontextualized in performance by the black rock group Living Colour).

It is precisely this fugitive spirit that informed Prince's politicized struggles with Warner Brothers in the late 1990s, when Prince became the Artist Formerly Known as Prince. After riding a crest of fame that included sold-out tours, multiple Grammies, two feature films, multiple spinoff groups, and five platinum albums, Prince fought to be released from his 1992 contact with Warner Brothers Records and to own the masters to his own songs. In his acts of rebellion against the studio, which included renouncing "Prince" as his slave name in favor of an unpronounceable glyph of his own creation, something akin to Malcolm's X, and in appearing in public performances with the word *slave* jauntily carved out in marker on his high cheekbone, signifying on his role as part of the Warner Brothers' "plantation," Prince placed himself in the history of African diasporic freedom struggles. He made this connection quite explicitly. He told *Jet* in 2004, "If you don't own your master tape, your master owns you. . . . And you might as well write slave on your face too. It's all about ownership."[21]

By becoming ♀, Prince evoked the erasure of history, of name and subjectivity, of the black diasporic slave experience—at the same time that he does so as an act of supreme self-naming and reclaiming of a place in history, creating a new line of descent—something like Michael Jackson naming himself the King of Pop and naming his children Prince Michael Joseph Jackson Jr., Paris-Michael Katherine Jackson, and Prince Michael Jackson II. Or George Foreman's brood of five sons named George. The "glyph" itself—sometimes called the "love sign" but actually a combination of male and female symbols—suggests, along with its unpronounceability, the insufficiency of language to capture the full spectrum of a fully emancipated, fully human self.[22] As the glyph both extends and postpones a determinate meaning, it also opens up the meanings of Prince's protest to future audiences—enacting what performance studies theorist Harvey Young characterizes as the ways that black performances are haunted by black projections of violence against the body and self, and in turn how those hauntings can be reimagined by creative acts that open up their meanings for the future audiences, who might experience these hauntings in changed ways.[23] Prince won his case in November 1996 and with his first record after the split, provocatively named *Emancipation*, earned the money that allowed him to pull himself out of a looming, if underreported, bankruptcy.[24] But most important, Prince gained control over his master tapes, and with it a chance to demonstrate, through this highly theatrical and "strange" tactic, the importance of controlling one's own creative work and ultimately claiming a more expansive space for the black body in public memory.

Such Post-Soul eccentric performances as Prince's play out the historical contradictions of the body and identity that were inaugurated by slavery, and are informed as well by debates within more recent political movements: the 1960s idea that "you are not your body" in theater, as well as the civil rights idea that you put your body on the line of your politics; and the movements of identity like the gay and brown and women's rights, as well as the opening up of what we think of as human embodiment by technology and Afrofuturism. To put all of these forces together, cook them up, and produce art is to make a claim to an expansive humanity. If the picture ends up looking quite different from conceptions of the Post-Soul Black Bohemian or "New Black" explored by recent Post-Soul critics, it may be because these conceptions underestimate the range of political and aesthetic influences, as well as the rage deep in the heart of Post-Soul eccentrics.[25]

Trey Ellis writes about the "cultural mulatto" that we "no longer need to deny or suppress any part of our complicated and sometimes contradictory cultural baggage to please either white people or black."[26] His conception of imaginative freedom is somewhat limited by his configuration of identity in solely racialized terms. I introduce a queered and eccentric politics of embodiment into our discussion of post-soul aesthetics in order to acknowledge the continued existence of prohibition as well as the possibilities of transcendence. Certainly, some of us continue to be more free than others in some black spaces.

Black Eccentricity, "Quareness," and Trafficking in the Authentic

As I consider Post-Soul eccentricity's departures from Soul, I've found it useful to combine recent theories of the "eccentric" by Daphne A. Brooks and Carla Peterson, together with E. Patrick Johnson's notion of "quare" to describe the performance of "excess" or outsiderhood from the already marginalized cultural boundaries of the black community.[27] Post-Soul "eccentrics" are located "in-between" and in excess of norms of sexual identity and racial difference, as well as musical practice. In Carla Peterson's foreword to *Recovering the Black Female Body: Self-Representations by African American Women,* she discusses the ways that black women's bodies have been figured as "eccentric" by the outside world, and the ways that eccentricity has been embraced and put to use by black women in their representations of themselves, from Sojourner Truth to Josephine Baker to Toni Morrison. She writes, "Here I have chosen to term the black female body 'eccentric,' insisting on its double meaning: the first evokes a circle not concentric with another, an axis not centrally placed (according to the dominant system), whereas the second extends the notion of off-centeredness to suggest freedom of movement stemming from the lack of central control and hence new possibilities of difference conceived as empowering oddness."[28] This eccentricity can be seen as both a response to voicelessness and an insistence "to reconcile body and spirit and represent the beauty of the African American self."[29]

Given the ways that both black men and women's bodies have been twisted, denatured, dehumanized, exploited, and objectified, I would like to extend Peterson's notion of eccentric bodies to consider multiple black sexualities, multiple black bodies in performance, including masculinities, femininities, and transgender identities. Eccentric performers' ability to locate themselves in a freedom of movement in an otherwise constraining situation—specifically, the constraints of a history of brittle racial, gender, class, and sexual stereotypes—is very important in my consideration of contemporary black popular culture, because it is in these moments of freedom that black popular performers can push the boundaries of identity and recognition. These "difficult" and sometimes controversial performances produce erotic energy that transforms the collective experience of black music. "Eccentricity" in this study implies purposeful oddness, and a simultaneous hijacking of our gaze and eardrums, jamming the system.

Daphne A. Brooks's *Bodies in Dissent: Spectacular Performances of Race and Freedom, 1850–1910* was the first scholarly work to take this concept of eccentricity posited by Carla Peterson and use it in a full-length scholarly study of black performance. Brooks's groundbreaking study intertwines with this one in its interest in strange pathways of black performance as a form of resistance—and in the importance of marginal and even alienated forms of blackness as a space for freedom—the space of the fugitive. Her study differs from this one in its focus on nineteenth-century and early-twentieth-century performance, informed by the first decades after Emancipation, and by early discourses of respectability and surveillance of "proper" performances of blackness. These are foundational moments of black identity. In my study, on the other hand, with its interest in Post-Soul eccentricity, the fugitive and strange are necessarily informed by the Post-Emancipation moment analyzed by Brooks, but these performances appear at a different point of inner community conversation—after and in conversation with and sometimes against the Black Nationalist and Black Art movements, the emerging Third World feminist movements and lesbian, gay, bisexual, transgender, and queer (LGBTQ) movements. There is necessarily a different and complexly historically informed space for eccentricity within the black community—in counterdistinction to the Soul moment, as well as considering eccentricity/fugitive identity as a response to white privilege and power, although these are certainly intertwined.

In myriad ways, these eccentric performances complicate discourse around authentic "black" behavior, politics, and art forms emerging from the "Soul" era, and continuing an ongoing conversation about black identity and unity that reaches back even further. In *Appropriating Blackness,* E. Patrick Johnson calls our attention to the ways in which blackness is multiple and has always been a contingent performance that has been arbitrarily awarded authenticity, dependent on our historical contexts and shifting subject positions.

> Indeed, if one were to look at blackness in the context of black American history, one would find that, even in relation to nationalism, the notion of an "authentic" blackness has always been contested: the discourse of "house niggers" vs. "field niggers"; Sojourner Truth's insistence on a black female subjectivity in relation to the black polity, Booker T. Washington's call for vocational skill over W.E.B. DuBois's "talented tenth"; Richard Wright's critique of Zora Neale Hurston's focus on the "folk" over the plight of the black man; Eldridge Cleaver's caustic attack on James Baldwin's homosexuality as "anti-black" and "anti-male": urban northerners' condescending attitudes toward rural southerners and vice versa; Malcolm X's militant call for black Americans to fight against the white establishment "by any means necessary" over Martin Luther King Jr.'s reconciliatory "turn the other cheek"; and Jesse Jackson's "Rainbow Coalition" over Louis Farrakhan's "Nation of Islam." All of these examples belong to the longstanding tradition in black American history of certain black Americans critically viewing a definition of blackness that does not validate their social, political, and cultural worldview. As Wahneema Lubiano suggests, "the resonances of [black] authenticity depend on who is doing the evaluating."[30]

Freed up from some of the constraints of a segregation era market, these are artists whose careers are distinctly irregular, unpredictable, and inventive, and whose self-presentations of body image and particularly of sexuality reflect an aesthetic of reinvention and change. At the same time, I'd argue that the condition of celebrity becomes a way for them to negotiate and sometimes circumvent the pressures of authenticity and respectability reflected in and sometimes perpetuated by the black community.

In this necessarily queered relistening to familiar and not so familiar black popular music, I challenge the idea of an "authentic" black sound, as well as a stable black identity, in these eccentric performances. Current discourse on authenticity around black music and culture in many ways springs from the Black Arts Movement, which certainly has grown in complexity and heat during the Post-Soul era. As Paul Gilroy discusses in *The Black Atlantic,* we see cultural discourse reflecting tensions around the diffusion/fragmentation of black music—whether from what is seen as "illegitimate" amalgamations of rock or other "white" musical forms into jazz and rhythm and blues, responses to the advent of the digital and other technological innovations,[31] or the continued appropriation of black sounds and traditions by white musicians and producers. Not coincidentally, the birth of hip-hop in the Post-Soul moment has also been accompanied by a reenergized Black Nationalist Movement for which music was a key force (including the Afrocentric rap of Queen Latifah, Public Enemy, NWA, and others). Gilroy points out that the continued presence of racism, including the denial of black cultural integrity and the "pernicious metaphysical dualism that identifies blacks with the body and whites with the mind,"[32] fuel the push for a black musical production that is recognizably "authentic" and black, and that might then be used to uphold the ideal of a black nation. We must necessarily understand the desire to claim a space for eccentricity in light of these reenergized fears of cultural contamination and racial purity and the resulting constraints.

The question "What Is This 'Black' in Black Popular Culture?" (the title of Stuart Hall's brilliant 1992 essay) has been pursued in a variety of ways in black cultural criticism, by looking generically at black popular culture's rootedness in the traditions and styles of the black vernacular, or by looking historically at black culture as shared responses to lived experiences, for example.[33] Embracing eccentricity necessitates that we claim as "black" precisely those performances in which community resemblance and recognition break down. Therefore, crucial to my analysis of eccentric interventions in the discourse of black authenticity is Gilroy's critique and deconstruction of the trope of "family resemblances" within black cultural criticism. This idea of a desired family resemblance between black cultural artifacts has been used as an interpretive filter to situate, periodize, and in some ways standardize and limit black cultural production. Gilroy uses this use of the "family resemblance" trope from Houston Baker's study *Modernism and the Harlem Renaissance* to frame his discussion.

My tale, then, to say again what I have said, is of a complex field of sounding strategies in Afro-America that are part of a family. The family's history always no matter how it is revised, purified, distorted, emended—begins in an economics of slavery. The modernity of our family's sounding strategies resides in their deployment for economic (whether to ameliorate desire or to secure material advantage) advancement. The metaphor that I used earlier seems more apt for such salvific surroundings—they are, indeed blues geographies that can never be understood outside a family commitment.[34]

Like Gilroy, I think it's important to intercede and complicate this ideal of "family resemblance" as "order words" for the ways that we conceptualize Post-Soul eccentric music, especially given the ways that the term authenticates the idea of an embodied blackness through this metaphor of the "natural" and socially sanctioned (as opposed to queered) body. This notion of black culture as family resemblance that echoes across time also directly or indirectly puts into motion ideals of respectability questioned by black feminist practice,[35] and heteronormative time, as opposed to queer time, in Judith Halberstam's sense.[36] In both cases, the family is used as a means of filtering what is or is not legible, and legitimate.

Certainly Post-Soul eccentricity is a continuation of the history of the survival and struggle of black people, which has produced the ongoing, successful production of new sound, movement, and generic innovation within the violently constrained spaces of slavery, Jim Crow, lynching, sexism, and segregation, as well as the fickle and often exploitative forces of capitalism. While this book focuses in particular on black performance in the Post-Soul era, it does not overlook the rich historical legacy of those creative, boundary-crossing performers who went before: the often imitated but irreproducible genius of vaudevillian Earl "Snake Hips" Tucker's shimmy, minstrel innovator Bert Williams's sly civility, Bessie Smith's split-tongued blues, Nina Simone's sneer, Little Richard's Queeny camp, and, as I'll discuss in the next chapter, Eartha Kitt's growl, as well as her purr. The shape these influences take is not static, nor is it linear. The Post-Soul family is not a finite set.

The success of Post-Soul eccentrics reflects a critical interest in what has in the past been censored and disavowed in black performance—

particularly quare black performance. This critical interest in censored black performance, I'd argue, is central to the political dimensions of what Greg Tate calls "post-liberation" identity.[37] The Post-Soul moment provides an unprecedented space of visibility for eccentric black musical identities, a new chance to stand up and both perform and be odd. The blossoming of rhythm and blues and soul in the 1950s and 1960s owes itself to highly theatrical innovators like Sister Rosetta Tharpe, Etta James, James Brown, and Little Richard,[38] performers whose combination of musical innovation, edginess, and often theatrical oddness had a key influence on the eccentric performers who came in the next decades. But for earlier eccentrics, this oddity sometimes had to be used strategically, and it often cost performers psychic and commercial freedom. What is it about the post-civil-rights period that has allowed for this space for eccentric performers to be as wildly popular as they sometimes were? We can't overlook how structural changes influencing the trafficking of black music might account for some of these changes: the integration of performances spaces like Las Vegas and, to some extent, an unsteady opening of mass media venues to limited black images and experiences; and the shaping hand of black musical innovators like Motown founder Berry Gordy and *Soul Train* producer and host Don Cornelius to provide new and wider spaces for black performance.

Artists in the Post-Soul era have reconceived of black music and black experience in a world where black identity is becoming increasingly cosmopolitan, where black music is trafficked increasingly globally, but also in an industry where generic risk has become increasingly narrowed and calculated. One of the key tensions that Post-Soul eccentrics have had to negotiate is their influence, embrace, and use by, and sometimes collaboration with, enthusiastic white audiences. Indeed, their sounds and styles often reflect a cross-fertilization with other streams of (white) oddity happening contemporarily. In Grace Jones's sound and style, for example, we see the influence of glam rock, and the shock/pop world of Andy Warhol. Michael Jackson dedicates his 1988 autobiography *Moonwalk* to Fred Astaire, who had died the year before, and credits him as one of his biggest influences in dance, although we might also note the ways in which Jackson's style reflects the hip-hop and particular break dance innovations happening on the streets of New York, Los Angeles, and other urban spaces. In his early days as a performer, Sylvester joined and performed with San Francisco's radical queer and mostly white per-

formance troupe the Cockettes. Every musician studied here has collaborated with white performers, and speak to the influence of rock,
folk, pop, and punk produced by white musicians. These collaborations
reflect an interest in tapping into national and global streams of musical experimentation, as well as markets previously earmarked as "white"
and off-limits to black artists. Significantly, these movements were also
sometimes conflicted sites of struggle for artistic control.

Nonetheless, black eccentrics' borrowings and movements into white
worlds call for an interpretive lens grounded in black musical and performance traditions. We would miss much from our understanding of
Stevie Wonder's musical experimentation, interest in spiritual transcendence, and sartorial androgyny in his *Journey through the Secret Life of
Plants* if we only interpreted him as a "black Hippie," for example. In
my chapter on Wonder, I explore his crossings into the realm of plants,
as well as the genres of opera, electronic music, and rock on that album
in the context of the history of representations of the black body and
the black intellect. Performers like Wonder (especially in this late 1970s
experimental phase), Grace Jones, and Michael Jackson challenge us to
rethink the terms of black authenticity and community membership that
we bring to our most visible cultural figures. Their work, in its intervention in the politics of black embodiment and authenticity, might be considered examples of organic intellectual work, challenging their listeners
to rethink and reexperience blackness through new, sometimes less familiar and comfortable positionalities.[39]

All of the artists discussed in this book must negotiate two key conditions in their careers, and these conditions are grounded in the Post-Soul,
post-civil-rights moment. First, these artists appear in a moment of potentially expanded notions of black identity within the black community.
These new notions of a heterogeneous blackness are in part enabled by
more porous cultural boundaries influenced by shifts in neighborhoods,
integrated working spaces, and the influence of African and other global
diasporic musical traditions. For example, the effect of shifting neighborhoods and schools on black musical performers who play rock is
captured profoundly by Maureen Mahon in *The Right to Rock: The Black
Rock Coalition and the Cultural Politics of Race*. Here, several of her subjects discuss the impact of bussing and forced desegregation of schools
on the kinds of music they listened to, danced to, and created—music,
especially rock, being both soundtrack and sometimes also catalyst to
social belonging—at the same time that they name the cross-effects of

black freedom movements like the Black Panthers, Black Nationalism, and black pride as shaping a complex and varied racial identity.[40]

We must also consider the impact on all communities of a slowing, changing commercial market in blackness that occurred, in part, as a result of these shifting social and spatial patterns. Taking the Jackson 5 as an example, we might note the release of albums with tours in increasingly large and spectacular arena halls or venues like Las Vegas at the same time that they appeared in black festivals and expos. (I first saw the Jackson 5 at the age of six in 1973 at the Black Expo in Nashville.) They appeared on black-marketed and produced shows like *Soul Train,* as well as *American Bandstand, Don Kirshner's Rock Concert,* and *Midnight Special,* along with Christmas specials, award shows, and other television appearances that reached wide international audiences, including a comedy sketch series and the Jackson 5 cartoon. They were publicized in both black and white teen venues like *Right On!* and *Tiger Beat,* along with adult magazines like *Time, Life, TV Guide, Jet,* and *Ebony.* Indeed, a significant social change to note in these early Post-Soul years is a growing mass media that included black youth as an audience—perhaps a direct outgrowth of Johnson Publishing and other black corporate ventures. The black-owned *Soul Train,* as the presiding "hippest trip in America," in its moment not only challenged but **changed** *American Bandstand.*[41] *Right On!* most likely changed who *Tiger Beat* included on its covers. Post-Soul eccentrics lodged themselves both within and between the spaces of white and black commercial markets, affecting black and white America.

With these changes came anxieties about the appropriation of black culture and style by white culture. While appropriation of blackness by white culture is by no means new, it has presented itself in new ways characterized in part by the visibility and glamorization of civil rights and Black Nationalist cultural heroes (e.g., Norman Mailer and the Black Panthers), increased white interest and consumption of powerful new aesthetic developments in black arts and music (including soul and blaxploitation), and the celebrification of certain black stars, including savvy commercial music producers like Berry Gordy and Quincy Jones.

And a final condition, rarely noted in terms of Post-Soul identity,[42] is the contested influence of new identity movements and politics that actively interrogate the past invisibility of gay and lesbian and trans sexualities. This same period is characterized by bursts of oppositional creative work and political and cultural activism. We see the blossoming of women of color feminisms, for example, exemplified by the publication of *This Bridge Called My Back: Writings by Radical Women of Color* in 1981; increased visibility and activism by lesbians, gays, bisexuals, and transgendered and queer folk, including vital work by authors like bell hooks, Audre Lorde, Barbara Smith, Cherríe Moraga, Joseph Beam, Marlon Riggs, and Gloria Anzaldúa; the energetic activism of Queer Nation, ACT-UP, and other queer activist groups; and the cultivation of black and Latino queer and other countercultural spaces, including the disco. These queer interventions create the space for pleasure and a vision for the future, a third space. Here, I borrow the concept of "third space" from feminist theorist Chela Sandoval's *Methodology of the Oppressed: Theory Out of Bounds.* Sandoval characterizes the Third Space as a practice of third world feminist oppositional consciousness, creativity, coalition and meaning-making that embraces ambiguity, contradiction and play in lived experiences.[43] Post-Soul eccentricity explores this third space through strategies of embodied and queered historical knowing. Eccentrics know that charisma, the elements of surprise, laughter, and sometimes even chaos can get things done and that taking up space in a queer body can change minds. Yet we know that the struggle for black LGBTQ visibility and inclusion within black communities is a difficult and ongoing one. The Combahee River Collective's 1977 "A Black Feminist Statement," Cheryl Clarke's "Lesbianism: An Act of Resistance" (1982), and Barbara Smith's "Some Home Truths on the Contemporary Black Feminist Movement" (1983) all document the ways in which the accusation of being a lesbian was used as a disciplining device to keep emerging black feminists from questioning patriarchy and homophobia within the civil rights and Black Pride movements. And, as Philip Brian Harper and Robert Reid-Pharr have pointed out, *faggot* and its synonyms have operated as shorthand for *political sell-out* in black men's writing, film, and music, from Eldridge Cleaver to Amiri Baraka to Spike Lee. These movements have called into question black community conversations about home and self, body and desire, struggle and the desire for change. The vision in black gay and lesbian writing, music, dance, and other forms of art is a vision of transcendence and possibility for the self and, for some, the black community at large. As Essex Hemphill wrote in his 1992 poem "Heavy Breathing," "I am eager to burn / this threadbare masculinity, / this perpetual black suit / I have outgrown." Eccentricity, as we will see, can be contagious.[44]

Eccentricity, Recognition, and Community in the Post-Soul Moment

I'd argue, then, that the Post-Soul era has seen visions of quare possibility in the midst of conditions of constraint, enabled in part by the shifting landscape of black identity and community. These moments are often overlooked by the critics because of their "strangeness"—and in particular, because of the ways that they exist outside of dominant modes of blackness, including normative heterosexuality. The Post-Soul eccentric's queer fierceness and potential for transcendence have been underplayed in most histories of the period. I think this is due in part to the ways in which the questions about gender and sexual subjectivity that I'm asking are relegated to the margins in a quest to create a linear narrative among Black Pride, Black Nationalist discourses of the civil rights movement, and hip-hop—perhaps the most commercially visible aspect of Post-Soul artistic production. Indeed, in some popular uses of the term *Post-Soul,* including music reviews and other popular discussions of black music in newspapers and magazines in the early 1990s, Post-Soul and hip-hop become interchangeable. This is not to say that there aren't powerful examples of femmecentric hip-hop, homo-hop, and other alternative aspects of hip-hop. This is more to say that when the term *hip-hop* is generally and popularly invoked, feminist and queer hip-hop are seen as marginal.

If we revise the post-civil-rights cultural landscape to foreground aesthetics that can be both black and queer, our conception of a Post-Soul identity might look quite different from earlier formulations of Post-Soul culture. In this book, I return to the voices and bodies left out in the quest to archive a recognizable and ultimately more heteronormative history of Post-Soul black experience. I offer a sustained analysis of a transgendered erotics/politics to transform the conception of a Post-Soul culture and aesthetics as they have been shaped so far in critical conversations about black music. *Sounding Like a No-No* links the transgendered erotics of Grace Jones and Michael Jackson, for example, to shifting conceptions of transexuality that bookend the late 1960s and the mid-1980s: the underreporting of the presence of black drag kings and queens at the Stonewall uprising and in other queer bars and spaces in the early 1970s on one end, and on the other end, the growing visibility and influence of filmmaker Marlon Riggs's work, especially his *Tongues Untied* (1985), which presents black-on-black gay and trans love with beauty, grace, and

▸ a new generation of black and queer writers, artists, and I'd argue that it is the music itself that has opened up new

In my formulation of an eccentric framework that is also queered, I resist the simple equation between queer performance and queer iden-tity. In many ways, these performers are queering what we think of as a "queer" culture or nation. Michael Jackson's, or George Clinton's sexual identities, though nonnormative, are not always clearly readable, for ex-ample; neither have they necessarily claimed a place in an LGBTQ move-ment. At the same time, I don't want to rely on an uncritical embrace of black or not-quite-queer exceptionalism. Even though these perform-ers might not always fit recognized codes of blackness or lesbian, gay, transgender, or queer identity, it matters that these performers are par-ticipating in an ongoing and always changing black aesthetic. Whatever their claims to identity might mean, their performances mean and mean intensely for other black and queer lives, as models, influences, and soundtracks to queer world making.

José Esteban Muñoz's influential concept of "disidentification" has been particularly useful in my conception of the ways that these black artists negotiate spoken and unspoken tensions around racism, gender, sexuality, and class in performance. Muñoz defines disidentification as "the survival strategies the minority subject practices in order to negoti-ate a phobic majoritarian public sphere that continuously elides or pun-ishes the existence of subjects who do not conform to the phantasm of normative citizenship."[45]

The artists I discuss are disidentificatory both in the ways they nego-tiate constraints of authenticity within the black community and in the ways their works explode the fiction of identity that they experience as commercially packaged subjects and subjects that circulate within white culture. We see in each chapter moments of tension between fixed/es-sential categories—ways of performing racial and sexual identity that are deemed authentic—and social categories, which are also "often format-ted by phobic energies around race, sexuality, and gender."[46] Especially important to my conception of the "eccentric" is Muñoz's conception of the ambivalence with which subjects disidentify "on and against" domi-nant culture.

As commercial success stories, Grace Jones, Michael Jackson, and the other eccentrics covered here, in their spectacular, look-at-me oddness, are neither "good" nor "bad" subjects, in Althusserian terms. They are unavoidably inside ideology. As Muñoz breaks it down, disidentification reveals the ways that the binary of identification and resistance, or counteridentification in Louis Althusser's thinking, still is in danger of recentering the dominant ideology, whether for or against it. Instead, these subjects work to transform dominant ideologies from within.[47]

These eccentrics do successfully package and sell their moments of oddness. They illustrate the growing ability of the marketplace to not only accommodate the new but also feed on the innovative tactics of these eccentrics. At the same time, eccentric figures are sometimes able to hijack or harness the modes of publicity and spectacle of capitalism, or at the very least, use past successes to finance less marketable projects. We might take, for example, Grace Jones's movement between subcultures and dominant cultures. If Jones began as a subcultural figure, a performance artist with her collaborator Jean-Paul Goude, she relatively quickly became a familiar face in Studio 54, on late night talk shows, in cameos on sitcoms, as a villain in James Bond films, and as an introducer at the Grammies. She even sang a duet with Luciano Pavarotti on Paris Public Television. Yet as she travels in these new venues, she does not alter her image, or performance, continuing to employ a mask of unreadability and surprise. This makes her consumption and reappropriation by others for subcultural ends all the more satisfying and possible. (I wonder, for example, if Jones being cast as God by the creators of the Church of Grace Jones website, a gay Edenic fantasy, was at all informed by the mysterious, dominating figure that she cut in commercial film releases like *A View to a Kill* or *Boomerang*.) As I comment in chapter five, Jones's choice of the title "Corporate Cannibal" as the first single for her latest CD speaks of the double edge of her and other eccentrics' work.

This Is What Eccentricity Sounds Like: Performing Imaginative Freedom

Familiar and strange, eccentric performance does a particular kind of work in relation to the center, by speaking to the condition of being highly visible and highly scrutinized, embraced and at times held at arm's length from the center. We see this dynamic in Joshua Gamson's description of Sylvester's early reception in the black community in his book *The Fabulous Sylvester*.

Sylvester opened for Chaka Khan at the Capitol Theatre, wearing a silver sequined robe, a feather boa, and black high-healed boots. "The drooping tendrils of nouveau afro framing his wide, subtly made-up, baby-soft face gave him that look," wrote Vince Valetti, "of a somewhat slimmed-down, somewhat freaked out Roberta Flack." At first, the mostly black, mostly straight crowd seemed to be at a loss. Unlike male falsetto soul singers they'd heard—love men like Eddie Kendricks or Donnie Elbert, say, or Smokey Robinson—Sylvester was clearly not trying to win over the ladies with feminine softness. Sylvester sang, as Guy Trebay put it, "like a street girl—sassy, hot, skirt hiked up, paying it no mind." That night, he took a look at the audience. "Sometimes folks make us feel strange, but we're not strange," he said. "And those folks—they just have to catch up."[48]

Sylvester is clearly making something new—a new black aesthetic that is at once nostalgic and futuristic (one part blues woman, one part space age funkster). In Sylvester's commandeering of the Capitol Theatre, he both courts a black popular audience and insists on his right not to explain his place there. Sylvester's use of pastiche draws from a vocabulary of images of black female sexuality and black male soulfulness that might be familiar to his audience, while switching codes, rewiring the circuits. Onstage he puts front and center a self that his audience might look right through if seen on the street, or even at a family reunion. But the space of the stage demands their participation. Sylvester is innovative but also still in trade or conversation with mainstream black culture, both odd and highly visible.

I find in Sylvester's performance and the other performances explored here a complex and sometimes awkward negotiation of communities that includes courtship yet always with the risk of rejection from both sides. Eccentric artists hold their audiences in an embrace that is both compelling and awkward. This awkwardness can reveal much about the potential and limits of black identity at this particular cultural moment.[49]

Through an analysis of eccentric sound and bodily performance, we can better understand the ways that black performers and black consuming audiences internalize and challenge laws of sexual and racial norms, even while those laws might be contingent and porous. How do eccentric performances push the codes of social laws around authentic race and sexual identity within the black community, even while they are also constitutive of that community and reflective of its traditions? As eccentrics disidentify with these norms, we can see how important they are for pushing and changing conversations within and outside of black spaces.

Central to my understanding of Sylvester's performance here are Judith Butler's theorizations of desire, recognition, and social intelligibility. If recognition is the code through which we desire and seek a place in the social order, our intelligibility is necessarily situated within a nexus of power relations influenced by the particulars of race and class within our community space.[50] The material effects through which we hope to be recognized by others, as "woman," "queer," or "black," for example, are contingent on history and ideology, and dependent on an unstable process of both reiteration and exclusion. Sylvester's reception by his black audiences exposes the dynamic of becoming intelligible, and the ways that recognition, while it rests on the internalization of these larger ideological forces, is also an open process. What is "intelligible" is always inherently contingent and unstable, and that in turn can be a productive and even erotic space, what Butler calls "a culture of democratic contestation" (Butler, *Bodies*, 221–22).[51] This deferral of recognition is the locus of desire. As Sylvester reinvents himself, he is reinventing his audience, feeding a hunger that they never knew they had.[52]

Moments of collaboration and contact are especially important for exposing and exploring the contingency of identity. For the artists in *Sounding Like a No-No*, the breakdown of essentialized understandings of blackness and other social roles can especially happen at moments of ecstasy—when performers teach their subjects how to understand their bodies differently, and interdependently, where "the discourses of essentialism and constructivism short circuit," as Muñoz puts it. Bodies need other bodies in order to short-circuit. We short-circuit these codes in relation to each other. This collaboration with the listener, with the dancers, with backup singers is potentially infinite; it is the place where ethical risks are engaged, including the risk of recognition. When, for example, Sylvester's voice intertwines with the orgasmic "female" backup voice in his last moments of "You Make Me Feel (Mighty Real)" the collaboration reorders the call-and-response tradition of leader and follower, as well as the heteronormative narrative of masculine musician/lead singer and feminized backup. In its melding of various femininities, the song leaves unclear whose voice is the "doer" and who is "being done"—and in fact, since the two feminine voices intertwine, we are unsure who is being made "real."

Music and other forms of creative pleasure making are produced out of the space of contingency, of not knowing. As Benin-born singer Angélique Kidjo has said, "Inspiration is in the domain of the unknown" (Barnett 31).[53] The often ecstatic experience of seeing and hearing the unknown is a refrain in each of my chapters: Eartha Kitt's geographically dislocated voice, the smile that might be a sneer behind the mask of Grace Jones, the gender fluidity of nonverbal sound in Michael Jackson's *Off the Wall,* and the secret life of plants that Stevie Wonder attempts to translate for us.

With these ideas in mind, I'd like to identify several markers of Post-Soul eccentric performance that will shape this book. Eccentric performance includes an initial off-centeredness, the use of not-so-ordinary means and often seemingly conflicting methods of theatricality: the crossing of generic boundaries of form or the crossing of gender or racial boundaries through twice-removed actions. For musical performance, this off-centeredness is particularly important in terms of sound: falsettos, growls, shifting accents, gasps, shouts, tones that threaten to veer off-key, improvised lyrics, breaks in the "fourth wall"—or silence. Eccentric body performances include gender code switching, facial gestures that might threaten a loss of emotional control one minute and then switch to a cool mask the next. This off-centeredness in many ways works against the grain of norms of black authenticity, or expectations of cuddliness or accessibility.

These sometimes unpredictable stylistic performances reveal the voice behind the Duboisian mask that hides the tensions between racialized and sexualized worlds. Fred Moten's groundbreaking book *In the Break* importantly highlights the ways that black bodies in performance have become a means of protest, giving voice to the unspeakable experience of black violence, and at the same time stretching the lines of genre. As he says in his opening lines, "The history of blackness is testament to the fact that objects can and do resist."[54] Ultimately, Moten opens up what has been figured as the history of black suffering, and this suffering's contribution to a radical black aesthetic of the avant-garde. He argues that this suffering produces pain as well as a blessing, "baraka"—a surplus of signification that must necessarily be understood not only through the lenses of the visual, but also through sound. Such protest is key to the pursuit of freedom. In *Sounding Like a No-No,* I follow Moten's insistence that in the roughness and edginess of black sound, "submerged in the broken, breaking space-time of an improvisation. Blurred, dying life; liberatory, improvisatory, damaged love; freedom drive,"[55] we can find political passion, even in commercial performance.[56]

This Duboisian mask can be the playful mask of the trickster (e.g., George Clinton), the childlike mask of the innocent (Michael Jackson), or one of brittleness and even cruelty, a gleaming or deflecting surface—one that is worked for its maximum effect (Eartha Kitt, Grace Jones). The mask of the trickster is one of the many ways that these performances use theatricality as a means of disrupting the pressures and constraints of "authentic" or true feeling, associated with blackness.[57] Within this mask lies the critique of the world of art and marketplace that is both generically savvy and historically informed—what some have called triple or even quadruple consciousness. It is in this spirit that I read Grace Jones's controversial image on the cover of Jean-Paul Goude's *Jungle Fever* (1982), naked, caged, eating a raw piece of meat, her face twisted in a snarl. Certainly, her performance of her sexuality, her race, her gender, her very humanity in this image, is in some ways still constrained by the social history of other images of black female sexual animality. Jones's use of the sexualized spectacle of her own body challenges us, tempting us to erase her humanity and skill as an artist by sheer force of sensation. Yet we must credit Jones's own role as cocreator in this production, and note the ways that her work engages contemporary movements in art and feminist discourse. There is always a risk involved in an eccentric performance, the danger of alienating your allies, cutting too close to the bone, or just trying people's nerves. Yet the *working* of this moment can produce the release of anger, an explosion of laughter, the joint between performer and audience, and perhaps even ecstasy.

Eccentric musical performance depends on a queered relationship between body and sound, one that through the heightened state of performance opens up boundaries and produces a state of vulnerability and change that can approach the ecstatic. There is an aspect of the spiritual in the state of strange. Simon Frith has commented on the ways that the state of the body in performance (singing, dancing, playing an instrument) is always in some ways unnatural and potentially risk taking in its exposure to and attempt to connect with the audience. For example, the mouth, as it is used to create the sound, is stretched abnormally large to create sounds, exaggerating syllables. Bodies as they work as musical machines are forced into unnatural positions. The body in performance is permeable in its readiness to be changed or transported by the act of producing music.[58] At the same time, this can be turned around to be powerful—to diva, work, overwhelm, to inspire and transform the listener. This heightened aspect of eccentric performance, its ability to both shift and make strange the body of the performer and to transform the listener's and collective audience's relationship to their bodies is a key aspect of the Jazz Aesthetic, as described by Omi Osun Joni L. Jones. Within the Jazz Aesthetic, both body-centeredness and virtuosity—"an individual's responsibility to bring forth her specific and idiosyncratic self into the world"—are key aspects of performance.[59] The body as it is both idiosyncratic and queered becomes a key instrument for shared knowledge and spiritual connection. Moten describes the powerful re-alignment of the black performing body as "the amplification of a rapt countenance, stressed portraiture. No need to dismiss the sound that emerges from the mouth as the mark of a separation. It was always the whole body that emitted sound: instrument and fingers, bend. Your ass is in what you sing."[60]

Eccentric sound flips the switch, splits the tongue. It highlights dissonance in terms of the relationship between body and expected pitch or register (here, echoing the sense of feeling "queer" in the old valence, to feel and/or sound odd). Eccentric sound can speak to the experience of one's body within the social body as changing, unclear, unintelligible. In "Walking in the Rain," Grace Jones describes this as dissonance among appearance, sound, and feeling, cut by experience of prohibition: "Feeling like a woman, looking like a man, sounding like a No-No."

While not every artist that I discuss here would describe himself or herself as queer (or gay, lesbian or bisexual), I argue that these performances not only queer traditional narratives of "authentic" black bodily presentation and identity, but have also shaped notions of what it means to "be" queer—to act or be seen or heard as queer.[61] These eccentrics, while not necessarily embracing a queer identity themselves, have presented a soundtrack and visual iconography in some cases for queer culture: for example, the choreography for Michael Jackson's video for "Beat It" has been appropriated by the femme drag queens the Queen Bees,[62] and Grace Jones's performances of high femininities and female masculinities make her a popular drag persona, lending her edginess to highly spectacular and sometimes muscular examples of butch and femme queen realness.

Generally speaking, popular music can be read as an audience-driven form of performance, consumed, queered, and transposed by its listeners, integrated into the most intimate aspects of fans' lives. Sheila Whiteley and Jennifer Rycenga, editors of the collection *Queering the Popular Pitch*, suggest that queerness's disentanglement of gender presentation from object of desire is important in the realm of popular music because "popular music . . . contains both hidden histories and iconoclastic figures that have long attracted devoted audiences who sense something quite different from what the mainstream thinks is being projected."[63] Pop music is a form shaped by the desires of its listeners, as well as its performers, from queer club remixes of Lil' Kim's sometimes homophobic raps in queer club spaces to my sister and me, obsessively listening and relistening to that one delicious line from Isaac Hayes's "Theme from Shaft" ("That Shaft is a bad mother—" "Shut your mouth!"). Post-Soul eccentric music is always shifting in its usefulness, always ready to be remade.

Coming Attractions

Chapter one, "Becoming Post-Soul: Eartha Kitt, the Stranger, and the Melancholy Pleasures of Racial Reinvention," explores more deeply the common threads of eccentric performance, including generic innovation, highly stylized self-presentation or theatricality, and "difficult" or queerly embodied sound in the work of Pre- and Post-Soul outsider Eartha Kitt. Borrowing Audre Lorde's concept of "biomythography," which combines biography, history, and mythmaking, this chapter considers the ways that Kitt's reinvention of her black southern self becomes a model for Post-Soul identity. At the same time, Kitt negotiates the ideal of "black exceptionality" as a flawed tool against racism and essentialism through sound, stage performance, and the autobiographic impulse in her work. Kitt's often mythic presentation of self that at the same time works against historical forgetting produces a sometimes slippery archive of oddness and familiarity that will become an important resource for performers and audiences in the Post-Soul moment.

Chapter two, "Stevie Wonder's 'Quare' Teachings and Cross-Species Collaboration in *Journey through the Secret Life of Plants and Other Songs*," turns to Stevie Wonder's radical performance of knowledge and possibility, in opposition to tragic and otherwise limited cultural narratives of "black male genius." One of the most powerful examples of Wonder's innovation is one of his most creatively risky pieces, his soundtrack *Journey through the Secret Life of Plants*, which redefines black humanity through inner lives of plants, opening up traditional constraints on the body, including those of racism, sexism, gender normativity, and able-ism. Through an exploration of cross-gender and cross-species groove, Stevie Wonder explores new directions of sensual knowledge and identity, musically charting the erotic power of collaboration.

Chapter three, "'Here's a Chance to Dance Our Way Out of Our Constrictions': P-Funk's Black Masculinity and the Performance of Imaginative Freedom," considers the ways that George Clinton's two funk projects, Parliament and Funkadelic, create new spaces for nonnormative heterosexuality and creative production. P-Funk's solidly funking, hallucinatory, and often politicized music, experimental cover art, and wildly theatrical stage shows create a new queer space for black heterosexual men. Most significant, P-Funk's music explores black experience, particularly bodily, sexual, and sensual experience at points of ambiguity, vulnerability, pain, desire, and laughter, using tools of music that speak to their listeners individually and internally, as well as collectively. This power to harness emotionally strong and sometimes inchoate feeling had a powerful effect on its audience—prompting some to find unity and empathy.

Chapter four, "Michael Jackson, Queer World Making, and the Trans Erotics of Voice, Gender, and Age," offers a new conception of Jackson's becoming—gender and age as experienced through voice in his first solo album, *Off the Wall*. Through his cries, whispers, groans, whines, and grunts, Jackson occupies an erotic third space of gender, one that often undercuts his audience's expectations of erotic identification. In this way, his vocal performances anticipate ongoing debates around transgender identity and essentialized notions of desire. Jackson's third space of sound complicates our reading of him as a desiring subject at later points in his career, as he moves from child-adult to man-child, and as he reinvents the terms of racial belonging through his always becoming body. The chapter frames Jackson's always becoming body in the context of shifting notions of Post-Soul black childhood and coming of age, including my own.

Chapter five, "'Feeling Like a Woman, Looking Like a Man, Sounding Like a No-No': Grace Jones and the Performance of 'Strange' in the Post-Soul Moment," considers disco and film provocateur Grace Jones, and suggests that Jones is often misread because of her effective contrariety and use of masking. In Grace Jones's work and that of the other black artists influenced by her, we see the wedding of disco and punk, art and fashion, male and female, animal and human, and human and machine to create new notions of black sexuality. Jones's use of drag puts her into the larger history of the ways in which performers of the African diaspora use performance in complex ways to lobby a critique of the dehumanization of black people. Yet Jones's use of drag and other techniques of performing identity poses challenges of readability. She is, in many ways, a trickster figure, sliding out of the grasp of both her fans and her critics. Like other trickster performers of color who rose to prominence during the same period of the 1980s and early 1990s, Jones uses an outsized, "strange" public persona—one that often risks caricature—to lobby critique and express anger and ultimately, agency.

Chapter six, "Funking toward the Future in Meshell Ndegeocello's *The world has made me the man of my dreams,*" draws from recent work on Afrofuturism in black music to consider the ways that funk musician Meshell Ndegeocello explores new forms of community and embodiment in multiple national and transnational/transworld spaces. Through Ndegeocello's "blaxploration" of gender, sexuality, religion, race, and nation in her seventh album, *The world has made me the man of my dreams,* I ask, "How might black artists engage multiple audiences while performing a dream of the future that is insistently black and queer?"

I end with a brief consideration of the recent success of performer/provocateur Janelle Monáe, and how her vibrant, expansive, and often gender-queer, sci-fi infused, punky funk gives evidence for a future of more explicitly collective Post-Soul eccentric music.

Ultimately, in eccentric performance, there can be celebration in resistance, creating the possibility for connection, community, and change, what Lucille Clifton alludes to in her poem "Eve Thinking": "Come celebrate with me that every day something has tried to kill me, but has failed." Ultimately, I am interested in the relationships between these eccentric performances and the production of queer and other counterpublics, where, as Muñoz suggests, "Communities and relational chains of resistance contest the dominant public sphere."[64] Eccentricity, though, is more than a critical intervention, in the academic sense, and it is about more than survival. Eccentricity creates a space for dreaming, a declaration of fun, funk, play, and pleasure.

ONE

Becoming Post-Soul

Eartha Kitt, the Stranger, and the Melancholy Pleasures of Racial Reinvention

I first come across Eartha Kitt in my parents' record collection when I am six, grouped with other female vocalists of the recent past. I add her to my gallery of "va-va-voom" ladies: glamorous, sequined, sultry performers like Eartha or Dinah Washington or Celia Cruz, women with elaborate Cleopatra eye makeup who wear their dresses tight like mermaids. They pose on the covers in midshout in front of microphones, caught in time. They enjoy a martini or a boogaloo in bachelorette apartments in unnamed cities. These album covers plant the seeds for my growing taste for camp and for my use of music as a space for dreaming up new selves. On the cover of *Down to Eartha* (1955), Kitt enjoys a good smoke with her trademark long Bakelite cigarette holder—the kind my sister and I liked to imitate with our candy cigarettes. She sits with her legs folded beneath her on a tiger-head rug, looking up at the camera through nylon-eyelashed eyes as if to say, "Who? Me?" Eartha's false eyelashes remind me of those of other people's mothers. When I come over to play dress-up with my friends, their houses are stylish in an unfamiliar, futuristic way, with plush white carpets and glass tables and plastic furniture. We are given old tubes of lipstick in frosted colors to play with, and pink plastic Mary Kay compacts with the dark, red blush worn down to the metal. In contrast, my own mother proudly never wears makeup, and wears her hair as a political statement, unstraightened and unbossed. Over the years I learn the natural processes of change that age makes on her skin and body, the laugh lines and freckles, the places where gravity wins. She rejects the devices that Eartha and her own mother used: wigs and eyelash curlers, foundation and foundation garments, to create her own funky, down-to-earth self. Watching my mother, I also plant the seeds of my own future rebellion, learning from her the insistence to be true to my own self. But sometimes I find myself traveling back (or is it forward?) to the land of nylon, sequins, and Bakelite. I discover in Eartha's voice, in her va-va-voom style, her own demand for liberation, something that bridges the future with the past.

Hear Eartha Kitt's "I Want to Be Evil" (1960) and listen for the echo of Zora Neal Hurston: "I love myself when I'm laughing, and then again when I'm looking mean and impressive." Hear "I want" and be pulled into the growl that some say is the purr of a kitten, but you know it is the growl of hunger barely held back, the trained muscular vibrato that starts deep in the stomach, traveling up to the throat. Hear in that "I" the shared story of a generation of black women up from the South, going about the business of remaking themselves. My grandmother, like Eartha, was one of these women, up from Waxahachie, Texas, to Chicago, like Eartha, who was up from the small town of North, South Carolina, to New York, the sulfur well water and no shoes and no daddy taunts left in that red clay dust. Hear in that "I want to be" wild yearning, homesick wanderlust, and remember those early Black Bohemians: Katherine Dunham, who trained Eartha to dance, Tommy Payne, Pearl Primus, bringing home the dances and beats, the isolations, the neck moves and the shoulder moves and full pelvic extensions from the homes that have been lost to us. Nod in recognition as Eartha whips ahead of those bongos, always anticipating the beat. (She knows that behind the mask of sweet flutes and Cole Porter jazz-wit are the ghosts of Africa: Chano Pozo, Cal Tjader, Afro-Latin jazz, the white-taped fingertips popping the tightly stretched skin of the drum.) Say it with me, "evil," and fully enjoy the stretch of lips into an almost smile, the soft scrape of teeth over lip, and then the roll of the tongue. Enjoy that tongue, stretch it out, and let it lick from the roof of your mouth to your lip. Love the pleasure of words, of "e-nun-ciation," of the mastery of the English language enjoyed best by self-taught women, and I'll think of my grandmother with her *Reader's Digest* books and dog-eared *Webster's* dictionary, beating us all at *Jeopardy.* Think of the secret pleasures of a southern accent that has been set aside, to be returned to when gossiping with a friend from down home, or the "Hey, now!" when your favorite Louis Armstrong tune comes on, or the cry of triumph with a winning hand of bid whist. Whisper with Eartha when she slips into "bahd" and "Nevah been kissed"—push that extra "ah" into it, and learn what she has learned, that "talking proper" is a hoax, or at best, a strategy that can win you a job, a role, a fight. This spirit will be a bridge to keep the selves united.

My own grandmother, Gwen, Eartha's contemporary, fought hard to be seen as proper and respectable. Moving to Chicago as a teen in the 1930s from Waxahachie, Texas, she had wanted to be a doctor, but was told by her teachers that she didn't have the physical strength to work a doctor's long hours. So, ironically, she cleaned houses, sometimes juggling two households at a time, mopping, scrubbing, and lifting for sometimes ten hours at a time, and later worked as a janitor for the Chicago public schools. She bragged that she could wring a rag so tight that it would tear in her hands. In summers, she'd clean out three floors of students' lockers, and would take home, clean, and "liberate" (she called it) what was left—hordes of abandoned dictionaries, pencils, notebooks, book bags, knit caps and scarves—to us, her grandchildren. She raised six children and on the side read science textbooks and *Gray's Anatomy* and medical prescription guides that she found in the student lockers or collected from used bookstores. Like Kitt, she also rebelled against her circumstances, expressing herself through extreme domestic arts: elaborately themed birthday parties squeezed out of paltry paychecks and food stamps; and slinky homemade dresses fashioned after Jackie O, and later, Lola Falana and Eartha herself. Her holiday dinners sometimes featured weirdly Dickensian experiments: a goose outfitted with white paper socks, plum puddings, or rabbit or venison, along with the traditional turkey and chitlins'. Fueling these heroic efforts at making a way out of no way was rage, which would sometimes be manifest in the form of drinking, and sometimes through the mask of bitingly sarcastic humor and commentary. "Don't try to be too hip," she'd warn us, "'cause you know what two hips make."

Kitt's "I Want to Be Evil" takes pleasure in the desire to be naughty, while also exposing this naughtiness as a fantasy, a mask, a code for something else that's harder to say. The speaker of the song is a contemporary working girl of the advertising age, at home with Ivory Soap and Rheingold beer, but always watched by the (white) eye of respectability. Most of her fantasies of revenge are laughingly toothless: throwing mud pies, stepping on folks' feet at the theater. But behind the coquettish opening rap, breathy and bored, the theatrically rolled *rrrr*s, there's the burst of laughter, head thrown back, teeth gleaming; there is a knowing, a full-on critique of washed out, prim and proper respectability, available for anyone able and willing to keep up. (Once she gets going, she can't be bothered to wait.) Eartha works us, spits out kitsch like she's spitting tacks, working those hard *t*s of "brilliant" and "sweetness" and "nasty." But we hear shadows in her lowering pitch. Coating the back of her throat, coloring her notes, is the phlegm of fury, disguised by speed. She alludes to the "dark brown mood" of the working world, too.

There are many kinds of work for this generation of women up from the South, with hopes of moving from cotton picker to chorus girl, from taking in wash to mopping up floors after hours at the Sears and Roebuck, or sometimes just from cleaning up other people's messes in Waxahachie to cleaning up other people's messes in Wilmette, Illinois. Inflicting her words with bite and a question, sometimes shouting them, letting the questions linger in this song, Eartha lets us know that there are many meanings of "work," and sometimes the demand for work of a particular and all too familiar kind from a high yellow gal translates from South to North, too. Eartha's so-called unreadable skin and voice have brought her to New York, and to Paris, and to Turkey and Leningrad, have delivered champagne and furs and jewels and a secret lover— the heir to an old money fortune, as well as a legendary bite on the ear by Orson Welles. My grandmother's unreadable skin gave her a seat in an otherwise all-white elementary school, and later, three darker-skinned husbands and six children of a rainbow of hues.

Kitt sings for herself and for a generation of black women. If we are lucky, those women might tell us more of what "I Want to Be Evil" only suggests: if we can make it backstage, to watch them remove the tight pumps from their worn-out feet, aching from dancing, or maybe waiting tables or scrubbing floors, they might let us in close enough to smell the undertow of bourbon in their sweat, or my grandmother's drink of choice, Fresca and Seagram's gin. But if not, we should listen out for the suggestion of bitterness, cut with neck-popping swing and the mocking shimmy come-on. Caught in time in this song, cynicism hasn't yet settled in her skin, hasn't atrophied her muscles, so when Eartha lets loose her final note and smiles her gleaming smile of satisfaction, she is still flexible, buoyant, becoming.

*

Singer, dancer, performer on film, television, and stage, and original writer of four autobiographies, Eartha Kitt was a multimedia performer— one of the first black celebrities, and one who, performing until the age of eighty-one, had an amazing capacity to reinvent herself. The title of the final book—*Rejuvenate! It's Never Too Late* (2001)—is emblematic of her ability to shape-shift and resuscitate her career. As a performer who continued to survive and thrive from the period of black migration from South to North in the 1930s through the Post-Soul moment of the late 1970s and into the twenty-first century, Kitt's often mythic and highly theatrical presentations of self produce a sometimes slippery, embodied

archive of racial, sexual, and gender "strangeness" that became an important resource for performers and audiences of the Post-Soul generation.

Kitt *is* strange, particularly in her oddly seductive, nasally voice,
which shifts unpredictably between accent, in her angular face, which
eventually softens into grace as she enters her eighties, and especially in
her stare, which seems to say less "come hither" than "Get over here!"
But Kitt is also strange in her very public explosion of mid-twentieth-
century community standards of American black femininity—as both
subject and object of sexual desire and need, in her insistence on professionalism and unabashed ambition, and on her political outspokenness.
In Farah Jasmine Griffin's analysis of narratives of African American
identity during the black migration from South to North, *"Who Set You
Flowin'": The African-American Migration Narrative,* she talks about the
importance of the "stranger" for emerging black identities in the twentieth century—a figure sometimes in opposition to the "ancestor"—who
offers a cosmopolitan alternative, a space outside of the everyday struggles of assimilation, a figure on the border. Griffin draws from the work
of sociologist Robert Park, whose theories suggest that human migration
produces a new personality, both emancipated and marginal.

> According to [Robert] Park, for this character type, "energies that
> were formerly controlled by custom and tradition are released. . . .
> [Such persons] become . . . not merely emancipated, but enlight-
> ened. . . . The emancipated individual invariably becomes in a cer-
> tain sense and to a certain degree cosmopolitan. He learns to look
> upon the world in which he was born and bred with something of
> the detachment of a stranger."[1]

Might Kitt have served, for all of the fans who saw her photos on the
walls of black barbershops and beauty salons in the 1950s and 1960s, or
who watched her on borrowed or newly purchased television sets and
at the movies, as the stranger who defied the borders of their own experiences—a sign of not-quite-yet-achieved freedom on the one end, and
scandal and exile on the other? And might she, in turn, serve as a prototype for the Post-Soul generation that followed, offering a recipe for how
to become a willful exile, leaving home, crossing racial, sexual, national,
or class borders to create something resistant, something beyond assimilation? As a part of the black migration herself, Kitt's experiences as a
celebrity and a black woman are both exemplary and eccentric, subject

to the constraints of institutionalized racism and sexism, while at other times seemingly able to resist and transform them.

Eartha Kitt's longevity as a performer, her fifty-year career spanning the 1950s through 2008, gives us the chance to view the shifts in the ways that odd or eccentric black performers are read and received over the course of the mid- through the end of the twentieth century. She was one of the first successful black performers associated with the turn of interest in African diasporic folk dance and music, performing with anthropologist Katherine Dunham's dance troupe at age sixteen, and traveling internationally with the troupe to Mexico, South America, and Europe. Kitt's internationalism would become one of her trademarks, and she would record multilingual hits with RCA records in the 1960s, including "C'est Si Bon," "Urska Dursa," and "Angelitos Negros."

Kitt is an important icon of contrariness and pleasure—a key, if often unnoted, source of inspiration for the formation of a queer black feminist sensibility seen in commercial and pop sources emerging in the early 1980s and 1990s. We might hear echoes of Kitt's sex-kittenish claim for sexual and economic control (in "Let's Do It," "Santa Baby," "Diamonds Are a Girl's Best Friend," "Love for Sale," and "All I Want Is All There Is and Then Some") in Grace Jones's demands for sexual satisfaction in "Pull Up to the Bumper." And her commitment to campy humor and visual outrageousness—showcased most provocatively in her role as Catwoman on the television show *Batman* in 1966–67—has echoes in George Clinton's sartorial outrageousness in his and Parliament/Funkadelic's stage shows. Kitt would later become a Post-Soul queer icon as an outspoken advocate for gay rights and same-sex marriage. Her disco hit, "I Want My Man," her first gold record, and her collaborations with Bronski Beat became part of the soundtrack of the New York gay club scene. She participated in multiple benefits for HIV/AIDS research, and she was widely imitated in local drag scenes. Her long-running cabaret show at the Café Carlyle became a mainstay of New York nightlife for fans, tourists, and connoisseurs of kitsch, performing there regularly until her death on Christmas Day, 2008, at the age of eighty-one.

At the same time, Kitt's performance of pleasure often includes the tinge of regret, pain, and loss that might well be informed by living through a period of transition in terms of sexual and racial politics and freedoms. Indeed, I choose to focus on Eartha Kitt as an example of a Post-Soul precursor not only because she was controversial and theatrical but because she uses her body in her performances as a sign of the cost of wrestling with racial and gender norms. I hear manifest in her sound, as well as in her stagecraft, the costs of the contradictory desires for recognition and freedom.

Even in the heat of her greatest acclaim, Kitt was often a figure of controversy. She was publicly reprimanded for lewd lyrics and dancing,[2] tailed by the FBI and the tabloids in connection with her romances with powerful white men like movie theater CEO Andrew Loew and make-up magnate Charles Revson,[3] and accused of not being black enough in her style and dating choices by the black press. Some of her early reviews in the black press see her as overly polished, calculating, and lacking "soul." In a May 1954 issue of the *Chicago Defender,* reporters George Daniels and Robert Elliot debated whether Kitt was merely a "stylist," basing her performance on sex appeal, or a soulful singer with the promised longevity of Ella Fitzgerald or Nat King Cole. The story was so popular that the debate opened into a larger one involving reader letters the following week. One *Defender* reader, a Miss Morris, wrote that "'Eartha must still meet the test when public taste changes. And when she does, John Q. Public will give the answer. Until then, there are those who like kittens and those who don't.'"[4]

Kitt took outspoken and often complicated political stands that often kept her stranded between groups. For example, her 1968 public criticism of the Vietnam War at a luncheon given by first lady Claudia "Lady Bird" Johnson gained the praise of Martin Luther King Jr., Jackie Robinson, and the Black Panthers, but others in the black community suspected her of staging a publicity stunt.[5] Many in the white press critiqued her as "brash," "rude," and unpatriotic. The *New York Times* ran two days' worth of letters for and against her, in which Lady Bird was often portrayed as Kitt's "victim."[6] She was blacklisted from performing as a result of this scandal and could not find work in the United States until 1974. In the early 1970s, when Kitt joined a handful of other black entertainers to perform in South Africa in the face of apartheid, she angered many in the black community.[7] When she returned, and denounced the racism she experienced in South Africa, she received a chilly reception from the black community.

Kitt provides a vocabulary for understanding the generation of eccentric black performers that follow her precisely in the ways that she makes her audience uneasy, and her embodiment and artistic exploration of that dis-ease within the space of celebrity. In addition to her political outspokenness, it might well be her theatricality of style that makes her audience uneasy, particularly in the ways that theatricality has historically been associated with excess, dissemblance, and lack of truthful representation—traits often attached to the feminine.[8] She, like Grace Jones, Michael Jackson, and others, explores what it feels like to be a "problem," suavely using not only her music but other forms of public performance, including interviews, political appearances, and most significantly her autobiographies, as a form of "blaxploration." Kitt, then, is an important model for the ways that black eccentric celebrities push and blur the boundaries of public and private, particularly in terms of sexism and racism.

Kitt's complex persona challenged norms of ideal black womanhood and black authenticity circulating in the 1950s, 1960s and 1970s and into the twenty-first century. To highlight Kitt's eccentric take on codes of black female respectability, we might contrast her performance of black femininity with those of two of her contemporaries: Lena Horne and Diahann Carroll. Horne and Carroll, actor-singers like Kitt, were highly visible, glamorous, and successful black entertainers in a period of tenuous racial integration in Hollywood, all beginning their careers in the early 1950s and continuing long career paths through the twenty-first century. (Indeed, Kitt and Horne often crossed paths and competed for the same roles in the 1950s.) In contrast to Kitt's aggressive, even predatory performances of female sexuality, Horne's and Carroll's dominant onstage and offstage images most often signified gentility, achievement, sexual restraint, and socially approved class mobility—respectable images of black womanhood.[9] Horne was cast as elegant ingenue (in *Stormy Weather*), a goddess (as Glenda the Good in *The Wiz*), or herself—a little bit of both! (in *Meet Me in Las Vegas* and other films); Carroll's roles included the less rambunctious friend to Dorothy Dandridge in *Carmen Jones*, fashion model (in *No Strings*), widowed nurse (in her TV show *Julia*), hardworking single mother (in *Julia* and *Claudine*), and eventually corporate magnate (as Dominique Devereax in *Dynasty*). In contrast, Kitt was often cast in roles associated with the sexual underground: prostitute (*Anna Lucasta*), nightclub performer (*St. Louis Blues*), cat burglar (*Batman*), and comic aging seductress (*Boomerang*). Think, too, of the differences in their voices and performance styles: Horne's warm, southern melodiousness and Carroll's clipped northern properness versus Kitt's oddly unpredictable vocal rhythms, "placeless" voice, and scratchy, nasally growls. Rather than taking roles that would reflect respectability for black women, Kitt took roles of the outcast. And within the small circle of other black female celebrities during this period of high scrutiny, she also stands out for the ways that her private life was often as much the subject of audience interest as her public one. Yet despite these differences in image, Carroll, Horne, and Kitt all struggled with the backhanded racial tactics of a still segregated Hollywood, and fought hard for their roles.

The Body and Its Secrets: Performing Racial Melancholy and Racial Shame

In Kitt's autobiographical narratives she takes as her subject her experience of exile within her own community as a "yella gal" and bastard child. These stories present a complex picture of black identity and community disunity in these years before the Post-Soul moment. She sheds light on her celebrity as a situation of both possibility and constraint, as she negotiates ongoing strictures of racism, and emerging standards of sexual respectability and authenticity. Kitt's experiences of tension, conflict, and grief, as well as her embrace of cosmopolitanism and "homelessness" in the quest to remake herself, serve as examples of the disidentification that is important to Post-Soul identity.[10] In Anne Anlin Cheng's pivotal study *The Melancholy of Race,* she discusses how the experience of racism creates patterns of grief that are often repressed, and reformed into a kind of melancholia—mourning usually banished below the surface of narratives about self and community.

Cheng uses Freud's melancholia to explore two important aspects of American racial construction: dominant white society's attraction/repulsion to the racial other and the ramifications of that paradoxical relationship that white society has for the racial other, placing the other in a suspected formation of self.[11] Such mourning processes can become the stuff of imaginative production, including performance. As Cheng suggests, "Even as racism actualizes itself through legal and social sanctions, it is animated through imaginative procedures."[12] Kitt presents her life as one of racial melancholia—and this melancholy in turn informs the tense, high-energy contrariness of her performance aesthetic. At the same time, we might think of her impulse to write and continue to rewrite her life and her documentation of her process of interpolation into racial, gender, and sexuality schemes, as well as her disidentification of it, as a form of theorization that is repeated and developed in her theatrical performance style: her denaturalized vocalizations and her pushing of her body and gestures into the extremes of gendered and racialized gestures.[13]

Following Audre Lorde's invention of biomythography as a new form of autobiography that allows for the melding of autobiography, history, and myth, Kitt aptly captures the yearning to reinvent a racial self, while at the same time dramatizing with explicit and sensual language the traumas of racial and sexual violence that led her to that point. And most important, in her drama of self-invention she implicates both black and white participants in the violence she suffers. While her autobiographies document a clear understanding of the institutionalization of white racism and the life-and-death impact of those institutions on her life, she is careful to also show how the black community has internalized these same racist hierarchies. She refuses innocence for herself and others, all the while reminding her readers, black and white, of the psychic costs of reinventing a racial self. In Kitt's autobiographies, we might see in action "interior patterns of grief and how they both constrain and are constrained by subjectivity. . . . How a racially impugned person processes the experience of denigration exposes a continuous interaction between sociality and privacy, history and presence, politics and ontology."[14]

If the body is a key site of racism and racial surveillance, through skin, hair texture, gesture, and movement, then it is also the container for racialized grief, and the drama of racial mourning. But bodily performance—onstage, in recorded song and film, and as recalled through written narrative—are powerful examples of the ways that the grief and shame of racism can be animated, and perhaps exorcised, through art. Kitt reclaims the body and its difficult knowledge in her autobiography as she does in live and recorded performance. In the same ways that Kitt's stage performances present an aesthetics of contrariety in the face of stifling norms of black female sexuality, her autobiographies chart the ways that racial and sexual oppression are experienced bodily in unpredictable ways. She takes the dual images of the black woman as "earthy"—southern plantation born, grounded in her body and nature—and as the exotic—the body reinvented, the fantastic body from "elsewhere"—and exposes the process of the formation of these identities in a shared history. Kitt's performances are powerful and perhaps also shameful to some in her audience—because of the wounds that they potentially open, reminders of the melancholic state of the racial other—here, black women. This shame might be one factor to account for the criticism and sometimes suspicion that Kitt faced from many in the black community. Kitt takes on the drama of black female shame through satire, as well as the direct tactics of naming and protest.

In her autobiographies, Kitt presents her racial and sexual formation as one marked by interlinked racial violence and sexual abuse. In the process, she performs a deessentialization of the process of racialization, reminding us of the structures of power in play. In a story that becomes more clear over the successive accounts of her life, Kitt was born in North, South Carolina, in 1927, the product of a rape of her mother Anna Mae by the white son of the owner of the plantation in which all of her family labored. The very circumstances of her conception—a rape whose secret is reinforced by the unequal power of white over black, owner over worker—are a repeated pattern in the shared history of black people in the United States, even as the shame and exile that she and her mother suffered in her family as a result made this act seem exceptional to her young self. This shame haunted Kitt throughout her life, and fueled her struggle for achievement and acceptance, adding an undertow of melancholy to the image of sexual experience and worldliness that she projected in her performances.

The violence is then reperpetuated by family members, who ostracize Kitt, her mother, and her sister, leaving them out of the circle of community. This act of violence not only marks Kitt racially—as "yella gal"—but also, it is implied, as sexual outsider, the inheritor of her mother's supposed sin. Kitt, her mother, and her half sister are left homeless and hungry, sleeping in fields and neighbors' yards. Eventually, Kitt's mother finds another lover, a black man, and she and Kitt's half sister, Pearl, move in with him on the condition that she leave Kitt's raising to others. (The lover tells her mother that Kitt's light skin will create contention and competition between his own children.) Kitt moves in with a neighbor, Mrs. Stern, who treats her like a servant and outsider, often punishing her for eating too much. Her position as outsider and scapegoat in this household leaves her vulnerable to teasing, beatings, and molestation by Stern's children. The rough treatment that she receives from the black community because of her lighter skin dramatizes the continuation of the dynamics of slavery, and the internalization of racial hierarchies within the black community. As Kwakiutl Dreher suggests, "Kitt informs us of an ominous post-slavery color hierarchy breeding abandonment, molestation, and abuse."[15] At the same time, Kitt's childhood of abandonment becomes an important staging point for her reclamation of a new, self-made, racial and sexual identity.

It is through Kitt's reclamation of embodied knowledge and voice denied her mother, that she counters the racial and sexual expectations that bind her. In the opening chapters of *Thursday's Child* (1956), I am astounded by her eloquent and frank descriptions of her sensual awareness as a child, and the ways that the codes of racism shape this knowledge. Kitt presents herself as being at home in the natural world, seeking solace and nurture from the sky, trees, and earth when her family and community fail her. Ultimately, her body becomes the source of knowledge when social bonds fail her. Bodily knowledge—pleasure and pain—shapes the memories that ultimately allow Kitt to understand how the community sees her body, and eventually allows her to assess and intervene in it. She begins *Thursday's Child* with her first experience of exile—reconstructed through the sense memory of a child.

> The wheat began to sway in the evening breeze and the cotton stood still and glared out at me with bulging eyes as we walked the narrow road through the fields.
>
> I couldn't figure out why we were way out here so late or where we had come from or where we were going. I wanted to ask Mama, but I was afraid I would get her annoyed. Mama heaved a sigh as she adjusted Pearl in her arms. She looked down at me with wet eyes and stroked my long bushy brown hair. Something did not rest right in me—I felt as though I had done something and was going to get a whipping for it, but I couldn't remember what it was.[16]

Kitt's encounters with nature here help her eventually to name what can't be said: the bulging eyes of the cotton speak to the suspicion with which her uncle and neighbors regard her as they seek shelter. And her awareness of the bushiness of her own hair shows her growing sense of difference from others, the ways that her body, skin color, and hair are seen by others as signs of the rape and shame that her mother has experienced. In her description of feeling like she's going to be punished, but without knowing why, we see the effects of internalized racism and shame.

At the same time as Kitt's sense of the world is marred by sexual and racialized violence, she insists on the importance of pleasure and sensuality as a means of survival. Kitt claims and discusses the development of childhood sexuality in the face of violence, complicating the image of black female sexuality as purely procreative and victimized. In the following passage from *Thursday's Child,* Kitt describes running away from the constant hard work and the surveillance of her guardians to find solace in a sandbank. Kitt's body becomes a resource, a place of self-soothing and pleasure in the face of the racism of her community.

> I was absolutely alone in a road that was pure white sand. I stopped to play for a while in the silvery, soft ground. I remember the place distinctly. It was on the edge of the pine forest. On one side of the road we had a patch of watermelon. At the edge of the melon patch was an old well. As I sat in this spot of glowing sand, I picked up a handful of dirt and licked it out of my hands like sugar. It became damp with the saliva in my mouth and seeped its way down my throat like honey. I sat crumbled up on my knees in the softness and gloated in the discovery of a new and different pleasure. I could smell the rain and the wonderful dust that is in the air before a rainstorm.

Kitt links her hunger for sand to the scarcity of food. Yet on some level she leaves her desire unaccounted for as pure pleasure—unattached to a particularized need or object—floatingly queer.

> A few days later, as my sister and I were playing in a ditch, I discovered an even newer pleasure, the taste of clay—red, yellow, purple, all the colors in the rainbow, all had that same rainy taste. Whenever I was alone, I would combine my secret feasts, and for dessert I'd suck my tongue and feel the middles of my breasts.[17]

This passage is a powerful model of self-soothing, but also transformation: sand becomes honey. Even in the face of starvation, Kitt claims the right to hungers that go beyond necessity. Pleasure and awareness of her body become the site for survival and self-assertion. As I'll discuss later, Kitt's "odd" or outlandish expression of hunger will become an important aspect of her performance style, and will become the embodiment of the tensions in her life between insider and outsider.

But Kitt's childhood expressions of desire are never uncomplicated. She represents her experience of her body as mediated by racial and sexual shame projected by her guardian, Mrs. Stern, who always reminds her of her precarious position in the household, and, by extension, her link to her mother's rape. Kitt writes:

> I'd hide behind the house, run my hand inside my shirt, and feel the centers of my breasts. At my age there was nothing there of course, but I wanted there to be. It seemed perfectly natural and harmless to me, but the Stern woman apparently thought it to be a sign of evil. I thought it no worse than eating sweet potatoes from the garden—for which I also got a sound beating.[18]

Kitt's insistence on her own pleasure in her body is in contrast with the sexualized violence that she experiences at the hands of her cousins, Mrs. Stern's teenage children, Willie and Grace. Indeed, it will take Kitt all three autobiographies to be able to name explicitly the sexual assault that she experiences at the hands of the Stern children. This reflects a shift in terms of the respectability of naming sexual abuse, especially the loosening of taboos of naming sexual abuse from within the black community. Kitt further complicates the issue of sexual abuse by linking it to her space on the margins of her family because of her light skin.

> "Eartha Mae, come here, let me see what you look like. Pick up your rags," he said, "More!" As the private parts of my tiny body became exposed . . . [Gracie and Willie] started laughing: "Damn, you're yella all over, ain't cha? Turn around," Willie suddenly said. As my body turned, the switch came across my backside with a sting that would make the devil cringe. I gritted my teeth.[19]

Kitt describes being assaulted by the Stern girl, who forcibly penetrates her with a dildo made from rags. The assault is interrupted by the return of adults, and this act is never repeated or spoken of again. Through this event, Kitt exposes the hypocrisy of the Sterns' self-appointed role as keepers of standards of racial and sexual purity. Kitt will continue to critique and expose other examples of such hypocrisy over the course of her career.

The experience of sexual exploitation and violence is important throughout Kitt's autobiographies, and we see that it is something she never escapes, even as she moves to New York, even as she flees the United States for Paris, London, and Istanbul. She tells of multiple violent encounters in part connected to her path as a woman who is trying to find her own sexual destiny. As a teen, a gang in New York kidnaps her and harasses her because she won't be the leader's "girl," ending in her nearly being pushed in front of a train. Later, in her travels as a dancer in Katherine Dunham's troupe, she and a friend are assaulted by two men. The autobiographies are rife with examples of racial and sexual harassment and abuse by lovers and fans. These examples become part of the fabric of Kitt's life and quest for sexual freedom, as well as artistic recognition. Kitt's identity as black and female informs her experience of both desire and violence.

Kitt doesn't limit herself to exploring the South as the place of sexual exploitation; indeed, her narrative shows the pervasiveness of sexual exploitation for black women. In many ways, the CIA's surveillance of Kitt in the 1960s is another form of sexual violation. It is clear from the language of the file that her sexual privacy has been violated, that she has been watched and then castigated for her quest for sexual freedom. The file accuses her of leading a "lurid sex life" and exhibiting "loose morals" and "sadistic nymphomania."[20] Kitt uses the opportunity of the autobiography to name the investigation as abuse, dedicating an entire chapter to the files in *Alone with Me*, and opening her acknowledgments with a slam against the CIA, which "should leave the writing of fiction to authors who don't write it at the taxpayer's expense."[21]

Kitt's insistence on using her autobiographies as a form of resistance—sometimes through humor, sometimes through the use of precise detail—is a key component of her complication of her public persona as black "sex kitten." While she coyly subtitles her autobiography *Still Here* as *Confessions of a Sex Kitten*, the autobiography offers a serious disavowal of this rather shallow description. An important legacy that Kitt offers to her Post-Soul kindred is her exploration and then refusal of shame, and her spirit of sexual resistance against the grain of the norms of other celebrities of the period.

Another important way that Kitt dramatizes the melancholy of racism is her complex relationship with the white gaze. Formative is Kitt's first and only encounter with the white man who was her father.

In my first or second year at the Stern house, I saw my father for the first and last time. I was behind the house by myself, as usual, when I noticed a white man leave the nearby road and trudge across the field toward me. I don't remember what I thought at his approach. Not fear. Perhaps curiosity. I was sitting on the ground

in the sun, my legs tucked beneath me, and I remember his paus-
ing, towering above me for a second and blocking the sun, before
he crouched slightly and gently cupped my face in his hand and
turned my face up to him. He studied my face for what seemed
like a full minute or two; then he turned, walked back across the
field to the road, and was gone.[22]

The white man's appearance and power to block out the sun is like a
planet. His attention, at once gentle and acquisitive, is curious to her in
its combination of intimacy and distance. Whiteness here is powerful
and inscrutable; distant, yet claiming its own undisputed right to touch
and possess. This scene echoes several other moments in the autobiographies where Kitt finds herself measured and assessed by the white gaze,
and where she responds with the need to justify her own humanity and
worth. Several decades later, at a club performance in London, she over-
hears a table of white men debating her racial origins and her beauty.

> "She is beautiful."
> "I wonder what nationality she is?"
> "She must be from Indonesia."
> "Ah, she's nothing but a nigger."[23]

Kitt is horrified and embarrassed. She finishes her set and then runs to
her dressing room. Eventually, her white manager convinces her to return to the stage. Not only does she complete the performance, but she
decides that she will charm the men. She allows them to wine and dine
her "until the wee hours of the morning," and even lets one of them es-
cort her home. Before parting, she turns to him and asks, "Now do you
think I am 'just a nigger'?" She boasts that her words are rewarded with
flowers the next day.[24]

On the one hand, Kitt describes the white gaze as controlling, and
often linked to violence. On the other, Kitt negotiates the need for white
approval and regard, even when the price of assimilation to standards of
whiteness proves to be a double-edged sword. She takes pride in her ability to speak to and reach multiple audiences, yet she depicts her growing
regard by a white fan public as arbitrary, and ready to turn on her. Kitt
describes many moments of compromise and negotiation in the face of
white supremacy. When told by her Jewish landlord that she must move
out of her New York apartment because they don't rent to blacks, Kitt
has other friends rent the apartment for her, in their name. When she

travels to South Africa in 1974, performing despite a boycott by other black intellectuals and artists, she engages in a series of acts of subtle protest: she takes her daughter to a whites-only amusement park; she causes a scandal by sitting on the lap of a white man in her audience; and she performs a number during which white audience members are invited to drink from her own personal bottle of champagne, breaking South African law.[25] Kitt simultaneously offers a critique of white institutions of power and describes and reflects on her own assimilation. This may give both white and nonwhite readers the chance to face their own racial shame.

Kitt's depiction of an unpredictable pattern of cruelty and sometimes arbitrary reward by whites is further complicated by moments of black betrayal and rejection. She recalls being punished for being late for school by her black teacher after she is attacked by the white kids, "the sting . . . sharp, leaving wide red marks where the blood had come to the surface, giving me visible evidence of another form of meanness."[26] Later, as her career gets under way, Kitt confesses to not being fully accepted by her black fans for her recordings because of her singing style and choice of material: "[T]he black people said, 'Oh, she thinks she's white,' which is ironic seeing as they accepted Elvis thinking he was black, until they saw his photograph on his records. I was accepted by the whites, the international whites, but it took some twenty years on the American scene before I was accepted by the blacks."[27]

Kitt's repeated public insistence that as a mixed race person she is "someone essentially without a race," as she puts it later, in an interview near the end of her life, anticipates recent and ongoing debates about "Post-Black" identity,[28] at the same time that she repeatedly publicly defends her loyalty to the black community.[29] In *Still Here,* Kitt writes about her first travels to Europe and how seeing the physical devastation of World War II helped her to better understand her place in a world of racial hate, from the perspective of someone "in between."

> Confusion and more confusion. Germany against the Jews—no place for them to rest their heads, no place for blacks to rest their heads. Is the whole world only for whites? And what about those of us who are in between, neither white nor black? My childhood experiences flowed through me. The more I saw of blitzed London, the more curious and confused I became. Where and to whom do I belong? Here? There? Everywhere? Nowhere?[30]

Kitt's self-conscious and often futuristic performance of her own racial identity as always in formation makes her an important figure in the history of black identity as "performed."

Throughout her autobiographies, Eartha Kitt conveys her experience of racism as an embodied experience in which loyalties are unclear and power can be unpredictable, irrational, and harsh. She exposes the painful moments of black and white community exile and rejection. That she doesn't leave out the cruelty of the other black children, as well as that of white racists, shows her willingness not to leave out the messiness of human experience, and seems part of her overall value of contrariness as a form of truth telling.

If, as Farah Jasmine Griffin suggests, the black South is figured in migration narratives as a place of pain, as well as a source of home,[31] for Kitt, the South stands for sexual pain and rejection that never becomes the source of a comfortable nostalgia. Kitt eventually finds community elsewhere, moving outside of the black community, but always circling back to reflect on the meanings of blackness in these new contexts: first through white friends and teachers at the School for Performing Arts in New York City, then movement to various diasporas through Katherine Dunham, and then through her travels to Europe, Greece, South Africa, and India. She returns to the South through her autobiographies, yet also claiming a more cosmopolitan self.

Kitt's response to the melancholy of racism, I'd argue, is precisely in the methods of disidentification and contrariness that we see as being central to Post-Soul performance. At times she is brutally frank and explicit about the everyday violence of racism; at other times she negotiates this pain through strategies of distancing, masking, and contrariness. Kitt's public performance of self, her shifting of accent, her performance of polyglot European sophistication on- and offstage, her severing of familial ties, might seem to be turning her back on the past. Yet, as I'll discuss below, Kitt's performance style embodies this struggle and tension in its very strangeness.

From Eartha Mae to Stranger: Sounding Strange

Kitt's success as a "stranger" for her black audiences, as well as for her larger audiences, is in part due to the ways that she presents her marginal identity as a point of tension, always still "in formation" or becoming.

Rather than suppressing the psychic costs of racial reinvention, she self-consciously embodies them, so that we hear this tension in her voice, in her movements, as well as in the palpable presence of anger in her writing.

Despite her cool persona, in her biographies and interviews, Kitt repeatedly represents herself as split between stranger, "Eartha Kitt," and home girl, "Eartha Mae"—the bastard child, the homeless "yella gal."

> My child is Eartha Mae: ugly, unloved, unworthy, and therefore a loner. The adult I've molded is Eartha Kitt: self-reliant, afraid of nothing, even defiant. Ironically, I think of Eartha Kitt as practically nothing. True. She is so far removed from the basic nature of Eartha Mae that I can—and do—think of her in the third person. She's she, not me. She's a name on a marquee. I'm curiously detached from her and yet suspended within her and totally dependent on her for my survival.[32]

Kitt's constant negotiation between black southern experience and pain and the demands of reinvention through celebrity informs her analysis of the social construction of blackness and the pressure placed on that blackness as it travels outside of home, as is evident in her writings and the performances themselves. It is the element that both keeps Kitt from ever fully being at home, or at rest—a shimmering energy that takes the form in her embodied performances of a kind of desire.

Perhaps it is this restlessness that critics hear when they call Kitt's performances "volatile," "combustible," and "incandescent." Certainly, there is something in Kitt's performance of sexual desire that has always been unsettling. As Kitt matures as a performer, she taps into the subversive potential of this restless homeless energy, converting it into a form of pleasure —and sometimes disruption and discomfort—for herself and her audience. *Los Angeles Times* pop music reviewer Dennis Hunt describes Kitt's stage persona as "an unpredictable, erotic temptress capable of romance, passion, humor, even aggression."[33] Critic John L. Scott describes one live performance of Kitt's that seems to border on sadism in its coolly punishing control of affect.

> As an entertainer Eartha Kitt remains the sex symbol, but her visual and vocal projection are so cool and her mannerisms so stylized that one begins to wonder whether she's putting her audience

on. . . . Regulars in the capacity first-night audience responded to her tactics enthusiastically, but I'm afraid newcomers to her art (or is it artifice?) never quite caught up with her. During one number she stopped singing and stared at the ringleader for an entire chorus, a ploy that convulsed some listeners and confused others. . . . She also danced in a quite remarkable fashion, seeming to move without much motion. In other words she has an almost perfect control of her body.[34]

Kitt has created a persona that is at once highly sexualized and closed, specifically rooted in the history of migration, and the epitome of the achieved ideal of assimilation: the stranger. Indeed, in *Alone with Me*, Kitt claims as her particular power, her "strange influence" over her audience, that of being mysterious, her disorientation from a particular time and place. She characterizes her voice as "placeless"—the expression of her distance from her black southern past, or more important, to a particular people or community.

I don't remember ever having a Southern accent. I don't remember speaking any differently from the way I do today—which someone once described to me as Continental, a British accent with American and French influence. How I could possibly learned this from South Carolina and Harlem is totally a mystery to me, as mysterious as that strange influence I had over my classroom and assembly audiences.[35]

Kitt's "rootless" voice, and cosmopolitan choice of homes and lyrics, becomes an important point of tension for both her black and white audiences. Yet the voice itself, in its strangeness and theatricality, embodies rather than erases the drama of reinvention. Kitt's voice becomes the site for yearning for another place and self, quavering between the familiar and the unexpected.

But like the other eccentrics discussed in this book, Kitt's masked distance is only part of the equation of her performances. Her ability to whip back and forth between the familiar and strange, restless desire and pleasure, emotional access and control, keeps her audience at full attention, while still keeping them at bay, sometimes making them squirm. Often her songs include a kind of build from slow to fast, cool to hot, distanced to connected, by means of a penetrating stare. This highly theatrical style itself mimics the construction of "Eartha Kitt" that she self-consciously deconstructs in her autobiographies: a polished, sophisticated, mediated self, under which lurks her "soul," signified by her blackness and her southern roots.

We see Kitt's performance of contrariety at work in *St. Louis Blues,* the 1958 film directed by Allen Reisner. The mise-en-scène is one seemingly set to highlight Kitt's contradictions between controlled and explosive, which become racialized and classed in the visual vocabulary of the film. Kitt is dressed formally and demurely in a long, white gown, white gloves, and tight, pointy-toed, white pumps. The song, "St. Louis Blues," is staged as a performance within the film, with tuxedoed symphony and an all-white audience dressed as if attending the opera. Kitt delivers the song "straight" at the beginning, making the most of her upright bearing and formal enunciation. She sings the first verse with a controlled, not quite operatic vibrato, carefully adding a hard *t* at the end of her *ain't*. Her hands are clenched, body still, eyes downcast, but in the second verse, she raises her eyes to show that they are smoldering. As the song gets to the third verse, Kitt closes her eyes, and her hands travel up to her throat—the site of vocal erotic action and feeling. Her body slowly melts into a shimmy that starts at her hips, and moves to her shoulders, traveling up to her neck and head, until by song's end her eyes pop open, and she ends in confrontation, staring bright and hard at the audience.

In the film's trailer, Kitt is billed as "The *Temptuous* Eartha Kitt" (my italics)—a conflation of her tempting and tempestuous performance. In this "St. Louis Blues" sequence Kitt provides a sense of an internal battle—between the power of maintaining a mask of control and the pleasures of losing it—that becomes a signature trademark of Kitt's delivery. The thrill of watching her slow burn in "St. Louis Blues" is both the voyeuristic pleasure of watching Kitt get hot under the collar and the subversive thrill that she has somehow infiltrated this scene of formally dressed whites and heated them up, exposing the lie of white propriety and distance. Since *St. Louis Blues* is a biographic film about blues pioneer W. C. Handy and his women, its depiction of the explosive powers of black musical performance have both intrafilmic and metafilmic significance. Kitt is both playing the wily temptress who lures Handy into the world of pleasure—and soulful musical creation—and playing herself, the temptuous Eartha Kitt, making her way into the hearts and heated-up imaginations of white and black theatergoers all over the country. She might be said to be performing Duboisian double-consciousness, the self beneath the veil. But there is also a third level of Kitt's mastery—

her ability to move between audiences *and* mediums, using her cabaret chops to master film, and creating a level of intimacy and pleasure for a multiracial audience. Here and elsewhere—as Kitt moves from kitschy cameo to serious film role, from live nightclub to record, from the *New York Times* to *Jet,* from talk show to a luncheon at the White House—we see Kitt's triple consciousness, a third layer of performance that is savvy about the mass mediation and circulation of images in a racially unequal world.

Kitt's performance of contrariety makes her an important precursor for Post-Soul performance and aesthetics. Like the other performers explored in this book, Kitt has a very theatrical and visually astute performance style—one that lends itself both to high produceability and circulation in mass culture and heart-stopping, one-of-a-kind live performances. (Think of Grace Jones's high-concept stage shows, or Michael Jackson wowing the crowd with the premier of his moonwalk on the *Motown 25: Yesterday, Today and Forever.*) She combines a high professionalism and knowledge of the business of entertainment with a perversity and willingness to turn expected codes of gender and race on their ear. Finally, she embodies the expansive musical and performance vocabulary that will be embraced by the Post-Soul generation later as cultural mulattoism.

Kitt's sound and vocal style reflect the complexity of performances of black Atlantic identity and counter more narrow conceptualizations of authentic blackness. Indeed, Kitt draws from a wide variety of black traditions and other influences: the tremulous hummingbird of a Fisk Jubilee solo, the charmed crooning of jazz icon Nat King Cole. She shares with Post-Soul singer Grace Jones the soulful, polylingual identity play of chanteuse figures like French songbird Edith Piaf and expatriate performer Josephine Baker; the shouts of both church and of musical theater; the bluesy, bent-noted wails of Bessie Smith; and, as transmogrified into rock, 1960s hipsters Grace Slick and Donovan. Likewise, Post-Soul eccentrics have a borderless approach to musical and performative influence.

In many ways, Kitt's complicating of authentic blackness is illustrated by her sound. Listening to a range of Kitt's music over the course of her career, I am struck that she is a musical magpie, picking up the brightest and juiciest—and sometimes showiest—trends in popular music. Kitt has covered and made her own virtually every pop style, from blues to Turkish folk songs, psychedelic to mellow Burt Bacharach, Duke Ellington standards to disco's Bronski Beat. Kitt makes these styles her own by pushing against expectations of performing race and gender—often turning on their heads interpretations of songs made by other, often untouchable "greats." For example, she takes Duke Ellington's jazz standard "In My Solitude," which, when covered so elegantly in the past by virtuoso Ella Fitzgerald, is delicate in its yearning movement along the scale, and instead performs it in a rough, naturalistic, almost "folk" style. She sings the song in a low register, the grain of her voice nubbly where Ella's is mellow and smooth. She extends each chord tone long, until she seems to run out of breath, sometimes wavering a little from the key. Her vibrato here is slow, and very basic, something like the folk style of 1980s performer Joan Armatrading. Her breath work in the song is audible, marking her effort. This work-song version of "Solitude"—sung as if sung alone while doing the chores outside, and seemingly unself-conscious in its inattention to vocal control—presents a rebuttal to Ella Fitzgerald's widely embraced aesthetic of beautiful jazz singing. On the other hand, she takes a more controlled and stylized approach to her cover of Donovan's "Hurdy Gurdy Man," lending it her deep, nasal, androgynous voice, and creating her own wah-wah pedal with a styled vibrato. If rock is, for many performers, the space of vocal "roughness" and seemingly off-the-cuff style, Kitt's rock voice is studied, thoughtful, even if haunting in its oddness. Kitt's contrariness becomes her signature—signally her "Kittness" in its very unpredictability.

Within this unpredictability is a tension between recognizable, historically rooted sound and a kind of iconoclastic individualism. Yet, as Brenda Dixon Gottschild notes in *Digging the Africanist Presence in American Performance*, contrariety is itself a primary premise of an Africanist aesthetic: "In a broad sense, the Africanist aesthetic can be understood as a precept of contrariety, or the encounter of opposites. The conflict inherent in and implied by difference, discord, and irregularity is encompassed, rather than erased or necessarily resolved."[36] Such aesthetic valuing in discord is key to the sounds of blues, Soul, and funk, as well in aspects like high-affect juxtaposition in dance and other forms of performance. Kitt takes this black aesthetic and expands it, applying contrariety not only to her vocal performance but also to her public performance of "self."

Conclusion: Eartha Kitt Unmasked

Though Kitt began her journey of deconstructing her stage self in the 1950s with *Thursday's Child*, it's the Post-Soul space that allows her to give full recognition to the forces of racism, sexual violence, and poverty that have haunted her and, by extension, fueled her performances. In her earlier autobiographies, she was willing to talk about internalized racism, sexism, and the patrolling of white men as financial providers—way ahead of her time. But her frankness was always with a cost: her books were often dismissed by critics as tell-alls (particularly in the white press), her sexual play was the source of scandal, and her "telling it like it is" confrontations of lockstep political and racial identities were persistently under suspicion. Like Little Richard, another contrary eccentric who is even now still receiving his due, Eartha Kitt's onstage and offstage deconstructions of her own persona and its limits are part of a Post-Soul turn.

The tensions between Kitt's highly theatrical performing style and her embodied voice in her autobiographies and interviews presents a particular style of balance between public and private exposure that we'll see taken up by other Post-Soul eccentrics. Kitt was constantly telling difficult stories, laughing at and naming her persona, and taking seriously the work of being in public while not taking herself seriously. Perhaps this is the way that she managed to stay alive for eighty-one years. This becomes clear in a 1989 appearance on a British talk show, *The Terry Wogan Show*. Kitt performs "I Want to Be Evil" in true Cruella De Vil camp fashion, and I see her scary stare, her hand as claw, her intimidating scowl and star-power legs. But she also keeps her hand on the piano player as if to keep herself steady, a quiet gesture of vulnerability. After the song, Wogan does his fried-by-the-sunlamp best to flirt, and Kitt turns up the heat, taking her stilettoed foot and resting it on Wogan's thigh, threateningly close to his crotch. But after five minutes of double entendre, this tone shifts to earnestness. Kitt begins to dismantle her invulnerable man-eater image, and suddenly the center cannot hold. Wogan watches with wonder as Kitt reveals being abused by her guardians and riding the subway back and forth all night as a homeless teenager in New York. She tells, voice breaking, of the racism and loneliness that she's faced. At first, Wogan seems nervous, then empathetic, until he finds himself talking to Eartha Mae, Kitt's down-home self. Suddenly, the space of the syndicated talk show gains intimacy and political heft. A throwaway interview becomes unforgettable.

In his 1996 essay "Cultural Politics and Black Public Intellectuals," Michael Hanchard includes Kitt in a roster of black public figures who have struggled, often in vain, to create cultural change from public roles that lack political power. While highly visible, Hanchard notes, some of the most significant figures in US African American communities—including Martin Luther King, Muhammad Ali, and Hank Aaron—haven't held public office. And while this underscores the ability of marginalized groups to make the most of spaces in the cracks of civic life, when more central roles are barred to them, these spaces in the cracks are often limited in terms of the ability they offer for direct political engagement and long-term impact, Hanchard suggests.[37] I'd like to suggest that Kitt's forty-year occupation of the public's imagination, her persistent insistence on edginess as a politicized act, must be accounted for. We must consider not only her role in terms of music, and style but her embodied rebellion against respectability. This, too, is "real" political work.

Outro: Eartha Kitt, *Live from the Café Carlyle*

Click on Eartha Kitt's *Live from the Café Carlyle* (2006) and become a part of the live audience. Forget the frustration of earphones, the hum of your air conditioner, children playing outside, the daylight from the window by your desk. Imagine your body now in darkness—knees, elbows, your white tablecloth, floating. You wait in the dark for the music to begin. The darkness gives you a sense of anonymity, but joins you with the others. You sniff whisky, cologne. Skin. The clapping tells you where the walls are, restarts time. The clapping makes her appear. Take the tiny icon of Kitt's album cover provided by iTunes and expand it. Remember all of those faces you've seen of her: as young dancer on the Paris stage with improvised thigh slit; as beatnik in black turtleneck; as Catwoman, masked and sly. As a centerfold in *Jet*. Add to this composite, Kitt's face at eighty as it appears on your screen. Imagine the conspiratorial gleam, the cocked eyebrow of Kitt looking just at you. Remember how beautiful you know black women can be as they age, rocking their crowns on Sunday. Remember watching your grandmother powdering herself, choosing her jewelry, insisting on earrings at the hospital; her care and her pleasure showed you that old age is still glamorous, the body still powerful. Still here. In the Post-Soul New York of Café Carlyle, cabarets are multiracial, queered spaces. Forget Liza in her bowler hat and think Vaginal Crème Davis and Carmelita Tropicana; think new burlesque, Kiki and Herb, and Julian Bond.[38]

As Kitt moves from song to patter, try to pinpoint her accent. One part Katherine Hepburn, one part Edith Piaf? One part Diahann Carroll, one part rolling-tongued Yul Brynner in the *King and I?* Give up. Pretend that you understand French. Feel sorry for those people who don't know what "C'est, Si Bon" means. Get seduced and code-switched from French to Swahili to Spanish and then English. "I may be 80, but I'm still hot!" she tells us.

Hear Kitt's laugh as it punctuates the end of each song and imagine how that laughter transforms her. Still here. Imagine shoulders rocking with laughter. Imagine shimmy and finger pop. Imagine laughing her laugh, growling her growl. Imagine yourself and others, a sea of black-brown-and-white-joined-shimmy, as seen from the stage. Imagine tapping your foot to the drum set's high hat.

The stage is so close you can feel the waves of heat from the lights and the musicians. You can see the horn player's steady, circular breathing, the rise and fall of his chest, the sweat on the drummer's wrists, the working of his forearms. Watch the piano player as he watches his singer; watch him cue the others with a nod to slow down the rock tempo to ballad. If Kitt rules us with her gaze, it's the band that keeps her steady, keeps her moving.

Hear Kitt's confessional whisper toward the end of the set: "I want to thank you for loving me. Because of you, I'm still here." Imagine her looking directly at you. Feel your heart leap. As she segues from "September Song" to "It Was a Very Good Year" to "Here's to Life," think a little about dying. And then admire the control of her breath and her volume. She can still shout, using the cage of her chest to hold the sound deep, then push it free. Imagine the grace of her body, and of all the parts needed for singing: stomach and spleen, diaphragm and lungs, rib cage and chest and throat. Snapping fingers, lilting tongue. Nostrils and lips and shoulders. Hips. Imagine breath and spit. Imagine her beating heart.

TWO

Stevie Wonder's "Quare" Teachings and Cross-Species Collaboration in *Journey through the Secret Life of Plants* and Other Songs

Lessons in Groove on *Sesame Street:* "Superstition" (1973)

I remember watching my father play drums in the park. Sometimes on a Saturday, he'd bring his congas and bongos out, his cowbells, his cuicas and shakares, and play for whoever wanted to come and listen. Other drummers would come, too, and they'd form a circle, and they'd play for hours, sometimes stopping to talk, or have a smoke. The music could go on and on for hours, circles of music, and sometimes women came and joined the drummers. They'd kick off their shoes and dance in front of the drummers, or take a tambourine or some sticks to keep time as they'd dance. They'd shake for us, wrapped in African cloths or the Indian blankets that they'd brought with them, and cry out, too, and that, it would seem, would make the music go on even longer. My sister Becky and I would watch my father enter the music, until he became someone else, and sometimes we'd grow afraid. He'd sweat right through the red bandana that he'd tied around his head. Sometimes he'd throw his head back, close his eyes and smile, or stare straight ahead, as if he didn't see us. But when the music ended, when the sun would go down, or when Becky and I would complain that we were getting hungry, we'd help my father pack up his drums again in their canvas cases, and he'd carry them, one on each shoulder. I'd smell his iron-sweat-smell of an athlete, and I would think that someday, I would learn to push past my everyday self and enter music like this.

This was different from listening to music at school, where we'd sometimes dance to the Folkways album of Lead Belly singing "Pick a Bale a Cotton" that my teacher brought in. We were taught to squat down and "pick" in time to the music, but we were always encouraged to keep in a neat circle, even as the music sped up.

But when I saw Stevie Wonder jamming with his band and a group of children on *Sesame Street,* I saw my own relationship to live music translated and broadcast on TV for the first time. Stevie showed us the power of live music, the power of funk, that it was okay to dance, that there was something good and right in letting it take us over.

A little after *Julia,* but before *Good Times,* right around the same time that *Soul Train* made its trip across the tracks of our minds, *Sesame Street* appeared. *Sesame Street* was a new place to expand the social horizons of kids of color, bringing aspects of black and brown life to the small screen. *Sesame Street* was radical in that it opened new worlds, at the same time that it made home lessons—the things you were sometimes discretely discouraged from remembering in school—official. Jazz, funk, and salsa infused everything, from the hallucinatory counting exercise whose animation looked like the cover of Miles Davis's *Bitches Brew* to Roosevelt Franklin's syncopated recitation of the ABCs, Roosevelt being the only Muppet with his own set of backup singers. Snippets of cinema verité joined animation, skits, and musical performance to create a collage of multiple narratives of urban realities. The stoop was a major meeting place, and so was the corner store, and the alleyways between buildings. That was where the Snuffleupagus would sometimes appear, after all. Laundry flapped proudly on the line, and Oscar loved that garbage can. The Muppets were all different colors—some you'd find in nature, some not—but their songs and voices, styles and worries spoke to many of us. I recognized in Kermit's blues, "It's Not Easy Being Green," the pain, frustration, and sometimes wonder of being born into a history of racism— sung by this most proper-talking frog. The adults in this world—Maria, Mr. Hooper, Susan and Bob and Gordon (Bald New Gordon, as well as Afroed Old Gordon)—expanded my universe of parents and grandparents, and I thought of them as my adult friends. Some of these adults were also famous ones, like Carol Burnett and José Feliciano. I remember watching, transfixed, as Buffy Sainte-Marie breastfed her baby right there at Big Bird's nest, imagining her nipple as a red, blooming sun.

And Stevie. Stevie Wonder's *Sesame Street* performance of "Superstition" took the music that I heard at home with my parents and mixed it up with counting and the alphabet, and with navigating new urban spaces. It's an example of one of the ways that *Sesame Street* spoke specifically to children of color, acknowledging the role that musical performances already played in many of our lives. This particular song, in its lyrics and Wonder's uninhibited performance, served as a way of unlearning the bodily lessons of assimilation into white culture. Stevie's *Sesame Street* "Superstition" is still available to us, archived (at least for the moment) on YouTube, and *Sesame Street*'s website (http://www.you tube.com/watch?v=_ul7X5js1vE). But it is also definitely a performance steeped in the hip, off-the-cuff style of its own historic moment. The band, in sunglasses and the funky duds of the era (colorful silk shirts and Apple Jack caps), is surrounded by the garbage cans and other bits of gritty urban debris that are a part of the permanent *Sesame Street* set. On fire escapes and risers made to look like back porches is a group of multiracial children, listening. Some are dangling their feet in time to the music, or swaying lightly to Stevie's jams. And one child dances wildly, light-brown-skinned, hair in exuberant curls, flailing his arms in time to the music, and most notably rolling his head back and forth with abandon, in a movement something like Stevie's own. Stevie refers to this trademark movement as his "blindisms," which he explains is a way of getting rid of the "excess energies" that are brought on by his music. The camera pans the clusters of young dancers and when it hits the dancing, head-rolling child, cuts away, returning quickly to Stevie. Stevie, too, rolls his head back and forth, smiling at his own singing. The camera never returns to a close-up of the wildly dancing child, but he is sometimes seen in the top left-hand corner, a little out of focus. What are Wonder's music and sound teaching this child and the rest of us about the body?

In Wonder's *Sesame Street* performance, he presents the right for his child viewers to take up the pleasures of black music in public space. In an interview included in Crescent Dragonwagon's biography about him, Wonder remembers his own desire to listen to and enjoy his favorite musician, blues legend B. B. King, without embarrassment, on the school bus as a child.

> I remember when I was little, I used to listen to this black radio station in Detroit on my way to school. Like I was the only black kid on the bus, and I would always turn the radio down, because I felt ashamed to let them hear me listening to B. B. King. But I *loved* B. B. King. Yet I felt ashamed—because—because I was different enough to want to hear him and because I had never heard him anywhere else. So freedom, freedom begins in the simplest things, even such things as feeling free enough to turn a radio to

a particular station. You have to seize that for yourself and then demand that kind of freedom from others."[1]

In the twenty-three-year space between Stevie Wonder's birth, in 1950, and his performance on *Sesame Street* in 1973, the public space for listening to black music freely had certainly changed. Black popular music's direct role in getting out messages of freedom at this same moment—Aretha Franklin's "Respect" (1967), James Brown's "Say It Loud: I'm Black and I'm Proud" (1968), and Sly and the Family Stone's "Stand!" (1969) are just a few noteworthy examples—all helped create this new context. And now the freedom for children to consume black music and openly express their own funkiness was happening in television space.

Wonder's lessons in groove teach the importance of beat and contrariness, the combination of paying close attention and getting lost in music. The ability to feel the "strange" in the groove requires listening with one's body, as well as one's ears. Grooving involves playing between the beats, working against comfort and expectation, the essence of funk music. On the opening of the recording of "Superstition," Stevie, on drum set, works the high hat and cymbal, changing volume, just before or behind the beat, adding extra taps, and hits. The pattern shifts just enough to keep us paying attention. As Wonder makes his drums speak, drawing from the Africanist tradition of the talking drum, he at the same time translates the speech of the drum into a language of the body—one that in turn creates a call-and-response with the audience. Wonder's embodiment of musical energy's power to transform—the "blindisms," as well as his own feedback loop of drum playing—might be linked to other traditions in black musical performance, like the "whoos" and nonverbal sounds of soul singers and gospel shouters.

Wonder's musical performances are protests against passing, and against the forgetting of the particularities of one's body, its strengths, its place in time and history. His performance is all of these things, and it is its own particularized thing, connected to the state of being blind but also to the state of being in music. It is significant that Wonder explicitly links his movements to his blindness, because he acknowledges the ways that his experience of the music and the experience of the body as a blind person have their own specificity. Wonder gives permission for his blindness to be performed as a whole body experience, expressed rather than "passing" as sighted. The rolling repetitions of his head mark the groove of the music, the arc and swing of it. It is a movement, like other forms of dance, that is both spectacular and infectious. Wonder's performance of musical pleasure is inherently social, and collaborative, connected to others. As Wonder's music-infused movements provoke and inspire audiences, he challenges the Western notion of the blind body as "being on display, of being visually conspicuous while politically and socially erased."[2]

Drawing from Nietzsche's understanding of the body as self-differentiated becoming, Foucault reminds us how the body is constitutively unstable, always foreign to itself—an open process of continuous self-estrangement in which "the most fundamental physiological and sensorial functions endure ongoing oscillations, adjustments, breaks, dysfunctions, and optimizations, as well as the construction of resistances."[3] In Wonder's performances of "groove," he puts at a premium the unknowability of experience, the sense of "wonder," of never fully grasping what's there. Wonder's blindisms physically chart the movement of sound as spatially layered, so that we who are watching visualize not only the ecstatic effects of music on the body, but also the ways that music shapes one's experience of space in a nonlinear way. The experience of sound in a basic way involves the pleasure of surprise—of being acted on from what Alexander Weheliye calls "multiple overlapping spatialities,"[4] and surrender. As Jody Berland describes it, in her *Locating Listening.*

> We surround the usual object, facing towards it as something other than ourselves; to look at something, even one's own image, is to constitute it as something separate. To listen to something is to forgo that separation. Sound comes at us from behind or the back from any direction, and surrounds us; we are constituted as listeners within its space.[5]

If we could map Wonder's blindisms, we might see them as the trigonometry of sound as it moves us. His is a theater of what it means to be "moved," giving evidence of music's power beyond the authorship of the artist.[6] Greil Marcus has said that "in its truest moments, songs like microbes—without intent, without brains—use people."[7] Another word for this, is, of course, *spirit,* but Marcus's use of the language of science gets at the anxiety that sometimes accompanies this experience of transformation. What Wonder's performances show us is the ways that music challenges the hierarchies of the body and its movements that have become normative in Western culture. And these hierarchies of movement are inherently political. Kodwo Eshun, in his essay "FUTURHYTHMA-CHINE," describes the ways that rhythm reacts on and re-creates the body, producing a new kind of intelligence.

> Your mother says: don't put your hand like this, don't put it like that. That's social law, which gets inscribed in the body. It becomes muscular, it becomes gesture, it becomes physicalized. A lot of music is about unlearning the mnemotechnics that have been inscribed by the social world, before you get the chance to revolt against them.[8]

The best moments in music force us to think about our bodies, movements, and gestures as socially politicized, scrutinized, and shaped. Music questions the boundaries of the body itself. Such powerful moments in music bring to light the ways that all of our bodies are potentially "quare," producing meanings and pleasures in excess of our immediate understanding. E. Patrick Johnson reappropriates this sometimes homophobic term as an alternative to *queer* to denote "excess incapable of being contained within useful conventional categories of *being*," as well as to describe someone who "thinks and feels and acts (and sometimes, 'acts up')."[9] As an expression of the ecstatic effects of music, and the pleasure of sharing, Wonder's performances blur the line between sexual and nonsexual, and have at their heart an exuberant appreciation of black musical traditions. This requires a certain level of vulnerability and willingness to exist between the space of sex object and spiritual resource. Such lessons on the embodiment of music, I'd argue, are an important, if neglected aspect of Wonder's performances. In Wonder's repeated return to the space of ecstatic possibility, his performances are "queer" or quare.

Wonder's Moral and Aesthetic Authority and the Revival of His Quare Teachings

My embrace of Wonder as a quare or eccentric artist pointedly goes against the grain of criticism about him. Perhaps because of his phenomenal success as both a crossover artist and one who speaks provocatively and directly about black experience, Wonder's fandom is both wide reaching and protective. It's difficult, in many ways, to see him as an outsider or eccentric. Indeed, for critics like Craig Werner, in his very quirkiness and originality Wonder is distinctly American, a sign for a new moment of black identity that would soon be shared.[10] In his strongest, Grammy-producing period, Wonder's songs compellingly captured what Werner calls "the gospel imperative": the turn away from self to spiritual, as well as civic, concerns.[11] *Innervisions* (1973), for example, featured warnings for the post-civil-rights generation of urban dwellers about the temptations and despair of the city in "Too High," "Jesus Children of America," "Higher Ground," and "Living for the City." The 1976 album *Songs in the Key of Life* combined an embrace of everyday black life (in "I Wish"), black pride ("Ebony Eyes," "Black Man," "Sir Duke," and "Isn't She Lovely"), community self-critique ("Village Ghetto Land" and "Past Time Paradise"), and spiritual renewal ("Love's in Need of Love Today," "Have a Talk with God," and "As"). Stevie's own life also provides a poignant model of integrity and achievement. Wonder's development from the "Little Stevie Wonder" of "Fingertips," a blind child harmonica performer managed by others, to the Stevie Wonder of *Innervisions, Talking Book, Songs in the Key of Life,* and other creatively and politically innovative works in the 1970s marks his ability to take control of his career, and more important, to use pop music as a space for teaching, for opening up how black people think about themselves, and their relationship to the rest of the world. In his period of increasingly independent artistic production, Wonder was able not only to open up his own aesthetic but to capture the public's attention, modeling a dynamic, hip, and also reflective mode of blackness. Moreover, although Wonder has also made songs that would seem to be blatantly commercial or formulaic (his contributions to the soundtrack to the film *The Woman in Red* [1984] come to mind), he has continued to stay politically engaged in the public sphere through music and public speaking campaigns, including his work to support the making of Martin Luther King Jr.'s birthday into a holiday and his public support of Barack Obama's campaign for the presidency, culminating in his performance at Obama's 2008 inauguration celebration.

In these discussions, there seems to be a hesitancy to discuss his performances as they are embodied—and none of his critics has framed him as "strange," "queer," or otherwise nonnormative. One unspoken reason for this might be the desire to look away from Wonder's body as it is disabled, to keep it hidden by piano or synthesizer, out of politeness, discomfort, or shame. This looking away allows his voice to be integrated into the normative trajectories of his romantic ballads. Instead, Wonder has been held up as the sometimes disembodied voice of a middle-class black community, the bridge between a pre-civil-rights dream of equality and the reality of a thriving black community. This often takes the form of praising Wonder as a "black genius"—a category of highest artistic praise, but one that often leads to a static and underexamined picture, or a tragic trajectory, as I'll discuss later. Werner, for example, praises Wonder's experimental soundtrack *Journey through the Secret Life of Plants* as "bafflingly beautiful,"[12] but he doesn't explore more deeply those moments of difficulty in Wonder's work or the ways that the album is performed by his powerful, if quirky, physical presence.

This chapter seeks to challenge what is already known about Wonder, to show how his generic crossing in *Journey through the Secret Life of Plants,* his quirky soundtrack to an experimental documentary about plant life and feeling, is a symptom for the ways that Wonder created for himself a space of freedom out of past successes. In the face of all of the ways that Wonder has been embraced as a moral and musical exemplar, I'm interested in moments when he doesn't as easily fit into this image of black belonging. How might Wonder's embodiment of the groove— and his application of these lessons of embodiment to the nonhuman— fall in excess of black community standards of black masculinity? And how might a project like *Journey through the Secret Life of Plants* provide Wonder the chance to explore embodiment and sensuality beyond such boundaries? In this discussion, I'll consider aspects of Wonder's music and performance that exceed the notions of respectability and "higher ground"—to explore the "quare" Stevie.

Unapologetically goofy, countercultural , earnest, maybe even a little nerdy,[13] Stevie Wonder's *Journey through the Secret Life of Plants* took fans by surprise. For many of his critics, it was seen as a detour from Wonder's run of classic hits that came after his declaration of independence from Motown: Bob Kilbourn called the album "courageous" but "odd" and "quite pointless" and "alien to the usual Wonder Style."[14] Stephen Holden wrote in the *Village Voice* that the album's vision is "as achingly sweet as it is profoundly foolish."[15] When he was first approached by film producer Michael Braun to score and perform the soundtrack, Wonder himself paused about its place in his artistic direction: "I hadn't given much thought to writing a score. Before writing, Michael approached me, but I'd always figured if I did one it would be for a film that would raise society's consciousness about black people. But this film interested me, being about plants, and it seemed to be a good place to start."[16] In many ways, a project like Wonder's *Journey through the Secret Life of Plants* reflects a new openness and possibility in the marketplace for black artists. But even more important, it embraces pop music as a potential place to explore new epistemologies of body, history, and being.

Wonder's soundtrack attempts to give voice to plant feeling and desire as a means of disrupting the powerful ways that popular music and culture hierarchize and normalize desire, body, and spirit. In an interview about the making of the film, Wonder comments, "Most popular songs . . . are about love and relationships: I want you—Do you want me? When are we going to get it on? I've written songs about that and I will again. But there is more to life—and love—than this 'up and down' business. . . . I'm dealing with love and life on a different level."[17] That we are a culture that puts a premium on normative representations of (human) sexuality, Wonder suggests, limits the spectrum of emotion and spirit that's available. In many ways, Wonder's work parallels that of blind author Rod Michalko in *The Mystery of the Eye and the Shadow of Blindness*. Michalko argues that sight deceptively presents a world of accessibility to everything—the rhetoric of vision implies that there's nothing that can't be known (a kind of imperialism of the gaze). Blindness for Michalko (like plants for Wonder) teaches us the shape of our own desires to know, as well as the insufficiency of our sight or other senses to fully satisfy those desires.[18]

Wonder's redefinition of black humanity through the inner lives of plants—and his embrace of the possibilities of new knowledge lent by plant intelligence in *Journey through the Secret Life of Plants*—is a bold claim to creative freedom. Beyond the project's sheer unusualness, I will consider the implications that this piece has for the ways that we think about race, sexuality, and disabled embodiment. If images of blindness in black popular culture are mostly heteronormative, from Jamie Foxx's depiction of Ray Charles in *Ray* to Lionel Richie's romancing of a blind art student in the unfortunately unforgettable video for "Hello," Wonder's sonic explorations in *Journey through the Secret Life of Plants* suggest the need for new epistemologies of the body and its boundaries. Through an erotics of cross-species collaboration, Wonder creates a radical performance of knowledge and possibility. Ultimately, we might consider *Journey through the Secret Life of Plants* as a queer offshoot of Wonder's ongoing exploration of the perimeters of black life, being, and freedom.

"Everybody Say Yeah!" Stevie's Quare Masculinity and Its Lessons for Black Freedom

Stevie Wonder was born Stevland Hardaway Judkins (later Stevland Morris) to Calvin Judkins and Lula Mae Hudaway in 1950. Growing up in Michigan, first in Saginaw and then in Detroit, Wonder was an energetic, highly musical, and mischievous child. He learned piano, harmonica, bass, and drums early on, sang in the church choir, and was known for his humor and love of practical jokes. Wonder was blind at birth, the result of premature growth of his retinas. First "discovered" by Berry Gordy at the age of eleven, Wonder was embraced for his exuberant energy, incredible drum and harmonica playing, tuneful songwriting, and comfort on stage. Perhaps most famously, Wonder's exuberance in his early career is captured by "Fingertips, Part 2" (1963), his first real hit. This recording of a live performance in Chicago begins in the middle, at what seems to be the moment of audience and performer frenzy during a Stevie harmonica solo. We hear the crowd already worked up, clapping and answering Wonder's call-and-response: "Everybody say 'Yeah!'" The audience cheers as Wonder answers them with a frenzy of blues harmonica, backed by a chorus of horns. Wonder works the crowd "just a little bit louder" and then rewards them with a round of harmonica that moves up to an even higher octave. The horns draw the frenzy to a close, and Wonder is escorted from the stage, but the audience continues to roar. In what will then become legend, Wonder runs back onstage and whips up another verse, apparently to the surprise of the next act. (One can hear in the background of the melee Joe Swift, conductor for the next act, shouting "What key, Little Stevie!? What key?") After a few more choruses, stage manager Clarence Paul manages to carry Wonder off the stage. According to Mary Wilson of the Supremes, this legendary performance "was a choreographed ploy to make the audience think that Stevie didn't know where he was,"[19] a play, perhaps, on Wonder's blindness, youth, and perhaps also the transformative power of his playing. Yet the fact that similar theatrical shows of enthusiasm became part of Wonder's stage shows suggests a conscious harnessing of black musical theatrical tradition that places the transformative power of music in the body. Stevie's being carried from the stage has powerful roots in the Black diasporic spiritual and cultural tradition, from African dance to "getting happy" in church to James Brown's live performances of "Please Don't Go" (as he is led off by attendants who gently cover his sweat-drenched body with a regal red cape) to Prince's orgasmic explosion at the end of "Little Nikki" in the film *Purple Rain.*

Likewise, Wonder's exuberant performance of "Kiss Me, Baby" (1965) at age fifteen, filmed in front of a live audience for the London pop television show *Ready, Steady, Go!* as part of the Motown Review, stands out in contrast to the other performances of Motown artists of the period: the Temptations' tight choreography; Smokey Robinson's contained if still smoldering crooning; the Supremes' tight, stylized hip shakes; and Martha Reeves's muscular Monkey. Instead, we have Stevie, jumping up and down, a much more straightforward expression of joy, head thrown back, wide smile. "Kiss Me Baby!" Stevie's wide claps leave his body open to our scrutiny, as if he's opening up his heart and lungs and stomach to us, or as if he's about to fly.

Despite their palpable links to black performance history and style, Wonder's performances of embodied pleasure and openness to music are risky. These expressions, rather than being taken as signs of inwardness, become further manifestations of the lack of self-consciousness and intellect of the black artist. The objectification of the black body and devaluing of black art are further complicated by the history of representation of the blind and otherwise disabled body, which has been figured as object, unruly to the gaze, and exceeding the grasps of knowledge, and at the same time open, available to be disciplined by the scientific/voyeuristic gaze.[20] When disabled bodies make moves in excess of "proper" bodily comportment, viewers tend to view them as accidents, or signs of loss of control, rather than as a point of distinction or particularity, says Garland-Thomson.

The success of Wonder's early performances of bodily "openness" and pleasure, as well as his struggles for artistic control, should be put into this larger history of the demonized black disabled body, as well as ongoing struggles for sexual freedom and full citizenship for disabled people.[21] Wonder has had to struggle against the constraints of artistic control imposed by his producers, and by a marketplace that has put a price on an aesthetic of black expressiveness and black joy. Looking back at his earliest work, Wonder reports, "The people who produced me used to say, 'Now come on Stevie, I want you to scream on this part of that song, 'cos that's you, man.' And I used to scream my head off. Then I thought, well, shit, maybe, maybe not. If I feel it, I'll do it, but don't make me scream before the break on every song."[22] In contrast to most of the eccentric performers in this study, Wonder counters the impulse of excessive black theatricality as a performative strategy. As Wonder developed as an artist, he crafted more strategically his exuberance and energy into his musical projects and political work. Wonder began to chafe under the diminutive "Little Stevie," and at age sixteen he dropped the title. At the same time, he sought to expand the breadth of his musical performances and generic packaging. While his early albums reflected trends that Gordy and the Motown executives chose for him (*A Tribute to Uncle Ray* [1962], a collection of Ray Charles tributes, or, less inspired perhaps, *Stevie at the Beach* [1964], a collection of surf music), Wonder also developed a stockpile of his own songs, including "I was Born to Love Her." This strategy culminated in Wonder's renegotiation of his contract with Motown at age twenty-one, as a result of which he was able to keep an unprecedented amount of artist freedom and ownership of his music.[23] Wonder's struggles to maintain control over the shape of his image, his sound, and his creative direction might be seen as part of his larger commitment to artistic and performative freedom, which we also see at work in his bodily presentation.

In much of Wonder's music that takes on sexuality explicitly, he is fighting against a discourse demonizing, or at best dismissing, the sexuality of the black disabled body, and is in itself a radical act. Wonder's performance of an exuberant sexual and sensual self might be read alongside narratives by black blind or sight-disabled authors like Ray Charles in *Brother Ray* and Audre Lorde in *Zami: A New Spelling of My Name,* which speak openly of sexual and sensual pleasure and awareness heightened by blindness and of a successful path to sexual and artistic fulfillment.[24] In *Innervisions* and *Music of My Mind*, Wonder includes songs about his marriage to singer Syreeta Wright, their mutual love, and an honest depiction of their struggles to maintain their marriage, while "Isn't She Lovely" paints a portrait of fatherly love. Wonder performs a nonnormative sexuality in his self-presentation, as well as in his sound and stage performances. In the liner notes accompanying *Songs in the Key of Life*, Wonder writes, "My mind's heart must be polygamous and my spirit is married to many and my love belongs to all. Sweets je t'aime." Then follows a list of no less than ten of Stevie's past lady friends with the eleventh in capital letters: YOULANDA. That's followed by "_____," with the notation "(There's an empty space for you)," and then his signature and thumbprint. After that there appears, again in caps, "PS TO YOULANDA, IF LOVE WAS WHAT I SOUGHT FOR THEN YOU HAVE GIVEN ME MORE THAN I EVER KNEW EXISTED!"[25] This carefree, polyamorous spirit informs *Journey through the Secret Life of Plants* as well, where, for example, in "Outside My Window" Wonder sings a love song to a flower.

In his live performances as an adult, Wonder balances the need to create a shared atmosphere of musical pleasure, spontaneity, and freedom for himself, his musicians, and his audience with professionalism and attention to detail. Despite the shield that the sunglasses provide, his posture and face are often open and relaxed, moving freely, rather than in explicitly choreographed dances. Whether singing or playing synthesizer or piano, harmonica, drums, or occasionally bass, Wonder projects exuberant energy, confidence, and humor: laughing between beats, imitating the flourish of a guitar with his voice, changing lyrics to add "Stevie" whenever possible, breaking into his trademark smile. While he is clearly the leader, he shares the stage with others with a spirit of generosity, making room for his backup singers and other musicians to have a chance to solo and show off as well, demonstrating their connectedness. Sometimes a performance will break into impromptu teasing, as when in a 1974 live performance of "If You Really Love Me" one of his conga drummers begins imitating his voice, or the whole band will get the spirit of church, clapping wide, stepping into extra solos, involving the audience. Wonder wears a wide range of flamboyant and sometimes gender-bending styles, from braids, dreadlocks, Afrocentric robes, and Indian shirts and beads to glam-rock- influenced glitter and sequins and ornate sunglasses.

Indeed, like the other performers discussed in this book, I see Wonder's sonic and bodily performances as opening up the spectrum of black sexuality. In his openness and fluidity, Wonder fits neither the extremes of black hypermasculinity nor femme divahood. Most useful has been E. Patrick Johnson's notion of "quare" to describe the ways that Wonder, in his braided, dashikied, and strategically vulnerable masculinity, might be read as "odd or slightly off kilter." I have also found useful Kobena Mercer's and Jason King's discussions of the sexually open and/or androgynous performances of sexuality in the works of Michael Jackson and Toni Braxton. Like Wonder's *Plants,* Jackson's *Thriller* in part performs an eroticized cross-species sexual/erotic collaboration (here monster and man). Jackson seeks and finds in *Thriller's* cross-species identification a route of sexual reinvention and ambiguity—a place in which to be "not like other guys."[26] And as Jason King discusses, Braxton's sexual "heat" combines masculine toughness and feminine fierceness to explode the constraints and packaging of pop Soul.[27] Likewise, Wonder's bodily and vocal performances challenge the codes of gender *and* genre. Neither cool nor fierce, Wonder remains difficult to fit into readily available continuums of black sexuality. He represents a space still not yet occupied.

The marketing of the black male performer has often favored an aesthetic of cool: distanced, beyond being affected by others, exemplified by Miles Davis, back turned away from the audience,[28] and Savion Glover's unsmiling face as he does his hip-hop soft shoe.[29] The stakes of remaining cool for the blind or otherwise disabled body remains prickly. Even though the blind male body might well be one of the most visible disabled bodies in the world of black music, we might see an impetus to "push past" blindness differences, either by translating them into spiritual knowing or by hardening them into a pervasive sense of cool. For example, in the film *Ray*, Taylor Hackford's 2004 biography of Ray Charles, we see manifest anxieties about the blind black male body: the fear of the blind body as nonproductive labor; the physical vulnerability of the blind body; the economic vulnerability of the blind body; and, perhaps harder to articulate, the ways that the blind body might posit new and unheard of forms of sexuality and sensual response. Are black blind bodies "freakish" both in the ways that they look and the ways that they access the senses? One response of control is to allocate the black blind body into the realm of the feminine, as a means of taking it out of circulation and control.

Even in *Ray*'s opening credits, we see the disciplining of the potentially vulnerable black and blind male body into this topos of coolness, which will continue over the course of the film. The credits show an older Ray Charles (Jamie Foxx), smoke lingering among his fast-moving fingers on the keyboard, to evoke the sensuality, heat, and power of his sound. This image is then reflected back in Ray's black sunglasses, effectively closing his face and eyes to the audience. The result is a "cool," closed performance that we learn has been hard-won. The younger Ray must contend with sexually and economic exploitative managers ("Come and get some of Mama's 'blackberry pie'!"), envious band members, and his own demons. If the younger Ray lacks the understanding and economic value of his own "mojo," by film's end, Ray has learned how to reshape his performances and masculinity to better fit these standard codes.

Stevie Wonder is the opposite. In his bodily performances, as well as in the political and romantic earnestness of his lyrics, he claims the right to openness—to wonder. His "blindisms" visually perform the effects of the music, in turn affecting others. The changing textures of Wonder's voice (from high and reedy to low growls), his closed-mic gasps and breathiness (e.g., audible in "Signed Sealed Delivered" and "My Cherie Amour"), and his willingness to play with his voice via voice bag and vocoder give a sense of his vocal style as reflecting a fluid embodiment, one that is varied in its presentation, open to collaboration, supplementation, enhancement, and inspiration. This openness is in fact the key to the power of the erotic. For Audre Lorde, for example, pursuit of the erotic in one's life work necessitates deep feeling and principled connection with others. It requires vulnerability and openness.[30] The display of such openness and expressiveness of feeling is hard-won, I'd argue, going against the dominant aesthetic of black male cool, and is always at risk of being attributed to black "naturalism" or essentialism.

Stevie Wonder, Eddie Murphy, and the Persuasive Power of Quare Performance

We see evidence of the power of Wonder's performances to challenge notions of black heteronormative masculinity in Eddie Murphy's imitations of him. For those of us growing up in the 1980s, perhaps Stevie Wonder himself was Eddie Murphy's imitations of Wonder. Frequently during that period, on *Saturday Night Live,* in guest star appearances, and in his concert film *Delirious,* Murphy's imitation of Stevie Wonder was part of his bag of tricks, along with those of Gumby, Mr. Robinson's Neighborhood, Velvet Jones, and James Brown.[31] Murphy's attempted mastery of Wonder, his ability to evoke what is most familiar and admired about him (his trademark vocalisms, visual iconography, and political and spiritual earnestness), is a strategy to establishing himself at the center of a Post-Soul generation. Murphy not only demonstrates his knowledge of key icons of an integrated Post-Soul culture; he can deflate them, remake them in his own image.

I see in Murphy's attempts to "do" Wonder a mixture of admiration, desire, and envy. (While Murphy aptly captures a recognizable simulation of Wonder's glissando, his own recordings, including *Party All the Time,* are more forgettable.) While Murphy describes himself as a fan and friend of Wonder, I think there is also more than a family resemblance between Murphy's parodic treatment of Wonder's "quareness" in these performances and Murphy's often present gay panic, reflected in the homophobic humor of his early work. What Murphy isolates in his Wonder imitations is the opposite of his own iconography: where Wonder's style is often androgynous and decorative during this period, emphasizing flowing Afrocentric robes and braided hair in beads, Murphy's is harder, slick, muscled, and angular in red leather pants and open shirt. Wonder's rhetorical style (at least in Murphy's imitation) is rambling and circular, while Murphy's delivery is the defensive one-two of a boxing match. If Wonder's voice, movements, and body are often feminized, Murphy's are macho, even femmephobic. As Murphy parodies Wonder in performance, he distances himself from a black masculinity that seems to be vulnerable, feminine, and at risk of being read as unselfconscious or "natural."

We might consider Murphy's parody of Wonder as an example of the ways that the policing of compulsory heterosexuality is also interwoven with a system of compulsory able-bodiedness, as Robert McRuer argues in *Crip Theory: Cultural Signs of Queerness and Disability*. If, in the past, "heterosexuality and able-bodiedness were wedded but invisible and in need of embodied, visible, pathologized, and policed homosexualities and disabilities," in our current postmodern and neoliberal moment, normalized (abled-bodied and heterosexual) selves depend on a performance of more spectacular examples. Normalcy is demonstrated through tolerance of the now more highly visible other. Rather than arguing for a space at the table of normalcy, McRuer's use of the in-your-face moniker of "Crip" in his *Crip Theory* attempts to push the envelope of this performed tolerance, to expose its larger function of containment.[32] But this dynamic of othering is further complicated as we think about the policing of queer and disabled sexuality among black male bodies, which, as Robert Reid-Pharr points out, have been consistently configured in modern culture "as an inchoate, irrational nonsubject."[33] The laughter that Murphy courts might be a way of striking out against this experience of being figured as "nonsubject" as a black man—as a way of maintaining his own subjectivity.

In Murphy's impersonation of Wonder, we must also note the high stakes of this form of humor, where to successfully perform another with a difference requires knowledge and subtlety. Murphy has clearly paid close, one might even say loving, attention to Wonder's cadence, the textures of his voice and breath. Murphy has watched and captured the ways that Wonder holds his head, the strength of his neck and shoulders, his open smile. In embodying Wonder, Murphy risks being haunted by him.

Indeed, I'd like to suggest here that Wonder teaches Murphy the potentiality of quareness, exposing what is similar between them. In isolation, Murphy's imitation of Wonder's "softness" bolsters his own "hardness"—both figurations of black sexuality that are "nonnormative," spectacular, and, as it turns out, highly lucrative. Murphy has constructed a stand-up style based on sexual outlaws Redd Foxx and Richard Pryor. His is a style that combines sexual charisma, mastery, and aggression. Yet as a moment of performance, Murphy's "read" on Wonder depends on the agreement of the audience on their differences.

Murphy's performance of impersonation attempts to control the startling effects of Wonder's performances. Through parody, Murphy produces a "looked at" Wonder who can never fully return his gaze, and therefore is suspended in the gendered dynamics of power. His performance of Wonder is a special version of what Garland-Thomson calls the "politics of staring" at the disabled, where "staring registers the perception of difference and gives meaning to impairment by marking it as aberrant."[34] Through imitation, he attempts to hold him steady in his gaze, in part owning and becoming him at the same time that he "fixes" him. Ultimately, though, as Murphy imitates Wonder, he is also seduced by him. In a skit on *Saturday Night Live* where Stevie Wonder is guest host, the show stages Murphy "caught" imitating Wonder when the real Wonder appears onstage. Murphy "teaches" Wonder how to be Wonder, and Wonder good-naturedly obliges. The skit ends with the two singing together. This skit not only reveals Wonder's good humor about being the object of imitation but also reveals the potential for the imitator to be transformed through the act of imitation. In the tightly regulated space of black male performance, Wonder gives Murphy a space in which to be open, even if that openness is caught between scare quotes. Perhaps what Murphy recognizes in Wonder, and distances himself from, is the ways that Wonder performs an examined life, exposing the constructedness of a masculinity dependent on the tyranny of the gaze. In the essay "Seeing Nothing: Now Hear This . . ." Martin Welton argues that "The dominance of vision, its range over a given situation, has long been linked to characterizations of male power and agency, to the power of the male gaze to see at a distance and command, and hence to be 'objective.'"[35] This drama of two competing forms of black masculinity is made even more poignant in its intersection with race, where black masculinity is always so closely watched and fetishized.

Stevie Wonder's *Journey through the Secret Life of Plants:* Wonder as "Quare" Seer

In *Journey through the Secret Life of Plants,* Wonder continues to expand the territories of black masculine performance. Though an album in part about the cosmos and spiritual connection to nature, like many progressive rock and psychedelic rock projects from roughly the same period, *Journey through the Secret Life of Plants* includes soul ballads, disco, funk and pop, classical, African, and Japanese orchestration, as well as ambient sound. In interviews about the project, Wonder insisted that despite its seemingly esoteric approach, it was in part about down-to-earth black life and love. For example, in a 1979 interview with the *Washington Post,* Wonder tells reporter Carla Hall that, like his other projects, this music "comes just from my life." At the same time, he insists that black life and love are of limitless potential as a subject. He tells Hall, "You see, I think that we cannot allow ourselves to put boundaries on what we do musically. An element of surprise is always good."[36]

Wonder's soundtrack, along with the film, exposes the disconnection between science and spiritual practices, united through the ecstatic effects of music and cinematography. Neither the film *The Secret Life of Plants* nor Wonder's soundtrack has had the cultural and scientific impact that it might have had it tempered the insistence of its message: plants have lively inner lives and emotions and, specifically, they feel empathy, pain and pleasure, and desire toward humans. Peter Tompkins and Christopher Bird's 1973 book *The Secret Life of Plants,* the film and soundtrack's source, suggests that we might consider the possibility of plant eroticism and sensuality, and among other things, that "plants and succulent fruits might wish to be eaten, but only in a sort of loving ritual, with real communication between the eater and the eaten."[37] The film documents the intrepid scientists and artists who attempt to locate and chart plant feeling and response: a scientific lab in the Soviet Union that attempts to show that plants "remember" when other plants are mutilated or cooked; a lie detector specialist who turns from the mean streets of San Diego to measure plant empathy and higher consciousness; and

George Washington Carver, who saw in the peanut a sense of "spirit" and an "invisible world," as well as potential for a lot of very useful products. The book, film, and soundtrack's exploration of plant spirit is in keeping with the practices of many cultures around the world, from indigenous cultures of North and Central America to that of the Dogon people of Mali.

Like Gil Scott-Heron's description of the blues mentioned earlier, Wonder and the filmmakers of *The Secret Life of Plants* use plants to further "the science of how we feel." But in its most powerful sequences, the film turns away from the humans who are obsessed with this secret life and uses its technology and craft to document the lives of the plants themselves: their movements; their emotions; and, it is suggested through Wonder's music, their "souls." The soundtrack and film's first sequences tell the story of evolution, in "Earth's Creation" and "The First Garden." Wonder's harmonica plays a duet with birdsong, backed by kalimba. A jazzy bass line is matched by the rhythm of crickets, broken by the synthesized rumble of thunder. This rich natural and synthetic combination of sound provides the loam through which leaves curl and reach.

The very question of plant knowledge asks us to rethink the ways we understand knowing and our language for describing that knowing. By reconfiguring the senses to foreground the shared experience of humans and plants, the project foregrounds a challenge to what we think of as bodily knowledge and pleasure. It forces us to face how our mechanisms for describing what and how we know physically or psychically are limited by human language.

Wonder's "sounding" of plant intelligence provides an aesthetic of expansiveness that captures the ways that plants become technologies for "seeing" and understanding. He does so by using the spectrum on musical instrument digital interface (MIDI) synthesizers, his own voice, and the voices of his backup singers to capture plant wit and sensuality. Critical theorist Richard Doyle, writing on the rhetorics of plant intelligence by naturalists and theorists of the nineteenth and twentieth centuries, suggests that we think of plants as technologies of sorts, for seeing and understanding, particularly in the ways that plants get human audiences to "pay attention"—through color, smell, and even limited movement. Indeed, we might think of the relationship between primates and plants as a form of seduction in which plants act not only on insects but on thought, "inducing visions of intoxication and ecstasy; activating, amplifying, and altering the mind."[38] Rejecting the idea of his own limits, Wonder presents himself as mediator of these experiences, forcing us to think about his body as a resource for communication with these non-human subjects.

Throughout *Journey through the Secret Life of Plants*, Wonder uses the range of his MIDI synthesizers to play with sound textures and rhythms, with crossings of human, animal, plant, and technology, sometimes including what sounds like the plants themselves: the whip of a leafy branch in wind or held in a moving hand. He uses the stretch between octaves to capture a sunflower's turn with the sun. Rather than playing into the Western splits between mind and body, and technology and human, Wonder demonstrates the facility of technology to move us to new relationships with the body, voice, time, and organism. For example, he offers a range of timekeeping: the traditional drum set and the tasty blues bass line but also the pulse of synthesized crickets, a clock, and the unpredictable bottom of thunder.

Wonder also reconfigures music and groove through the positionality of plants themselves. For example, in the instrumental version of "Send Her Your Love," we hear a sound collage as if from the point of view of flowers on a table. We hear a strangely muted collection of tones and rhythms: laughter, the clinking of glasses, the strumming of a Spanish guitar, all entering the earphones from multiple, intertwined directions. We are flooded with sensation, the melody of the original version lost to the textures of the other noises.

If, as Richard Doyle suggests, plants, despite their apparent passivity, are able to capture human and primate attention through multiple mechanisms, including smell, bright color, stickiness and other textures, and movement, this would seem to mimic what Wonder is also doing stylistically in *Journey*, layering styles and devices. The expansiveness of technique itself a proof of its beauty. This becomes especially evident in the album's finale and its rapid shift between styles and sounds: pop ballad, classical, traces of Indian and Japanese, African rhythms, and also popular instrumentation. As we consider Wonder's capturing of plant intelligence, its "secret life," we might return to the ways that Stevie himself is attempting to produce a supplement to vision in this soundtrack project, sound creating the color, texture, movement, smell, and even taste of plants—through synesthesia.

The secret life of plants turns out to be a lesson in collaborative, complementary existence and adaptation, something along the lines of Wonder's lessons in "groove." The song "Race Babbling," for example, suggests that the speed and sound of every day life obscure the simple lesson of interconnection and need, told in the voices of the plants: "Can't you see that / Life's connected / You need us to live / But we don't need you." The song's funky disco stylings—evocative of George Clinton, Sly Stone, and also perhaps Giorgio Moroder—capture the pressures of urban life at breakneck speed. And layered on top of the song's rhythm sections, melody, and harmony are a ticking clock in the left speaker and a plane landing in the right. But as the guitars stand back and the song breaks into a meditative three-minute sequence featuring the rhythm section, perfect for dancing, we experience the trance effect that dance music's repetition can provide, creating space within motion for thought and transformation. (Here I'm reminded of the midsong meditative effect of Donna Summer's "I Feel Love.") The song disturbs the neat distinction between "nature" and technology.

In a radical move of "blaxploration," Wonder claims these issues of interspecies communications as specifically black concerns. As *Journey through the Secret Life of Plants* openly questions the splits between mind and body, human and technology, it in turn pushes the boundaries of black identity on a national, species, erotic, and aesthetic level. We watch in the film a fly rapping to a Venus flytrap with the seductive style of a George Clinton ("Hello, Flower. Boy, do you look juicy"). One-celled organisms groove to a funky bass line. We watch flowers unfold, captured by Ken Middleham's time-lapse cinematography, Wonder's harmonica and synthesizers giving voice to their yearning. Wonder not only creates a soundtrack that counters the hierarchy of image to sound in film (where his music creates the heart of the film, it *is* the secret life of plants),[39] but he is claiming for black musical production the space of experimentation and intellectualism, as well as spiritualism, at the same time that he is claiming that at the root of all life is funk, which writer and Bay Area Funkateer Rickey Vincent defines as "an aesthetic of deliberate confusion, of uninhibited, soulful behavior that remains viable because of a faith in instinct, a joy of self, and a joy of life, particularly unassimilated black American life."[40] In this Post-Soul moment, "Soul" can include a plant subject, and groove and improvisation are the movements of evolution, the soundtrack of life on this planet.

In his infusion of "funk" into this depiction of the life of plants, Wonder suggests that black music is synchronous with the roots of all life. This runs counter to the status of black life and sexuality as social death, the legacy of slavery.[41] Indeed, a running theme of the soundtrack is the restoration of black life/ aesthetics' connection to the natural world, estranged by African removal and enslavement, as well as migration from South to North. Both "Come Back as a Flower" and "Outside My Window" treat the themes of rediscovery and connection to plants as a form of spiritual healing. "Come Back as a Flower" explores the beauty of rural life and rhythms with a sense of childlike wonder and immediacy, which builds into an increasingly complex and alive composition. Wonder begins first with basic singular instruments and voice: piano, bass, the sound of hand-clapping, and Syreeta Wright's sweet soprano. As the first verse is completed, and the melody repeats, the arrangement builds, and other sound elements join and intertwine with the first ones. Wright's voice is now accented with ghostly dove call, the bass joined with the groan of what could be the creak of wood against wood. As the patterns repeat themselves with a difference, the song explores the possibility of an Edenic return, though one that acknowledges the inevitability of change.

"Outside My Window" considers the possibility of reconnection to the natural world and its rhythms in an explicitly urban space, where nature is clearly framed through the lens of the human. Stevie's singing in this bouncy ballad is accompanied by what sounds like a synthesized whip of a branch in the air, water, the rustle of leaves, and the sounds of children playing just outside. Here plant life is not disconnected from human life.

In "Black Orchid," a midtempo ballad cowritten with Tammy Wright, plant life and beauty are specifically linked to the desire to heal black womanhood, postslavery: "In a world / with need for a change / A touch of love in fear of hate." In the "Black Orchid" sequence in the film, the black orchid is literally a black woman (performed by Eartha Robinson), the adult version of Wonder's sturdy-legged young protagonist in "Living in the City," perhaps. Robinson moves in an Alvin Ailey–inspired dance from a burned-out tenement building to a field, until she merges with a tree. Wonder's plea for the appreciation of the black orchid and a renewal of her power parallels the defense of black womanhood devalued by slavery, in keeping with early black feminist writings by Anna Julia Cooper and Maria Stuart: "Black Orchid, Black Orchid / Why did they criticize / when they knew your love could cast its spell and consecrate their eyes?"

In "A Seed's a Star/Tree Medley," a song combining lyrics in English and Bambara, plants become a route for African return: "I gradually burst through my shell / Pushing down into the ground / The root of me is homeward bound." The song is the energetic apex of the album, structured something like a rock opera, with Wonder taking on the persona of "Tree" in deep vocoder, with Tata Vega's honeyed mezzo-soprano in response. Trumpets, a chorus of African drummers, and two guitars, as well as the claps and other responses of a live audience, add the texture of liveness and drama. In this and each of the songs of the album, Wonder explores and merges the sensuality of plant life with the exploratory and yearning elements of the erotic.

It makes sense to me that Wonder's *Journey through the Secret Life of Plants* project occurs simultaneously with the blossoming of hip-hop culture, in 1979. Both share a sense of urgency, drawing from the expressiveness of black cultural traditions in the attempt to capture through sound and beat and shape black aliveness and struggle. And while Wonder's *Journey* doesn't sound at all like the dynamic, pared down aesthetic of much early rap, both emerge out of a context where "social alienation, prophetic imagination, and yearning intersect," in Tricia Rose's words.[42] Despite the characterization of *Journey* by many of its critics as (only) airy or otherwordly, we might, in particular, connect Wonder's exploration of *return* in this project, in addition to its other themes, to rural landscapes and knowledge, and to Africa, as a response to the deindustrialization and burned-out city landscapes that have also influenced hip-hop graffiti, breakdancing, rap, and DJing.

Stevie Wonder as Post-liberation "Black Genius"

Wonder's quest to create an art that links black life and spirituality to plants and all life creates a line of flight from what Greg Tate calls "the looming shadow of black failure." Tate writes:

> For too long black genius has been just another word for black existential suicide. How did Samuel Delaney put it: "I have come to wound the autumnal city. So howled out for the world to give him a name. The in-dark answered with the wind. All that you know I know." Yet, even in the face of all the light that has been shed on blackness before us, in this generation, on the eve of the millennium, we remain dark to ourselves, setting up shelter in Plato caves of our own immaculate design, black holes situated in Arc-

tic wastes where no other black soul can hear us scream, because, to paraphrase the poet Ninety Nine, we're cool like that, we're sold out like that, we're played like that, we're lost."[43]

Wonder's willingness to reimagine that living as a sensual/erotic connection beyond species is one of the ways that he expands the notion of the black genius, releasing him from the constraints of black genius and black masculinity as tragedy, as well as from the idea of blind sexuality as invisible.

Over the course of Stevie Wonder's career, he has been labeled as a black genius, a term that is limited in its conceptualization of black male identity. *Journey through the Secret Life of Plants* is Wonder's gentle rejection of the reductiveness of the formula of packaged pop, but it is also an engaged "blaxploration" of black humanity and expression, looping in on past texts—including Wonder's own—and moving beyond his own genus as well as genius. Whimsical, goofy, meditative, the album is a response to the often limited parameters of black intellectualism and "genius." *Journey through the Secret Life of Plants* is very much in keeping with Greg Tate's characterization of the "postliberationist," Post-Soul moment. Postliberationist art is deconstructive, reflective of its own workings and its relationship to white power, says Tate. Absorbing and reaching beyond the lessons of the Black Art Movement, these artists demonstrate a love of blackness, while keeping in sight a wide horizon, free to draw from all cultures for its "gene pool."[44] In this case, however, Wonder widens the notion of "cultures" to include nonhuman ones.

In popular culture (and often played out in everyday life), black male genius has its limits concerning where it can go and what it can do. For one thing, the term *genius* in the world of black music is almost always used synonymously with *male* (with the exception of Billie Holiday, thanks to Farah Jasmine Griffin),[45] and its most embraced and best-known models are reassuringly and zestfully masculine, deeply loyal and embedded in the world of men. Black male musical genius is often connected to sex and the seductions of power. Trumpeter Freddie Hubbard tells this story about Miles Davis: "Miles would hit a low note with that Harmon mute in his horn and the girls would move their legs like they had just got too hot to keep their thighs together."[46] The stories we tell about black male genius are bigger than life, mythological. These geniuses are arrogant, charismatic. In these stories, black geniuses are exceptions to the rules of racism, or else they are victims, man-children, brought down by the limits of the flesh: sex, poverty, drug addiction, loneliness (as in Clint Eastwood's image of Charlie Parker depicted in the 1988 film *Bird*).The stories that we hear about black geniuses are that they are misunderstood and therefore doomed. They die of loneliness. They die of not being able to do their art. Or else that they die from the difficult knowledge their art yields. They are martyrs to the black creative spirit. These tragic stories of genius are so powerful, in part, because they are also lived, and speak to the limited place in the world for black creativity and radical thought.[47]

What might be missing, perhaps, in black genius cultural narratives is the impact of fundamental aspects of empathy and transcendence that are nonetheless at the heart of music's power to affect one's humanity— the possibility, even in the exploration of one's blackness, of leaving behind one's own pain and struggle to touch and understand another's, outside of one's own gender, race, tribe, or even species . Spoken word and jazz artist Gil Scott-Heron alludes to this element of empathy when he defines the blues at its best as "the science of how things feel."[48] Music critic Stanley Crouch hints at it when he describes the jazz geniuses of his youth, their ability to satisfy the often unspoken "need for beauty" in black life, and his own desire to transcend "the mediocrity, oafishness, and stupidity" that loomed in his life and in those of his community.[49] These aspects of feeling, empathy, and connection are often underplayed because they don't fit into traditional notions of black masculinity, perhaps. But I am reminded of the wide psychic reach of the work of black male geniuses when I remember a bus ride home from the 1992 March on Washington for Women's Lives. Someone had put Marvin Gaye's song "Sexual Healing" on his or her mixed tape, and the whole bus joined in singing, mostly women and some men, many of us survivors of sexual assault, maybe all of us with the desire to get beyond just surviving in our thoughts. Maybe this was against the grain of the original vision Marvin Gaye had in performing the song, maybe not.

What Stevie Wonder models in his work are the limits of these past conceptualizations of black male genius, by centering empathy, and the transcendence of the historical, social, and even physiological constraints on one's body through openness to others', through music. Wonder's genius is in his fundamentally democratic configuration of groove. Groove for Stevie is the elemental and human and also plant and animal force of desire, which moves all of us to show our faces to the sun. Groove is the life force, and the force of connection. What Wonder offers to the ongoing story of black genius is a fundamental investment in living. Each of the

eccentrics discussed in this book use strategies of off-centeredness to re-
but the forces of history that shrink the creative spirit in black life. As we'll
see in the next chapter, for Grace Jones, this revolt against black spirit kill-
ing takes the form of satire, a mask that momentarily hides critique and
rage; for George Clinton and Parliament/Funkadelic, it takes the form of
a goofy embrace of sexual pleasure. For Stevie, wonder, openness, and
vulnerability, along with the communal powers of groove, are the forms
that his strategy takes. In *Journey through the Secret Life of Plants,* Wonder
explores new directions in sexuality—the erotic power of cross-species
collaboration—as a means of escaping tragic trajectories of black masculinity. This has implications for the ways we think about the constructions
of sexuality, race, gender, and ability in the Post-Soul moment.

Wonder pushes these limits, but he does so while also enjoying the
fierce loyalty and protectiveness of his audience, as we see in Eddie Murphy's confession about him in his 1983 film *Delirious.*

> I remember I did Stevie Wonder in a show once, and black people
> lost their muthafuckin minds! I had brothas rolling up on me, go-
> ing, "Hey! You the muthafucka that be doing Stevie Wonder? . . .
> Don't ever let me see you do that shit again! I'll fuck you up! Stevie
> Wonder's a musical genius!"

Perhaps this very protectiveness keeps us from recognizing Wonder's
radical quality as an artist, and as a performer of eccentric blackness.
In his thoughtful study of African American musicians and blindness,
The Songs of Blind Folk, Terry Rowden suggests that for blind musicians
"the attribution of genius has functioned as a way of countering the
deindividualizing narratives to which blind African American performers have frequently been subjected" while also mystifying the political,
economic, and historical factors shaping authorship.[50] Keeping Rowden's
thesis in mind, I'd suggest that the term *black genius* obscures what's often "strange" about Stevie's work, in particular in terms of gender and
sexuality.

There are some very powerful parallels between the trajectory of
Wonder's career at this stage and that of another performer often figured
as a "black genius" from the same period, Jimi Hendrix. Cultural critic
Steve Waksman, in "Black Sound, Black Body: Jimi Hendrix, the Electric
Guitar, and the Meanings of Blackness," writes about Hendrix's desire to
create a sound without limits (intellectual, technical, and social).[51] Like

Wonder, Hendrix found in the Electric Lady studios a place of safety, and innovation through technology.[52] Hendrix, like Wonder sought to expand his sound and audience by listening to and collaborating across genre and race, stretching blues and gospel traditions and taking them to new places.[53] Waksman suggests that toward the end of his life, Hendrix sought an escape from the traps of a highly spectacular and objectified black masculinity perpetuated by white rock audiences: "For Hendrix, as for Fanon, a sight of blackness in the eyes of others had become oppressive, and so he expresses a desire to be heard, not seen; listened to, not watched. The most 'visible' of black performers, he yearns for a sort of invisibility . . . a realm of pure music where both he and his audience can lose themselves in the power of sound."[54] Unfortunately, in his shortened life, Hendrix was unable to fully occupy this space of creative freedom. I'd like to suggest that one of the ways that Wonder has been able to escape some of the creative constraints experienced by Hendrix is by resisting the temptation to become invisible and instead reclaiming new spaces for creative collaboration and production. Wonder has been able to achieve a flexibility of sound and genre that has influenced other Post-Soul chameleons, including Prince, Michael Jackson, and India.Aire.

In the last sequence of the film *The Secret Life of Plants,* in a performance of the title song, Stevie Wonder appears for the first time in the flesh. Wonder walks through a field of sunflowers without his sunglasses. His braided hair and gown, following the style of the cover of his *Talking Book,* make him both androgynous and mystical—a "seer." As he travels through the sunflower field, and then a stream of lily pads and a finally a forest, he is the only visible human. As the camera slowly pans the fields we realize that we are watching a view of nature as Stevie might have seen it, had he been sighted. This moment is indicative of the ongoing practice of collaboration between Wonder, technology, and humans (as well as plants) that has made the soundtrack possible.[55] As he floats through the field, singing, we get a profound sense of yearning, an acknowledgment of his own limits. Wonder's soulful and earnest voice is cushioned by the lush, classical Spanish-style guitar arpeggios of Ben Bridges and Michael Sembello. At the same time, the sequence demonstrates the possibility for connection, and for new ways of being in the world. The lilies, connected by a rhizomic network of roots under the surface of the water, are an ideal metaphor for the image of symbiosis and connection between plant and human life throughout the film and soundtrack. In the idealized figures of the blind of the classic past—Blind Tiresius, for example—the blind person is an oracle, disconnected from the everyday problems of the flesh but for an androgynous, if shell-like body. This end sequence demands that we consider both Wonder's body in the flesh and his capacity for transcendence. And parallel to Marlon Riggs's final naked run through the forest at the end of his *Black Is, Black Ain't,* Riggs's last film before he died of AIDS, Wonder's disabled black body performs both vulnerability and strength, singularity (a celebrity among a field of repeating flowers) and collaboration. He is, like Riggs, reclaiming the green world, its expansiveness and freedom, for black people.[56] At the same time, he does so in collaboration with human and nonhuman others, vulnerable, open, and insistently quare.

THREE

"Here's a Chance to Dance Our Way Out of Our Constrictions"

P-Funk's Black Masculinity and the Performance of Imaginative Freedom

Growing up, I took pleasure in and an example from the funky sartorial experimentations of my uncles Kevin and Chip: cutting each other's hair in my grandmother's pink bathroom in preparation for a Saturday night and the care they took to shape each other's muttonchops and goatees with the small electric razor they had ordered from Service Merchandise. I secretly hoped that my uncle Chip would pass on to me his stylishly worn army jacket with the magic marker sketch of Jimi Hendrix, fist raised, that he drew on the back, but I'm still waiting. Understated men, they were well liked in Parkway Gardens, the South Side Chicago housing development where my grandmother lived, for their good humor and style. I'd watch them go out with their friends from my grandmother's fifth-floor window and admire the brave way they'd laugh together, throw their arms around their friends, take up space on the sidewalk. Dashes of style: well-shined Stacy Adams shoes, a yellow knit shirt, wide-legged jeans with silver rivets up the side, or a leather cap tilted just right, added color and texture among the rust and weeds, as they stood in clusters alongside the railroad cars that sat abandoned in back of the buildings. Someone might be smoking, the orange glow of Kools lighting up the gestures of their hands. And somewhere someone would have a boom box playing a bass line of deep funk: Ohio Players, Slade, Parliament, and Funkadelic. Sometimes I wanted to be them.

In Funkadelic's *Cosmic Slop* (a short film directed by Armen Bolodian, Westbound Records, 1973, as found on YouTube), I see the spirit of my uncles and their friends as teenagers, out on the street.

The men, funky in their sartorial grooviness, arms raised like birds, run from a city park tunnel, this everyday space of darkness and transition. The underpass is true in its particularity: an underpass somewhere in Central Park, a space in which to write graffiti, make love, share an illicit smoke. The urban park underpass, a dark pause in the middle of the green, the city turning in on itself, ripe with damp earth smells that seep into the concrete, along with the piss and smoke. It's the space where the wildlife of the park (animal, vegetable, mineral) takes refuge. Castaways and survivors. Broken glass and pigeons. The men fly from this space, and they come running toward us, like children playing airplane, like Busby Berkeley dancers on shrooms, like serious visionaries, transformed in ceremony, this unclaimed black and brown and white tribe.

Released by the squeal of guitar, they take over the park and the streets beyond. The city, for once disinterested in them, becomes their playground.[1] They congregate in front of a fountain, climb over park benches and into the streets like a wave, still steady in tight leathers and platform boots. Rhythm guitar driving them ever outward, they create a *Soul Train* line in the middle of Times Square. They move like birds do, in parabolas, looping, then circling away. They dance in mirror to each other, shoulders, hips, and long thighs in call-and-response. Sometimes the men turn their backs to the camera, disoriented, lost in their own experience of beat; they close their eyes to follow internal geographies. They turn, stoop, and crouch toward the camera, as if engaged in capoeira with it, as if ready to pounce. The camera matches them, meets them, slows down their groove into a tasty syrup. They do slow splits, they are superhuman in their flexibility. Loose and tight. Flow and the force of drums felt on the back of the neck. Laughter. The beat stays right on The One.[2] Faces squish up in the nastiness of the stank of it. The men heat the air of the city, defy gravity, take flight.

In this film made to accompany the album *Cosmic Slop*, produced before the age of music videos, we see the vision and ethos of Parliament and Funkadelic's lead and cofounder, George Clinton, in action: playful sexuality expressed by a tight beat and theatrically citational, body-conscious style; eccentric, exploratory individuality, as well as the power of the collective; a grounding in the everyday grittiness of black street culture, combined with the quest for imaginative freedom. P-Funk's Post-Soul "blaxplorations" enact a liberationist black sexuality funking up traditional codes of masculinity. Together with his ever expanding band, which over time included such luminaries as guitarist Eddie Hazel, bassist Bootsy Collins, lead singer Gary Shider, keyboardist and arranger Bernie Worrell, and cameo appearances by Sly Stone, Clinton changed the face and the feel of funk music, making it visionary, dangerous, hallucinatory, hilarious, and very hot.

And they are beautiful, these men, in Afros wild and defiant, shirtless, unmasked and masked. They are a parade of tricksters, all moving with the antidiscipline of funk: Wolf meets griot, King Tut meets spaceman, Sly Stone meets Afro-Kabuki warrior, Pierrot meets Pimp. They wear found shirts as headscarves and flags, carry branches from the dying trees found along the avenue as their walking sticks. They have holes in their pants. They are dirty. They have painted on themselves, on their faces and chests like children do, playing in their mothers' makeup. They have marked themselves with mud and clay as their paint, like warriors do. Before Kiss, before Iron John, alongside Bowie and Iggy, they have returned to the land of make-believe and to the lost feminine with serious intention—at stake, their own freedom.[3] They have returned to this city park to funk. And, as the lyrics tell us, to hear their mama call. (George Clinton once said that funk can save your life. And so can listening to your mama.)

What do we make of the fact that this dance of masculine dreaming, of freedom and future and found community, is all to a song of lost women, mothers whose smiles mask the fact that "life is really tough"? The singer remembers his mother, and the things that he as a child is not supposed to know—that she had to "turn tricks" in the neighborhood in order to hold things together.

> But always with a smile, she was sure to try to hide
> The fact from us that she was catching hell, hey!

As the men seek solace in the beat, and in the sloppiness of the cosmos, their future mixes with things and people left behind, found objects and the lessons they never wanted to receive. As they seek rebirth, they are haunted by their mothers' late-night calls of grief: "Please, please don't judge me too strong."

The song is a series of countergrooves: the heavy downbeat of The One, played by drum set and bass, countered by the extending riffs of the bongos; the high sobbing of Worrell's lead guitar versus the gruff, tight forward shuffle of the rhythm guitar; Gary Shider's earnest falsetto and the street realism of his leading lyrics, countered by the mystical "Hoo Ha ha" of the chorus, a dance with the devil. The psychedelic aspects of the song: the chanting, the fuzzy blur of the guitar's tone, the deep hypnotic repeating of The One, might invite us inward, where Shider seems to be, possessed by the spirit of his mother. But ultimately the song keeps bringing us back to the present, to the experience in our bodies of the beat, right now. In "Cosmic Slop" we hear performed in the lyrics and sound the lesson that will be revisited again and again by P-Funk. We hear the lesson that haunts P-Funk's roster of others, and links them to other Post-Soul eccentrics, an acknowledgment of the complexity of desires, the funk in fucking: "And then the devil sang, / would you like to dance with me? / We're doing the Cosmic Slop." A song of empathy, a song of vulnerability, with a dance of yearning and flight. Haunting and the exorcism of judgment. The voice of mother becomes woman becomes self.

In this dance, in this cross-gender joining, they take pleasure in the movements of all of their parts. Polymorphously perverse, their pleasure is in the call of mother as it is in the join of skin to fabric; in the mystery of the mask; in the crouching, the shimmies, the pop of the bass against fiberglass; in the move of air through nostrils from dank to clean and then funky again; in the peal of the guitar; in the heat of other men; in the dance of other men; in being watched, in dancing alone; in nature, in the confines of man-made concrete. In the fetish of leathers, headbands, and feathers, in a cold metal saxophone on bare chest. In The One, in bass and drumbeat matching the beat of the heart, in blood rising and insistent. In the hush of cymbals and the chant of the singers; in the mystery, raising the hair on the back of the arms; and, yes, in the crying of the man who in his falsetto becomes the voice of Mother, a pain in the solar plexus, the tear in it so much like her or your own voice, for that matter, when you wake yourself from dreaming.

"Cosmic Slop" appears in 1973, early in the life of Funkadelic, the funk collective orchestrated by George Clinton. Clinton, singer, songwriter, as well as bandleader, was born in 1941 in Kannapolis, North Carolina. His family moved to Plainfield, New Jersey, a predominantly African American community not far from New York City, when he was still in his teens. There he formed his first group, the Parliaments, which used to practice in the back room of the barbershop where Clinton straightened and styled hair. The Parliaments were inspired by many of the successful doo-wop groups of the 1950s, including Frankie Lymon and the Teenagers, but they set themselves apart with their protofunk sound (heard in their hits "I Wanna Testify" and "All Your Goodies Are Gone,") and often eccentric lyrics and performance style, including costume changes at the ends of their gigs in which the all-male group became visibly pregnant, and "in titties and wigs."[4] The Parliaments evolved into two entities, Parliament and Funkadelic, in the 1970s and kept going until the early

1980s. These groups moved from underground sensation—performing in local clubs in Detroit, producing the edgy music that most radio stations were afraid to play—to become one of the most influential forces in black sound and performance, including huge, sold-out, highly theatrical stage shows.

In their innovative oddity, Parliament and Funkadelic's songs became the bedrock of the hip-hop aesthetic, sampled by Snoop Dog, Run DMC, NWA, De La Soul, Digital Underground, Public Enemy, Dr. Dre, L.L. Cool J, and Outkast, to name only a few.[5] They've also influenced other genre—and sometimes gender-bending—artists, including most notably Prince, Living Colour, Fishbone, and the Red Hot Chili Peppers.

Under the artistic direction of Clinton, Parliament and Funkadelic shared and swapped musicians, representing the yin and yang of Post-Soul aesthetics. If Parliament became more associated with black music's commercial side, including dance and disco, Funkadelic was the voice and body of the critique of the commercial. Funkadelic has been characterized by its critics and by Clinton himself as the more hard-rocking of the two projects, more driven by the experimental sounds of psychedelia and Clinton's genre-pushing vision of a black music that reembraces rock as one of its own—as the heat left out in black music's recooking of the blues by Motown and other, more commercial black music ventures. Together they have a complex relationship with the commercial and mainstream, critical of the music industry's tendency to eat its young, reflective of the history that has already shaped black music and the black bodies that produced it, but also pushing to create sounds to capture more ears.[6] The bands evolved into several entities, including Bootsy Collins and His Rubber Band, the Brides of Funkenstein, and Parlet. And Clinton, Collins, and some others of the band still play their three-hour sets in venues like Lollapalooza and the Pitchfork Festival as the P-Funk All Stars. (Here, unless speaking specifically about one of the groups, I'll refer to the groups collectively as Parliament/Funkadelic or as P-Funk.)

Funking Up Nationalism's Divisional Gender Logic

In the song " Cosmic Slop," as in many other P-Funk's songs, we see at work a process of political and aesthetic reconfiguration, taking stories and aesthetics from black ghetto culture,[7] and also braiding them with other influences, ultimately transforming what is considered "authentic" black culture, especially in the wake of Black Nationalism and the Black Art Movement. "Cosmic Slop" unapologetically combines elements of avant-garde and psychedelic rock culture with the existential, historical, and aesthetic aspects of black working-class life, addressing the urban poverty that continued to haunt African Americans in cities like Plainfield, New Jersey, as well as the struggle to maintain community and black love in a changing social scape. It combines the hard guitars of white rockers like Vanilla Fudge and the prepunk of Iggy and the MC5 (friends and coconspirators with Clinton), or the exploratory openness of psychedelia, with the driving rhythm of James Brown, as well as the soulful falsetto of a Curtis Mayfield or Marvin Gaye. Westbound records' film for "Cosmic Slop" might be said to be informed by the happenings and be-ins of the 1960s, and perhaps the experimental theater of Augusto Baol—particularly in Baol's attention, through theater, to the politics of bodies in space. Yet, as the song's lyrics concern black tribe, nation, and family, the realism of poverty and the sex trade, we might consider the influence of the Black Art Movement in its interest in creating politicized art about black life. In its exploration of black clothing, hair, and gesture, as well as urban cityscapes, I also see echoes of blaxploitation films of the same period. Yet rather than creating a glamorization of black street life, P-Funk definitely lets loose the weirdness and the unexpected. The terrain is never what one would expect from watching *Superfly*. The album *Cosmic Slop* presents a series of eclectic references and layered identities in its lyrics, from the neighborhood prostitute who is also a mother in the song "Cosmic Slop" to a new lover who might be a transvestite in the song "No Compute." This particular album's sound and lyrics shift wildy in tone, from soul aching to wickedly sly to surreal.

P-Funk's embrace of outsized, "funky" expressions of desire, its subcultural reference points, as well as its bringing together of cross-racial artistic aesthetics, might be one reason that the band in its first years had trouble securing stable airplay on black radio stations. P-Funk album cover artist Ronald "Stozo" Edwards talks about the group's difficulty in attracting black audiences in its early days.

Niggas have always been a little scared of Funkadelic. My cousin bought that *Maggot Brain* album, it was the scariest shit I had ever heard. You had to be, like, a freak to be into them. It was the same trip with niggas liking Jimi Hendrix. It was almost a sellout to be into anything that had too much rock-and-roll guitar going on. Plus *funk* was still a bad word. If a mug was "funky," niggas would call you out on that shit. I'm not talking about the music, I'm talking about the odor. So there was just a select crew of some whites, but predominantly some blacks, who were willing to take that walk on the wild side.[8]

P-Funk's sometimes hard rock sound, combined with its challenge to political and cultural orthodoxies, set it apart from much of the soul and funk of the period. Song-writing partner Sidney Barnes describes the early band as having "a young, black militant kind of weirdness that people just weren't associating themselves with."[9] The very kinds of experimentation that P-Funk trafficked in, and in particular the melding of black nationalist and black hippie worlds, were sometimes thought to be socially and artistically dangerous, especially in their fluidity, at least by some in the Black Art Movement. Take, for example, poet Haki R. Madhubuti's castigation of the black hippie Clean in his poem "Move Un-Noticed to Be Noticed: A Nationhood Poem."

> Clean, u is the first black hippy I've ever met.
> Why you bes dressen so funny, anyhow huh?
> I mean, is that u, Clean?
> Why u bes dressen like an airplane, can you fly,
> I mean,
> Will yr/ blue jim shoes fly u,/ & what about yr/ tailor made bell
>   bottoms, Clean? Can they
> Lift u above madness,/ turn u into the right direction. & that red
>   and pink scarf around yr/
> Neck what's that for, /Clean,/huhn? Will it help you fly, yea, swing,
>   siwinging swing?[10]

Madhubuti's poem paints a portrait of the black male hippie as one who has abandoned proper blackness—and, by extension, himself. The poem's coy jabs at Clean's tailored bell bottoms and pink and red scarf imply his refusal of proper gender as well. Phillip Brian Harper suggests that some of the poems of the Black Power Movement depend on a "divisional logic" that betrays an anxiety about ambiguous gender identities. This binary is exemplified by an "authentic" model of black masculinity, including self-determination, righteousness, black identification, and hardness, on the one hand, and on the other, a "failed" masculinity: assimilationist, effemininate, mixed-up, and too influenced by the standards of white culture.[11] It's what Eldridge Cleaver describes in *Soul on Ice* as being "fucked."[12] This surveillance of sexuality and gender conflates body politics and desires with political vision, so that, for example, Amiri Baraka's "Civil Rights Poem" calls Roy Wilkins "an eternal faggot"—perhaps by suggestion—because of his perceived assimilationist politics.

This policing of black masculinity by some in the Black Art Movement has had a lasting effect on the ongoing discourse of black nationhood, authenticity, gender, and sexuality. Black feminist theorist Barbara Smith has commented on her own experiences of some of these constrictions of gender and sexuality in her introduction to *Home Girls*.

> I will never forget the period of Black nationalism, power and pride which, despite its benefits, had a stranglehold on our identities. A blueprint was made for being Black and Lord help you if you deviated in the slightest way. How relieved we were to find, as our awareness increased and our own Black women's movement grew, that we were not crazy, that the brothers had in fact created a sex-biased definition of "Blackness" that served only them. And yet, in finding each other, some of us have fallen into the same pattern—have decided that if a sister doesn't dress like me, talk like me, walk like me, and even sleep like me, then she's not really a sister. Conformity.[13]

These tensions within nationalist black political movements around sexual and gender codes become particularly vexed in the context of art making and performance in particular—perhaps because poetry, music, and other forms of performance are so emotionally powerful—at the same time that some nationalist writers have feared performance as being politically diffuse. For example, in his highly influential book *The Crisis of the Negro Intellectual* (1967), Harold Cruse betrays a growing discomfort with art, and particularly performance, as a reliable medium of black politics. Although Cruse repeatedly embraces the creative intellectual as vital to the black community, and talks about his own experience in theater as the first place where he realized the potential for community, he distrusts the radical potential of nonlinear thinking, and the importance of *feeling* and other often ambiguous or fluid ways of knowing that accompany creative work. For example, Cruse gives Langston Hughes faint praise for his "extraordinary faculty for defining the confused sensations that constitute the collective conscience of simple minds'" but adds that Hughes is "not a thinker."[14] He says that James Baldwin fails to address "black reality" in his novels.[15] In his commentary on Paul Robeson, Cruse reveals his discomfort with performance and its accompanying forms of feeling as knowledge as the site of intellectual work.

> He [Robeson] exists in a world of illusion and there is little dividing line between his relationships with the world behind the footlights and the world of living reality. As an actor-performer, it was remarkable that Paul Robeson essayed an actual leadership role. But he never was to escape, fully, the world of make-believe.[16]

Overall, Cruse suggests that because the performer's work is inherently and physically collaborative, "he is in many ways the most ethnically unstable, or the most *aracial* of all Negro artists."[17] The actor must embody and interpret with others. Cruse here seems especially concerned about the performing body as open, making physical his suspicions about the ambiguity and potential vulnerability of the act of interpretation that also reveals itself in his discussion of Hughes. It would seem that for Cruse, the body, theatricality, sensation, feeling, and cross-racial collaboration are dangerous as sites for intellectual work because of their unpredictability and lack of pure or stable answers to political problems.

P-Funk was often willing to explore black experience, particularly bodily, sexual, and sensual experience, at these points of ambiguity, vulnerability, pain, desire, and laughter, using tools of music and performance that spoke to bodies individually and internally, as well as collectively. Yet this power to harness emotionally strong and sometimes inchoate feeling had a powerful effect on its listeners—prompting some to find unity and empathy with other black men. Take, for example, P-Funk lead guitarist DeWayne "Blackbyrd" McKnight's description of Eddie Hazel's guitar on *Maggot Brain*.

> I was listening to Funkadelic for as long as I can remember. "Maggot Brain" fucked me up. It was emotion—the sounds that Eddie was making, and the way he was playing the notes that he played. I don't know where he was at the time he was doing it, but damn! That's what I think got me—just emotion-wise. I don't think I had

heard a song like that with, like, no drums, no bass, and playing like that.[18]

Hazel's guitar models a kind of vulnerability, emotional immediacy, and transformation that becomes the nexus for a new form of community between the black men—and others—who listen. As I'll discuss below, in everyday acts like hanging out and listening to the radio, record collecting and exchanging, going to concerts, or learning and imitating Hazel's guitar solos, black men have found powerful routes of transformation.

The black hippiedom and funk experimentation of P-Funk pushed boundaries of black culture and sound, as well as sexuality and black respectability. George Clinton, as a kind of trickster figure, deliberately courts images that risk abjection and rejection. Clinton's recounting of his experience of the 1967 race riots in Plainfield, New Jersey—a narrative that one might expect could be the place to solidify one's political status in the black community—is playfully contrary, countering an idealized view of the properly masculine, properly righteous, black nationalist warrior.

We couldn't get in or out of Plainfield for a while. They let us in, and we ended up in our apartment for the next two days. And like everyone else, you ran around and got whatever was laying out in the street. The only thing I tried to take was big boxes of tissues and sanitary napkins. My stealing days or my riot wasn't that profitable.[19]

Here, as well as elsewhere, Clinton identifies himself with not only femininity but abject femininity. In interviews, in public appearances, and onstage, Clinton and other band members risk the notion of proper black masculinity, not just by cross-dressing but by playing with dynamics of humiliation, abjection, and exposure: wearing diapers or soiled bed sheets for robes; wearing see-through women's black lace panties; or creating the outsized and sexually anxious persona Sir Nose, with his pale, floppy, rubberized, and (somewhat thinly) phallic schnoz, for example, to disorient prevailing views of black masculinity and open up new spaces for creation. In these campy moments, we see Clinton and his band mates performing an intentional and arguably feminist masquerade of male and female gender, in that their performances foreground and consciously play with the rules of gender.[20] In their particular work of foregrounding in P-Funk, gender is always deeply connected to the history of race, yet it travels, and is multiple, linking the objectification and criminalization of black slavery and segregation to a surreal yearning for the future. Whether in Hazel's open displays of emotion or Clinton's self-parodic, shame-shedding laughter, P-Funk's performances embody and embrace nonnormative forms of desire, and rage, as well as the unspoken loss that punctuates black male histories of embodiment in public space.[21] In P-Funk's performances of eccentricity, and especially gender and sexual eccentricity, we might find a project of "creative historical knowing," to use Kathryn Bond Stockton's phrase,[22] which exposes, among other things, the racist logics of social debasement.

This disorientation, as a form of disidentification, can have critical as well as pleasurable effects. As John Corbett suggests, P-Funk's disruptive, disorienting take on black masculinity shares with black eccentric musicians Sun Ra and Lee "Scratch" Perry the strategic use of alter egos and personal mythologies in their performances to support an overall aesthetic and politic of disorientation or "unreality."[23] Whether we look at George Clinton's elaborate staging of "The Mothership Connection"— complete with rebirth from an onstage pod, or the comic book struggles of good and evil between Sir Nose and Dr. Funkenstein, Clinton and P-Funk embrace the unreal as a space of critique. Disorientation is not just a moment of confusion but a performative command to look at the world in a decentered way—indeed, to embrace a constant position of critique and dis-ease. Clinton not only asks his listeners to disorient themselves from normative modes of pleasure but he presents disorientation itself as a form of pleasure. This embrace of disorientation will become the fuel for transportation to new worlds in the futurist and gender-bending work of Meshell Ndegeocello as well. Both artists ask their audiences to see and hear freshly through forms of beautiful confusion, in the process expanding the spaces of black identity.

P-Funk's performative reconfiguration of normative black sexuality, as well as its nonessentialized rethinking of gender and nation, contradicts at least some tenets of black sexuality in the nationalist rhetoric of this period. If, in the Black Art Movement and Black Nationalist rhetoric, we see the solidification of a particular kind of heterosexual black manhood, and the importance of art in policing that notion of black manhood, as I've previously discussed, P-Funk then complicates matters, even as it presents its own rhetoric of a populist nation. Here the nation is formed not specifically by race but by "One Nation under a

Groove." And while such a nation is founded on the love of funk, a form that Clinton and P-Funk explicitly link to black musical and cultural forms, drawing from the call-and-response of gospel,[24] the bent notes of slave calls, African polyrhythms, the soulful harmonies of doo-wop, and the on-the-street storytelling of black life, "groove" is something that anyone, guided by funk, potentially can enter, "just for the funk of it."[25] Nation, under the P-Funk banner of groove, is both culturally specific and fluid, embodied and inviting transcendence. Such rethinking of nation as new potentiality—constructed by desire ("Do you promise to funk, the whole funk, and nothing but the funk?")—is reflected in Eve Zibat's description of the Chocolate Jam, an all-day celebration of music and black pride that took place in Washington, DC, in July 1978, which featured the music of P-Funk and bassist Bootsy Collins as headliners.

> The dark heads and bright clothes of 10,000 young Washington-ians on the field of RFK Stadium break into the fragmentation of a vast Impressionist painting. A simmering effect over the surface gradually resolves itself into the bobbing groups of tightly packed dancers and the shaking of thousands of upraised arms. Driven by the insistence of the disco beat, couples bump hips, knees and elbows; on the edge of a giant platform, a roadie dances in exact tandem with a girl 10 feet below.[26]

Here we see funk's potential to unite its audience precisely in the experience of disorientation,[27] as Clinton and Hazel tell us in their 1970 song "Free Your Mind and Your Ass Will Follow."

Queering P-Funk: Music as a Space of Nonnormative Black Self-Fashioning

I'd like to suggest that the musical space of P-Funk—whether it is the space of the live concert or the space between your ears or headphones—might exist as an important space for improvising and performing non-normative sexual desires for black men. And while these moments are at times inchoate and contradictory in terms of a critique of sexism and homophobia, they do at least advance an "elsewhere"—a fantasy space for new formations of self. This is particularly poignant in a historical moment that saw increased surveillance of black men's bodies in public space, reflected in a reported rise in the black male prison population.[28] As this book argues, in general in the Post-Soul moment—a moment that is arguably still with us, if we can look beyond the rhetorics of unity and racial uplift, which tend to flatten sexual identities—we might well find more examples in which seemingly normative male spaces serve as places for more fluid sexual and gender self-fashioning, identification, and desire. We might think of music as this space—sometimes a space within a space tightly patrolled by others.

While black feminists, gays, and lesbians have—perhaps by necessity—created a visible public space in which to talk about and practice nonnormative sexuality and community, such a community space for nonnormative heterosexual black men is missing. Here I'm thinking of the formation of nonnormative sexual communities through clubs and other social spaces, the founding of feminist and queer journals and other publications, and political activist movements. Where are the spaces in which black men who are heterosexual can talk about their desires—particularly nonreproductive sexual desires—and claim public space in which to talk to each other about those desires? If, as many have argued, the black family is the space in which to be productive citizens,[29] where are the spaces in which to be nonproductive? I'd argue that we have to look with a queer eye at the narratives, creative practices, and performances of black masculinity otherwise deemed "normative," looking in high school halls, straight bars, and spaces for style and self-fashioning, like barbershops. Interestingly enough, George Clinton's memories about his first job in the Silk Palace as a hair stylist, in a New Jersey barbershop, give a very different construction of this mostly male space that we see in the dominant media. If in films like Ice Cube's *Barbershop* we see the barbershop as a space where playing the dozens, hair styling, and even physical violence allow men to keep each other "in check" about their masculinity, Clinton's descriptions of the over- and underground economies at the Silk Palace hint at a more chaotic and perhaps layered and fluid space of male self-fashioning, and pleasure.

> Processing hair. We had two or three older barbers who had their clientele, playing checkers and shit. Then we had the younger guys, who may be nodding, you know what I mean? I might have a girl in the back there. Somebody's head might be burning, talkin' 'bout "Get this shit out of my muhfuckin' head?" Congolene—fry

that muthafucka! Just put it on your head with a comb or brush, grease your head to death, then wash your head out while you pat your feet and holler. Or you might get: "I'm going to audition for my record thang, I'll tell my boy to comb you out. I put the waves in, so you gon' be cool."[30]

Clinton's barbershop here is both a real space (a particular and indexible place in a particular historical moment located in the black community in Plainfield, New Jersey) and a space linked to the other Chocolate Cities that P-Funk sings about (Washington, DC, New York City, Cincinnati, and Detroit), as well as an imaginative space of laughter and experimentation.

To locate P-Funk in a queered discourse of eccentricity requires listening for what is unnamed, unrecognized, and perhaps unclaimed—what Phillip Brian Harper calls "Critical speculative knowledge" of what seems to be hiding in plain sight:[31] "For how else can you capture a boogie, if you don't attack from the back?" (lyric from P-Funk's "Theme to the Black Hole"). P-Funk's spectacularly freaky funk, its enthusiasm for booties, and its almost Irigarian call to surrender to the pleasures of underwater aquaboogieing seem to these eyes as queer as it gets.[32] Kodowo Eshun, Ricky Vincent, Anne Danielsen, and Amy Nathan Wright discuss the erotic pull of P-Funk's music but have less to say about the implications of their eroticism in terms of gender codes of black masculinity.[33] A queered reading of P-Funk goes against the grain of much recent cultural and music criticism, which has been primarily focused on P-Funk as a place in which to imagine an Afrofuturist utopia (or dystopia),[34] or P-Funk's interventions in the politics of sampling, copyright, and other aspects of black cultural traffic.[35]

A queered reading of P-Funk faces the strong sense of ownership of the band by (straight) fans, blogs, and other commentary. Perhaps this is because P-Funk's rhythms have, especially in this hip-hop age, become the gold standard of (heterosexual) black male cool. We see the power of P-Funk as a sign of cool and black male normativity in cultural critic Robin D. G. Kelley's autobiographical essay "Confessions of a Nice Negro, or Why I Shaved My Head," in *Speak My Name: Black Men on Masculinity and the American Dream* (New York: Beacon Press, 1996), where he claims Funkadelic as having been important to his own Post-Soul—and insistently nonnerdy—coming of age in the 1980s.

Never an egghead or a dork, as a teenager I was pretty cool. I did the house-party circuit on Friday and Saturday nights and used to stroll down the block toting the serious Radio Raheem boom-box. . . . Those of us who had cars (we called them hoopties or rides back in that day) spent our lunch hours and precious class time hanging out in the school parking lot, running down our Die Hards to pump up Cameo, Funkadelic, Grandmaster Flash from our car stereos. I sported dickies and Levis, picked up that gang-sta stroll, and when the shag came in style I was with it—always armed with a silk scarf to ensure that my hair was laid. (13–14)

But while Kelley includes listening to Funkadelic as one of the many initiation rites that marked his place in the world of black male cool, his description at the same time implicitly reveals how black male self-fashioning and performance have some room for fluidity in their appropriation of feminine gendered signs—certainly something explored by Cameo, as well as P-Funk. These standards of black male cool are not naturalized or stable: five or six years earlier, that silk scarf would have labeled him a "black hippie" and a decade later the shag might have got him teased in the hall. While the costs of a "bad performance" of black masculinity can be high (to borrow E. Patrick Johnson's notion, expressed in his article and performance *Strange Fruit*), black masculinity can and does often have elements of the "silly" or "queer," if put in another context, or is pushed into excess.[36] As I'll argue at more length a little later, P-Funk takes the inherent aspects of silliness/excess in black male style and embraces them, pushing them to the edge. By exposing what is inherently queer about black male sexuality and style, P-Funk can show us what in other circumstances must be masked, or encoded, in normative black male identity and performance. At its most fundamental level, in the music and live performances of Funkadelic and Parliament, we see a rejection of fear, loathing, and shame of the black body and the embrace of sexual and imaginative freedom.[37]

The implications of P-Funk's work as potentially feminist and queer gets drowned out by, first, the dominant of conceptualization of funk as a stereotypically masculine sound and scene, including primary emphasis in some musicologists' working definitions of *funk* on The One, as opposed to what musicologist Anne Danielsen calls the "extended ambiguity" of funk.[38] Funk scenes locally and nationally have been dominated by men—despite some amazing examples of female musicianship in the funk scene, including Sly Stone's trumpeter Cynthia Brown, Labelle, Betty Davis, female P-Funkers the Brides of Funkenstein and Parlet, Meshell Ndegeocello, and others.[39] Despite this, P-Funk's "militant kind of weirdness" makes room for a new and nonnormative masculinity. As George Clinton once told *Rolling Stone* magazine, "Funk is anything that you need to be to save your life."[40]

P-Funk, through its sound, lyrics, and use of theatricality on- and offstage, makes room for a more exploratory and decentered notion of black male identity. I'm interested in the ways that we might think of a queer heterosexual black masculinity as a means of giving voice and visibility to black masculine self-fashioning that is often "bred out" of the traditional neoliberal subject. Cultural Historian Rinaldo Walcott suggests that narratives such as heteronormative conceptions of family, or the overall idea of the triumph of black men over slavery through economic achievement and traditional notions of power—what he calls the "from victim to victor" narrative—are often lobbied to root out less coherent, and ultimately less economically useful, notions of black masculinity (at least according to a postliberal state, one that was definitely in formation in the United States in the Post-Soul moment.[41] I'm particularly interested in the ways that P-Funk might be read as an opposition voice in this context, presenting performances of black maleness that play "chicken" with codes of respectability.

As George Clinton takes some of the discourses already in the air, including psychedelia and black nationalism, and makes them his own, he creates a space for something strange, outlandish, and new, particularly in terms of gender. Many fans and critics have praised and theorized Clinton's funk as a means of space travel—an important tenet of an Afrofuturism that nonetheless reminds us that we cannot escape our origins. As Michael C. Ladd writes, "Funkadelic focused on flight, but not escape."[42] But I think there's room for more thought on how Clinton's Parliament and Funkadelic make us think about this "something new" as a distinctly embodied experience.

Funk, with its hard-driving rhythm, is very much about the body and pleasure. As many recent theorists on funk have written, you cannot have funk without the sweat, without the labor of the body at work (and play). Clinton asks us to think about the funky body as one that challenges the order of the ways that the body is patrolled and controlled in space. In the song "Aquaboogie (A Psychoalphadiscobetabioaquadoloop)," for example, Clinton imagines an underwater escape from this history of control where, "With the rhythm it takes to dance to what we have to live through / you can dance underwater and not get wet." The song offers under water as a place to speak back to history, to defy the rules of nature. Critics Tony Bolden and Cheryl Keyes speak to the West African etymology of the word *funk* as meaning both "bad odor" and "bad order"—a tantalizing combination.[43] Clinton and his Parliament/Funkadelic crew are not just interested in outer space but also in reconceiving inner spaces—the spaces of desire and the performance of those desires for others—through the creation and sometimes deconstruction of "personae" of blackness. In performance, P-Funk commandeers the nightclub, the stadium arena, or the city park to perform sexual freedom and exploration outside of the familiar discourses of courtship and family.

In spite of the often crudely sexualized terms in which male and female relationships are represented lyrically and in terms of the icons of its covers, Parliament/Funkadelic's ultimate vision of black humanity seems to be one in which men and women are equal and connected in struggle. This is captured well in Pedro Bell's cover for *One Nation under a Groove*, where men and women plant a Black Nationalist flag together. P-Funk represents that struggle, though, as an ongoing and imperfect one. Much of P-Funk's album cover artwork provocatively represents black women's bodies as contested territories, and as the locus for political and psychic frustration. The cover for *Cosmic Slop* features an image of a naked, chained black woman that echoes some Black Nationalist art in which the enslaved women become the icon for black struggle,[44] or where the head or body of a nude black woman is used to depict a lost "Mother Africa." But these P-Funk images utilize a more dominant note of the surreal. The woman's left nipple is circled by a map of the United States and Latin America and the Caribbean, the nipple itself seeming to be the waters of the Caribbean. Her left breast has been transformed into a combination lock. These bodies are mediated objects, where scopophilia and touch are linked to colonization and capitalism. Rather than the nostalgic use of the black female body as a sign of lost Africa that we see in some popular Black Nationalist iconography, these images present the black female body still entangled in political battles and the economic exploitation of others. The lettering on the album is punctuated with spurts of what seem to be representations of blood, sperm, and/or milk, linking the album's artistic production and creativity to the material products of the body and sex. On the cover of *Maggot Brain*, the bodies of women even more actively express their frustration. Here, a woman, screaming and surrounded by maggots, becomes the icon of frustration and dis-ease explored in the songs—the visual equivalent of Eddie Hazel's crying guitar in the song "Maggot Brain." In this way, the album features an image of collective frustration and struggle.

Yet these album covers do sometimes implicate P-Funk in their participation in the objectification of black women, and in the trade of sexualized black bodies that they would seem to be critiquing. The controversial cover for *The Electric Spanking of War Babies* skirts the line between critiquing and exploiting the objectification of women's bodies. The back of the album depicts a nude black woman (or cyborg?) on all fours, transformed into a machine in which money goes in and sound comes out. Her body is punctured with knobs, wires, and bolts. The critique is somewhat ambiguous. Is she meant to be the personification of the exploitation of black people? A "tar baby" produced by the powers that be to distract us all from our own exploitation? A gullible consumer? P-Funk's placement of itself as an increasingly successful commercial band, straddling underground and mainstream success, is also unclear. In my reading, the cover seems to extend its critique of the institution of slavery to consider how the exploitation of black bodies and labor continues through the music industry—perhaps here a not so veiled critique of commercialized black music such as that of Motown (the target of George Clinton's ire and critique). This reading is reinforced by the fact that the woman is shown shackled and seems to fit an ongoing critique of the music industry as a form of exploitation of black labor leveled by Clinton and the group. Whatever its intention, the cover was boycotted by the group Women against Pornography (WAP), and Warner Brothers was forced the group to alter it. But in a rebellious move against the company, P-Funk created a cover that allowed the viewer to peek at the shackled female legs, and bits of her torso, with slashes and slits, and the words "Oh Look! The cover 'they' were TOO SCARED to print! Peek Here. And Here, too." Perhaps this new "peep show" cover is meant to suggest that WAP and Warner Brothers' emphasis on the nudity overlooks the political critique of the original cover. In any case, we see here, as in the case of many of Grace Jones's performances, for example, that sexual spectacle often risks misreadings, an ongoing tension in eccentric performance.

Many of P-Funk's songs explore the politics of relationships and sexual conquest in wry, and sometimes self-critical, ways. Male sexuality is often the source of gentle and not so gentle mockery and critique. Consider the nasally, weaselly, potentially parodic chorus of Clinton's otherwise pretty celebratory ode to "doggin'" in "Atomic Dog": "Why must I be like that? Why must I chase the cat?/ Nothin' but the dog in me."[45] In the later, Afrofuturist concept albums of the mid-1970s and into the 1980s, including *Mothership Connection* and *The Clones of Dr. Funkenstein,* the evil institutions of oppression are depicted as exaggeratedly phallic: Sir Nose and his bop gun, the dookie squad, which chases after its enemies with "pissgun rays" on the inside cover of *One Nation under a Groove.* And I think most significantly, the group's constant return to and sometimes critical image of the pimp as both a site of great style and cool and a figure of economic oppression returns over the course of their work as a trouble spot to negotiate. (See, e.g., the song "Trash a Go Go" on the *Cosmic Slop* LP, which features a judge shaming a man who pimps his girlfriend to feed his drug habit.) Rather than settling these moments of contradiction in black sexual politics and desire, the group embraces moments of ambiguity in black life. So, according to "Funkadelic Bylaw No. 19": "It is better to open your eyes and say you don't understand . . . than to close your eyes and say you don't believe" (credited to O. J. Rodney on the cover of *One Nation under a Groove*). In other words, according to P-Funk, it is better to acknowledge the complex and contradictory aspects of black love, sex, and politics as they present themselves to you in the flesh than to pretend you're beyond them. This is the hard-learned lesson taught to Sir Nose by Dr. Funkenstein, the personae created by Clinton and featured in songs like "Theme from the Black Hole," "Gloryhallastoopid," and "Flashlight." Sir Nose always claims that he is too cool to sweat, funk, swim, or dance, until he is taken over by the music.

Clinton lends his skills in the theatrical to engage in an ongoing conversation about the masks of blackness, and in particular, the experience of double, triple, and even quadruple consciousness.[46] This conversation gets pushed into a new form by Clinton, by getting us to think about such masks playfully and critically. His is also the mask of the trickster. The mask is both burden and boon, a way to escape, re-create oneself, trip on out. The masks of trickster, space alien, hippie allow for an exploration of the black imagination, and with it, gender and sexual freedom.

P-Funk does not posit as the solution to full humanity and black freedom the suppression of desires, in all of their sticky, complicated, and funky forms. Instead, we are encouraged to dance our way out of our constrictions. P-Funk chooses subversive and nonnormative tactics: cross-dressing and transvestitism (from performing as a pregnant doo-wop group to the consideration of a mock marriage to Iggy Pop); scatology;[47] fluid lyrical movements between male and female voice; depiction of the fluidity between masculine and feminine desire; the melding of human and machine, and sometimes with it, the fetishization of nonhuman objects as sites of desire (including a gyrating dance with a huge flashlight in a 1978 stage show in Houston); the mind-expanding ethos (and sometimes ingestion) of psychedelic drugs; the embrace of nonreproductive sexuality, and especially praise of the "booty" as a site of desire (in "The Theme to the Black Hole"); and, through it all, an embrace of silliness as an aesthetic.

Black Men, Black Cool, and the Aesthetic of Silliness

Anyone who has seen a photo of George Clinton himself—bursting wide-legged and smiling out of a spaceship on the cover of *Mothership Connection* or more recently, pumping up the Lollapalooza crowd in a large African gown—must be struck by Clinton's propensity toward outrageous, original, and gender-bending style: hair extensions (always at least shoulder length, and in unearthly Day-Gloorange, acid green, or platinum blond); his rocking of oversized sunglasses and hats (even before Flavor Flav thought of it); and his willingness to switch from spandex and spangles to long white ermine coat to wedding gown. These outfits are often bricolage—Clinton might be wearing an African dashiki combined with raspberry beret covered in political buttons, under which he might be rocking a long blond wig. He might bring together a shiny pimp "cane" with silver thigh-high platforms. Gary Shider, inexplicably, is almost always wearing a diaper (and in a 1978 live performance in Houston, a diaper and silver leather chaps). The Brides of Funkenstein, the women of the group, sometimes are in everyday street wear, sometimes in the space-age glamour favored by Labelle, and other times in what looks like their panties. During the Dr. Funkenstein era of the early 1980s, the Brides and Clinton himself wore "big booty" fat suits—referencing, perhaps, the Venus Hottentot. At play seems to be a sampling of historical moments and influences, textures, and most definitely genders. In interviews, Clinton has reflected a strong interest in black style, and especially the creative and sometimes over-the-top impulse of black cool, especially after his experience as a barber and hairstylist in New Jersey.

"After you've done other people's hair for so long you know the concept of doin' hair," he says, wrapping a bright braid around his index finger. "The garbage man looked just as cool as the pimp and the singer when they left the barbershop. Really, style is just a bunch of bullshit, it's just how you carry it. If you is safe with that concept, then you can be ugly as you wanna be or cool as you wanna be and know that neither of them mean shit! No matter how cool you are, you can go someplace where you look corny as hell to somebody. . . . They thought that to have your doo was the corniest stuff in the world when you got around hippies. And then a few years later, the afros came out and then the black people started lookin' silly. So it means that styles just go 'round and 'round and ain't nothin' permanently cool or corny."[48]

Clinton's deconstruction of black style flies in the face of one of the beloved commandments of Soul: that black people are just naturally cool. Black style, then, and the accompanying command to be cool are freed up as a space for play, for silliness. As Dr. Funkenstein (with dripping white ermine, hat, sunglasses, and cane), Clinton captures the image of the pimp, but it gets transformed and transmogrified. Clinton takes what's already over the top and pushes it further, shows us the potential queerness of it. Stepping out of the mothership, and surveying the crowd, he captures the hypervisibility and command of this image, but he further denormalizes it, lets us laugh, too. He gives the pimp a blond wig, puts Superfly together with Foxy Brown, and then adds some silver chaps from the Village People, to boot. Change clothes, change places. Perform it for the people on the street and the club. Perform it for white college girls and bourgie black men. Perform it for the black hippies who have always wanted to have a stage of their own. Perform it for Led Zeppelin (members of which apparently did go to their shows, too) and the white Soul crooners, learning black sound. Resteal the sound, and their guitars and amps, borrowing their new twists and adding your own. Perform it for Berry Gordy and show him what he's missing. Play it for Aretha and the music executives. Strip off your clothes if you have to.[49]

Silly sartorial style—especially outrageous, outsized style: the nattier-than-thou suits of the black dandy, the boxy bold shoulders and outrageous colors of the zoot suit, hip-hop's oversized bling, are part of an everyday evolving performative history of the adorned black body using innovations and appropriations in fashion to claim collective freedom in white-controlled spaces.[50] We might also put P-Funk's signifying on the black body through silly style into the historical trajectory of black tricksters and comics such as minstrel performer Bert Williams, Richard Pryor, and Dave Chappelle, who, as Glenda R. Carpio suggests, use humor to both conjure and ultimately exorcise black stereotypes and a history of violence. P-Funk's music, and in particular the rhythm of the funk, as well as their highly theatrical forms of gender masquerade, might be means of ritualistically entering into and riding the spirits of the past.[51]

Embracing perversity for all that it's worth, Clinton's improvisational and sometimes whacked-out style performs his body's status as free—as the property only of a boundless black imagination. As Clinton tells John Corbett:

> The Temptations and the Pips had their type of thing wrapped up—the choreography, the outfits. . . . Instead of wearing suits we'd just gotten pressed, we'd wear the bags that they came back from the cleaners in. We'd just bust holes where the legs and arms would go. If we were on the road and we didn't have the costume, I'd take a sheet from the hotel and just dump whatever I had around it.[52]

Certainly, in Clinton's description of their improvisational tactics, we see a rejection of the codes of respectability pushed by Motown and others. Though Motown's Berry Gordy and George Clinton at one time collaborated in Clinton's early days, the relationship between the two devolved into heated competition, mutual influence, and/or stealing of riffs, and sometimes playful animosity. Clinton's commentary on Motown might be seen as part of the band's ongoing critique, or at least complication, of the image of the black male entertainer, along with the minstrel, the pimp, and the hypermasculine gangster, interrupting and reconfiguring the ways that black masculinity has been sold for others' pleasure. And we might think of the crazy stagecraft—the wildly oversized flashlights, the ingenuous doobie-smoking skull, and, of course, the mothership itself—as other expressions of creative freedom. Indeed, Clinton designed and paid for these sets himself, taking the profits that other performers might have used for Cadillacs or houses for their mothers, and used them for costumes, spaceships, and birthing pods.

Queering Black Cultural Traffic: P-Funk and the Entertainment Industry

Through his sometimes gentle, sometimes pointed critiques of Motown, disco, blue-eyed soul, and other commercialized forms of black music, George Clinton makes black cultural traffic one of his central points of political concern in his music and interviews. In "P-Funk (Wants to Get Funked Up)," he sings about appreciating the blue-eyed-soul sounds of artists like the Doobie Brothers and David Bowie but razzes, "Sounds like it got a Three on it though, to me." Clinton does not attempt to place P-Funk above the forces of commercialization and other aspects of black cultural traffic and trade. Instead, the band allows for messiness, including cross-influence across lines of race, genre, and power, as well as corniness and cool. In answer to the high number of unacknowledged samples of his music, Clinton has both gone to the courts and produced an album of frequently sampled songs called *Sample Some of Disc, Sample Some of D.A.T.,* which includes an application form for the use of copyrighted materials. This acknowledgment of the messiness of musical influence can also be seen performatively in the songs themselves. The band sometimes dared to "Doobie" its funk, taking on consummately "white" pop standards and lending them a hard funk edge. Band manager Bob Dedeckere describes one late 1970s P-Funk set as that which moves from "Dixie" to "Do You Think I'm Sexy" to their own "Maggot Brain." Indeed, the band's relationship to white rock in some ways acknowledges cross-influence, as well as the borrowing and reborrowing of black sound.[53] I hear in Clinton's rerecording of Cream's "Sunshine of Your Love," featuring Brian McKnight's one-man multiple guitar workover, as a form of (loving) revenge. Each return to the bridge keeps topping itself, reaching higher and higher, betraying the calm, steady beat of the drums. Clinton says of the song, "We took the motherfucker and roughed it up."[54] At the same time, Clinton has enthusiastically collaborated with a new generation of white performers influenced by P-Funk's songs and style. Since going solo, Clinton has performed live with Phish and the Red Hot Chili Peppers, and has produced and recorded with a variety of other artists.

P-Funk is not afraid to situate its music in a history that is both violent and comical, and that can completely transcend the politics of race, even with a mothership. P-Funk bassist William "Billy Bass" Nelson acknowledges the multiple influences of acid and psychedelic rock on his sound.

> Sgt. Pepper's Lonely Hearts Club Band, that motherfucking re-cord turned me the fuck out, for that direction—more like a pop-rock type of thing. Blue Cheer and Jimi Hendrix turned me out for acid rock. And Cream turned me out for the bluesy kind of rock. And I listened to those albums diligently, every day, until I knew all the songs, note for note. After I heard that stuff, I knew that I couldn't just play rhythm and blues constantly. I had to be able to branch out and play it all.[55]

I find the repeated use of the phrase "turned out" in Nelson's descrip-tion to be significant and suggestive. Not only does the term refer to an extreme and perhaps ecstatic reversal of previous thinking—having one's proverbial mind blown. It also has more visceral, even sexual connotations—literally being turned inside out. In some sexual slang, the term refers to being "turned" in terms of sexual orientation,[56] or of being raped, or prostituted. Nelson's choice of words speaks to the ways that his view of black music was turned inside out—the ways that white rock forced him to think about the relationship between white and black sound, not as opposites but as being of the same family. It also recalls a deeper cultural memory—the "primal moment" of sorts of the "rape" of black sound and labor—the history of abjection of black performers in the United States as unacknowledged sources of rock and pop. Indeed, we might think of this history of rock as entwined with the deeper his-tory of "love and theft" of black labor, creativity, and sexuality.[57] P-Funk resists complete erasure of this history and interestingly conceptualizes music listening and musical performance as a mixture of pleasure and pain, abjection, and remastery.[58] Ultimately, then, P-Funk's quest for imaginative freedom is informed by the history of the black body as it works and reworks history.

In his foreword to the book *Speak My Name: Black Men on Mascu-linity and the American Dream*, playwright August Wilson writes, "Re-duced to its most fundamental truth, black men are a commodity of flesh and muscle which has lost its value in the marketplace. We are left over from history."[59] P-Funk, with its interest in grooving, vamping, and being turned out and reanimated through sound, presents an extraordinary realignment of the black male body in labor. As Clinton describes it, "We had a groove that was religious. We could vamp forever."[60] Instead of the image of the black male body used up through the labors of nation building voiced by August Wilson, P-Funk offers up a new relationship to work, one where sweat leads to pleasure and exploration, where the black male body might be viewed under new terms of value.

Yet P-Funk's style is not meant to be a complete escape from reality and the more familiar struggles of home. We are meant, I think, to consider the work that goes into the production of P-Funk's musical performances in the same way that we are meant to see them (and ourselves) sweat as we dance. For Michael Ladd, P-Funk's dirty costumes and other less than perfect aspects of stagecraft were part of its political vision, the ways that the fantasy was not meant to be one of escape but one of return.

> They got their image from everywhere but primarily from the broom closet or the trash. They were beyond their world; they were out of this world. My friend Michel, horn player and flutist, remembers seeing them at the Apollo Theater in 1977; "Shider was wearing a diaper like he always did, and he had these elevator boots on but they weren't fly, they were worn, like really worn. Then out comes George in a baby-blue sheet with Roadrunner and Wile E. Coyote on it and the sheet is not clean. He's got a bike chain around his waist for a belt. I mean, it looked like he grabbed the first thing he saw when he was walking out the door and was like, 'Fuck it, I'll wear this.'"[61]

For Ladd, P-Funk's creative style marks its travel produced from a history of struggle. Struggle graced with silliness. This creative refashioning provides an important way for black men in the Post-Soul era to reexperience their bodies in history. P-Funk acknowledges both the costs of history and the funk of a history of struggle, as well as a way out, a possibility for something new by way of humor, vulnerability, and emotional openness.

Take, for example, some recent eruptions of P-Funk in writing about black men's coming of age. In all three of these examples, the sounds of P-Funk provide an entryway to new ways of being for Post-Soul men, where gender, sexuality, and class prove constrictive. While the paths that P-Funk offers are inchoate in their advice on how to proceed, they serve to encourage each speaker to create something new, to rebel, and especially to dig deeper into modes of desire and embodiment that may have been otherwise ignored by their families and communities.

Poet Kenneth Carroll, who grew up in the Montana Terrace Projects in Washington, DC, remembers the profound impact that the music and cover art of Parliament/Funkadelic had on him and his male friends, as a space where he and his friends found a rare pleasure in critical interrogation, imaginative freedom, and self-fashioning.

> "Guys who literally could not read would be interpreting the pictures, the art work, and they would come over my crib. We'd be in my living room, going over what it meant." Kids played hooky from school to line up in front of a downtown record store on the day Parliament *Mothership Connection* LP came out, he says. A crew of older kids carried P-Funk albums from party to party, and invented dances, and became a self-styled "funk mob." "Part of the thing was that, for a lot of us in the inner city, they literally kind of opened the world up," Carroll says. "In the framework of their music, there's a possibility of being beyond. That you can literally exist as a Child of the Universe somewhere, where color and class and none of that really matters. That people could be something else besides, you know, po' niggas."[62]

Carroll and his friends' critical "funk mob" might be the visual and aural model of bell hooks's "oppositional gaze"—the practice of critical looking (and listening) as a form of pleasure and power, the key to a decolonized mind.[63] She writes, "By courageously looking, we defiantly declared 'Not only will I stare. I want my look to change reality.'"[64] Along with the pleasures of disorientation, P-Funk's music and visuals offer space in which to imagine new possibilities for oneself and each other.

For writer-critic Michael C. Ladd, Funkadelic, and especially the early music of *Maggot Brain* and *Cosmic Slop,* becomes a space of escape from the normative pressures of black middle-class men coming of age in Boston: dressing "seditty," combing one's 'fro, or keeping it cut short, nice and tight.

> My mother, like any sensible black woman of her age, was big on appearance. Getting me to dress well was a constant struggle. At-

tempting to drag a comb through my afro was near impossible. I'd pull a William and Ellen Craft and just start running. I would run until I had exhausted my mother and aunt's energy and the pick would slip from their hands. But I felt like the world was against me on this one. Everyone was snap tight UpSouth. Needless to say, when I saw the Funkadelic covers I felt I had finally found some company—big, bushy muthafuckas. They were the masters of the margin, right in the middle.[65]

While Ladd doesn't talk specifically about the link between Funkadelic and sex, the music becomes his alternate soundtrack for the politics of gender and (sexual) coming of age around him, and is a part of his own awareness of his body, and his fashioning of it, as a site of contested ownership.

Grit, and nappy and ashy kneecapped grit is what I needed. I didn't wash already, that's whom I was, a complicated black kid bouncing from a faux ghetto to suburbia and back, in the same town. . . . I found *Cosmic Slop* at my cousins'. It did not save my life. It just gave me the map so I knew how.[66]

Finally, we might consider P-Funk bassist Bootsy Collins's narrative of discovery and becoming a part of George Clinton's band, in this interview with Thomas Sayers Ellis, as an example of how the blaxploration that P-Funk offers its audiences also works internally, for its creators. Bootsy offers another example of the ways the band opens up the constraints of normative black masculine performance. For Bootsy, his collaboration with George Clinton becomes a way to move beyond the musical and sartorial aesthetic of respectability and high style embraced by James Brown's band to something more experimental. Bootsy describes showing up at his first James Brown session in 1969, with "tied died jeans, my afro was leaning to the right. And we were wearing them little round eyeglasses from back in the day. Just cool."[67] But he was out of step with the aesthetic of smooth soulfulness of James Brown and his review.[68] To be asked to hold down the bass in the Godfather of Soul's band was an amazing professional opportunity. Bootsy describes his apprenticeship with Brown as a time when he learned discipline and, in some ways, a route of respect as a fatherless son. But Bootsy also describes his yearning to play outside the bounds of Brown's direction.

"Son, listen to me now. I'm the Godfather of Soul." He always had to lecture me and it was cool because, like I said, I didn't have a daddy back home, so I guess he felt like he had to fill those shoes. And he was like my dad. "Son, you got to stop doing all them things and just give me the One." So when I started doing that, he started to like it and I could tell. So I figured, if I could give him this One and play all them other things . . . I think he'll like me.[69]

When Bootsy is introduced to George Clinton's clearly more counter-cultural style, he finds a way out of the disciplining framework of family and patriarch.[70] He goes to visit Clinton in his apartment and finds a new mode of blackness, a (post?) soul mate for the self that he had to sacrifice in order to play in Brown's band.

I remember walking in the house. I'm kinda semi-trippin' too. Walk in, and George didn't have no furniture, got no furniture in none of them. And he sittin' in the last room, in the corner, got his legs in like, a Buddha thing, you know, with his head down. He got a star on one side and a moon on the other shaved in his head and the rest was bald. He got a sheet on, his feet you know, he got these big "Boy, I say Boy" feet. You know who I'm talking about. Foghorn Leghorn! . . . And I'm like Dang, this is going to be fun.[71]

For Collins, Ladd, and Carroll, P-Funk's music provides a means of seeing around corners to a future that others can't see, and to provide new answers to those basic questions of desire and funk and freedom that plague them in the present. P-Funk shares its lessons in how to occupy the spaces of city streets, schoolyards, and concert stages in the full-on beauty of a new black masculine weirdness: ashy knee-capped, 'fro leaning to the side, playing to the One to the pulse of your own magnificent body. For its growing collective of Funkateers, P-Funk awakens otherwise unheard frequencies. Please do not adjust your set.

FOUR

Michael Jackson, Queer World Making, and the Trans Erotics of Voice, Gender, and Age

Off the Wall (1979) was the first album I ever bought with my own money. Thirteen years old, seventh grade, size ten feet, finally convinced to wear a training bra only after my gym teacher tactfully suggested it to me after a particularly vigorous game of kickball. Our family moved back to Chicago after eight years in Nashville, and, an Afro-puff wearer in a sea of Jheri curls and Farrah Fawcett press and flips, I was way behind the curve of sophistication. In Nashville, my friends and I competed over our standardized test scores and played with our gerbils. I was the happy-go-lucky-only-black-girl in circle of 4-H Club geeks. Sex was all around me, of course. Lured by the smell of Gee Your Hair Smells Terrific and sun and Bubblicious, I did give up my neon yellow plastic pocket comb to Rebecca Evans for the chance to watch her use it, but those desires were floating, inchoate, and I enjoyed my state of suspension.

Writer Dale Peck says of his own queer thirteenhood:

> Desire was still a single urge then, undifferentiated at its core but beginning to ribbon apart at its edges; like an octopus, it reached out in so many directions that it came to seem like several different desires. Though we came up with a thousand different answers, we continued to ask the same question, over and over: What do I want? But we dismissed each answer we came up with—*I want a sandwich, I want to write a story, I want to kiss LaMoine Weibe*—because the one thing we thought we knew was that we didn't have a name for what we wanted. Indeed, we suspected that it might not even have a name.[1]

In hindsight, of course, it seems to me obvious that my own awkwardness that year after our move to Chicago, and my panic at participating in the rituals of heterosex readiness around me: straightening hair, shoplifting lip gloss, endless note passing and rating of boys—was because I was—

am—queer. But are sexualities always so clearly retraceable? Maybe, as Peck says, at thirteen we're all queer; if "Queer was the desire to live in another time, queer was the dream of traveling to another planet, queer was the need to do something."[2]

In *Off the Wall*, I found a soundtrack for those desires that were floating around me, but for which I didn't have a name. Yes, Michael Jackson sang of "dancing into sunlight," "putting that nine to five up on the shelf," and other bright, simple fantasies, but he also spoke to something deeper in the moments when he didn't use words, "ch ch huhs," the "oohs," and the "hee hee hee hee hees," fueled by mysterious elements like "the beat," "the force," "the madness in the music," and "a lot of power." Listening to Jackson at home or at our end-of-the-year dance, boys and girls grinding with determination around me, I ignored the romantic stories of the lyrics and focused on the sounds, the timbre of his voice and the pauses in between. Listening to those nonverbal moments—the murmured opening of "Don't Stop Till You Get Enough" or his sobbed breakdown at the end of "She's Out of My Life," I discovered the erotic, described by Audre Lorde as "a measure between the beginnings of our sense of self and the chaos of our strongest feelings."[3]

Born in the heat of the civil rights movement and coming of age in its transition to the post-civil-rights, postindustrial age,[4] Jackson's ever shifting voice and body provided a model and soundtrack for a generation of Post-Soul children and their desires for an elsewhere: to both claim blackness and being "more than a color," to be both bold on the dance floor and eccentrically shy, to be sexually unreadable, to be neither/nor or both. Michael Joseph Jackson was born August 29, 1958, in Gary, Indiana, one year after the signing of the Civil Rights Act. That same year, hip-hop icon Grandmaster Flash was born, too, as were Madonna and Vernon Reid of the band Living Colour, all arguably Post-Soul trailblazers. That same year Martin Luther King Jr. published his first book, *Stride toward Freedom: The Montgomery Story*, and survived a freak assassination attempt via letter opener. Back in Gary, U.S. Steel slowly began hiring more black workers. Elvis went into the army, Chuck Berry recorded "Johnnie B. Goode," and Ella Fitzgerald and Billie Holiday together recorded *Live at the Newport*.

Jackson's parents, Joseph, a steel worker, boxer, and sometime musician, and Katherine, a housewife with her own interest in country music, had come up to Gary from the Mississippi Delta—Joe from Fountain Hill, Arkansas, and Katherine from Barbour County, Alabama. Whether as a child or as an adult, Jackson's voice has always had a searching quality, perhaps spawned by his parents' own searching spirits. Like Eartha Kitt's placeless accent and Sylvester's high femme gospel melisma, Jackson's voice takes us from familiar to unfamiliar spaces; he is at once nostalgic and future seeking, combining soul man falsetto and jazz scatting along with his refusal to fully occupy the space of meaning and familiarity. For example, we might link Jackson's falsetto voice to the tradition of the male falsetto in Soul, blues, and gospel music. Singers like Frankie Lymon, Jackie Wilson, Smokey Robinson, Marvin Gaye, Al Green, Prince, and more recently D'Angelo all use a high masculine vocal range and yet are often connected to (sometimes) heterosexual masculine seductiveness. In the falsetto tradition, there can be tremendous power, as well as vulnerability—a crack in the macho posture, the expression of need. In Jackson's voice, there were these aspects of the tradition, as well as something else—the suggestion of being on the verge of something we haven't yet heard, a spirit of fugitivity, claiming what Nathaniel Mackey calls "the obliquity of an unbound reference" both forged by and breaking away from histories of black struggle.[5] Jackson's vocal and often highly theatrical embodied performances capture the contrariness and resistance of the eccentric, pushing our expectations of gender and racial authenticity.

For Jackson, *Off the Wall* marks the transition between child performer and adult. Although it was not his first solo album (his first, *Got to Be There*, was in 1972, followed by *Ben* [1972], *Music and Me* [1973], and *Forever Michael* [1975]), it was the first solo album to mark his independence from Motown, his new creative relationship with producer and mentor Quincy Jones, and his increasing artistic freedom in the crafting of his songs. In *Off the Wall*, Jackson takes new creative risks, particularly in his forays into disco sounds, experiments with instrument arrangement and dubbing, and the widening of his vocal range and technique. Yet, while Jackson was twenty-one when he released *Off the Wall*, it still captures the prepubescent mood of his earlier work, which I'll explore later in this chapter. Glimmers of sexual knowledge are there in his sound, as well as in his lyrics, as they were in childhood songs like "Who's Lovin' You" and "Got to Be There." But those moments still manage to take us by surprise, framed as they are by relatively innocuous romantic situations, like taking a spin on the dance floor. It was this element of suspended sexuality, I would argue, that I found so seductive.

Much has been made of Michael Jackson's Dorian Gray–like evolution of image. Jackson's celebrity, especially as a solo performer, has been greatly enhanced by his use of music videos to frame each new transition in his image. Writing about Jackson as a figure of becoming in an earlier study, I've suggested:

> From the little boy who sang love songs like an adult, to the adult who hangs out with children and animals on Neverland ranch; from his rumored associations with mummification—including his taste for sleeping in oxygen chambers and his collection of the bones of the original Elephant Man—to his alleged experiments with his own visage through plastic surgery, makeup and acid washes for the skin, Jackson, shape-shifter, style-changer, thriller, is the ultimate figure of becoming.[6]

I don't think there has been enough theorization of Jackson's becoming gender as experienced through less material modes like voice, however. Through his cries, whispers, groans, whines, and grunts, Jackson occupies a third space of gender, one that often undercuts his audience's expectations of erotic identification. In this way, his vocal performances anticipate ongoing debates around transgender identity and essentialized notions of desiring bodies.

Voice, because of its link to the theatrical, and because it is both embodied and disembodied, can operate in a way that allows gender transgression and play differently from full body performances. The throat is an erotic space that can both encode and undercut gender. It is the site of performative expression where desire becomes manifest—where desire is transformed into communication. The larynx shapes the air, turns it, warm from our mouths, and shapes it into expression. The larynx is a collaborative part, polyamorous, working with teeth and tongue and diaphragm and lungs, but sometimes it has its own ideas. It can be temperamental. A diva. Many performers treat it as if it has its own mind—coaxing and coddling it after a particularly difficult night. Throats are part of the erotic act, commanding, whispering, swallowing. Like the brain, the throat is a sexual organ that both genders, all genders share. It is not surprising, then, that the throat has been an important site for rituals of sexual identity and the surveillance of gender codes, from Renaissance castrati to Freud's Dora to Linda Lovelace.

Jackson's vocal style betrays an intelligence of the throat's strengths and its limits. His chucks, grunts, clicks, rasps, groans, gasps, and stops, as well as his use of emotional expressiveness, vocal range, volume, and pitch, provide a depth that often adds layers to the sometimes simplistic lyrics of his songs. Roland Barthes talks about the "grain" of the voice—the aspect of authenticity that speaks of a combination of body(the "muscles, membranes, cartilage," the rasping of the throat, the state of the vocal cords) and its relationship to the symbolic: "The 'grain' is the body in the voice as it sings, the hand as it writes, the limb as it performs."[7] While Jackson's voice conveys the embodied nature suggested by Barthes's notion of "grain," it does so in a way that reconstructs our notion of a stable or "authentic" physical self, particularly in terms of age and gender. In this way, Jackson forces us to think about the ways that the grain of the voice can be counterintuitive, and never fully describable or known.

The grain of the voice is not just its physical quality but also the friction of the body against meaning, against language. Cultural critic Kobena Mercer suggests that the grain of Michael Jackson's voice not only adds a subtext of sexuality to his lyrics but also is ultimately about a larger "eroticization of the body" that "transcends the denotation of the lyrics and escapes analytic reduction."[8] For Mercer, this eroticization queers traditional notions of black masculinity. In this chapter, I'm particularly interested in the ways that Jackson's queer erotics extend our notions of gender and age, and the ways that Jackson performs this queering strategically, to complicate his body's own readability as a child star and afterward. The space of "refusal" that Jackson creates through song and dance, as well as the construction of his star icon, becomes a space of dreaming, the desire to create a place where we haven't yet been.

If, as Monique Wittig has observed, "the first, the permanent, and the final social contract is language," bodies as they read and are read are a primary element of that contract. Trans activist and poet Riki Anne Wilchins writes:

> Our bodies—as signs in that language—are the first and most permanent element of that linguistic contract, and in order to participate in the social space of language, we agree to be our "selves" as we are seen by others, that is our particular physical selves—fat or thin, black or white, young or old. The most basic part of that linguistic contract to which our bodies are apprenticed is to be sexed, and being sexed in this context does not mean agreeing to mouth the words "I am female" to answer the name, or to mark the box next to Male with an X. It means agreeing to feel and look and act

your sex, to participate in society as a meaningful member within the matrix of expectations that go along with your sex.[9]

Yet, thanks to the work of gender theorists like Judith Butler and Elizabeth Grosz, we know that the body and the gendered meanings it communicates are *not* permanent, and as it is altered, so, too, is our relationship to language. Indeed, transgender theorist Leslie Feinberg describes her gender identity as a "work in progress."[10]

In trans activist Kate Bornstein's writing in *Gender Outlaw*, we get the chance to think about what a transgender aesthetic and transgender "voice" might look and sound like. Bornstein uses "cut-and-paste" techniques of the flotsam and jetsam gathered from a life lived on the borders, the baggage from a culture that does and does not see her: bits of theory, songs, passages from novels, unwitting insults from others. These are transformed by her placement of them. She calls this work "sewing sequins onto our cultural hand-me-downs."[11] She says that she wants her writing voice to capture the process of integration and reintegration that her life has become: "I keep trying to make all the pieces into one piece. As a result, my identity becomes my body which becomes my fashion which becomes my writing style. Then I perform what I've written in effort to integrate my life, and that becomes my identity, after a fashion."[12] Ultimately, Bornstein says, her goal in her writing voice is to make sense of her own life, to perform her "view" of or "take" on the world, and perhaps, too, to create a "transgendered" experience in the reader. She speculates, "Will the identification with a transgendered writing style produce an identification with a transgendered experience?"[13]

While coming from different historical and political trajectories, we might be able to link the transgendered aesthetic of Bornstein's "sewing sequins onto our cultural hand-me-downs" with the expressionism and "blueing" of music from the African diasporic tradition that we hear in Jackson's work. Both present an aesthetic of transformation of performer and listener; both attempt to capture the beauty of a lived experience in the body; both counter dominant narratives and makers of meaning. And both can move the reader/listener into a form of transcendence. In the African diasporic musical tradition, singers like Louis Armstrong, Billie Holiday, Sonny Terry, Al Jarreau, and Bobby McFerrin are praised for their ability to imitate the sound of the instruments—the wah-wah of the trumpet, the staccato of the chikere. Musicians are also lauded for their ability to make their instruments sound like the human voice, sometimes crossing gender boundaries to become male or female, imitate animals, or become spirit. Expressionism, cultural critic Philip M. Royster says, is

> The "dramatic" value that prefers vocal and instrumental performances delivered to convince the listener that the performer has actually experienced the content of the performance. This value probably has its source in African religious experiences of spiritual possession, as well as ceremonies involving the periodic return of various spirit entities to the village and in African-American religious experiences in "getting happy," that is, becoming filled with (or anointed by) the Holy Spirit.[14]

What Jackson's vocal performances offer is a way of extending our understanding of his voice's transformational quality, to see how its spiritual project speaks to and opens up the possibilities of expressiveness beyond the limits of the secular and spiritual. As a blaxploration project, Jackson's "trans" aesthetic of expression challenges our notions of where and how and by whom we are moved. It is one of many ways that eccentric performances prove to be collaborative, rather than merely isolated.

In many ways, we might think of Jackson's "Don't Stop Till You Get Enough" as a secular expression of "getting happy." In this song, we can hear aspects of expressionism: Jackson's voice imitates percussion instruments like the cuica and kalimba, and he alters his voice to create his own "female" chorus, all to create a building energy and persuasive power to get the listener to similarly push the limits of desire, to "get enough." At the same time, we might think about the cut-and-paste aspects of the production itself as similar to Bornstein's transgender writing aesthetic. Consider Jackson's description of his production process.

> "Don't Stop Till You Get Enough" had a spoken intro over bass, partly to build up tension and surprise people with the swirling strings and percussion. It was also unusual because of my vocal arrangement. On that cut I sing in overdubs as a kind of a group. I wrote myself a high part, one that my solo voice couldn't carry on its own, to fit in with the music I was hearing in my head, so I let the arrangement take over from the singing. Q's fade at the end was amazing, with guitars chopping like kalimbas, the Afri-

can thumb pianos. That song meant a lot to me because it was the first song I wrote as a whole.[15]

In his description we see that Jackson conceives of his voice as a collaborative or adaptive tool, making the other performers and instruments stretch from their natural or past abilities, even imagining another self with which he collaborates. Jackson combines the deep resonance of the bass with his own mumbles and trembling whispers at the beginning—vulnerability and threat all at once, to create drama and mystery, exploding into the "whoo" and swirl of strings. He overdubs his voice to become a group with himself, a collaboration with selves, at the same time making the self "other," heightening the already feminine aspects of his voice. He stretches his own range by fitting his voice "into" or in between the strains of the instruments. And in response the other voices and sounds around him are affected, adapting, becoming something new and not yet defined, so that the guitar moves from melody to percussion, from swirl to chopping, from rock to African kalimba, moving diasporically from present to past and back again.

In *Off the Wall,* Jackson's performance is at the cusp of expansion that will take his play with identity even further—from gender fluidity to monster, alien, and space dweller, as Victoria Johnson, Kobena Mercer, and Jason King have suggested. We can certainly trace elements of identity play through expressionism in *Off the Wall* that will show up more developed in *Thriller* and *Bad.* For example, we might connect his stylistic use of overdubbing in "Don't Stop Till You Get Enough" to the use of vocoder in *Thriller*'s "Pretty Young Things," which transforms his voice into a ET voice, his use of whisper-heightened suspense in the opening of "Don't Stop Till You Get Enough" expanded on an epic scale and ventriloquized into the body of Vincent Price in "Thriller." The rebellious "Hee heee heee heee heee" of the "party people" in the opening of "Off the Wall" is also linked to the spooky "Thriller" and that unearthly, androgynous howl—something like what Peter Pan might sound like if he spent the night drinking whiskey and smoking cigarettes—that he performs in "Bad," and the controversial extended end sequence to the video for "Black or White." Jackson uses his nonverbal voicings to express a state of outsiderhood in songs like "Beat It" and "Bad." In these songs, in fact, the nonverbal elements act as a kind of bridge between singer and persona, one fueling the other, allowing Jackson to move from the position of shy, androgynous observer to interpreter of the power and angst reflected in the dancers and actors around him. In "Bad," for example, Jackson seems to be split between two voices, performing both the call and the response: the sneering "Bad" braggadocio voice, which makes its claims of toughness, and the intertwining chorus, which encourages with squeals, "whoops," whip snaps, and, my favorite, "Ch'mon." Through voice, as well as other forms of performance, Jackson offers the promise of movement, of creating a world with the always-existing possibility for change.

Jackson's Queer World Making: Becoming Gender

So much of Jackson's performative persona has been analyzed as being about either concealment and revelation—the glove, one off, the other on; the surgeon's mask, the sunglasses, the military uniform, even the crumbling nose, all costumes that signal their artificiality and their potential for being taken off. But the model of becoming tells us more about Jackson's performances in terms of its imaginative and erotic link to audience. Like me, Jackson himself cites a transgendered performance as marking one of his first realizations of the erotic relationship between audience and performer.

> When we did the Apollo Theater in New York, I saw something that really blew me away because I didn't know things like that existed. I had seen quite a few strippers, but that night this one girl with gorgeous eyelashes and long hair came out and did her routine. She put on a *great* performance. All of a sudden, at the end, she took off her wig, pulled a pair of big oranges out of her bra, and revealed that she was a hard-faced guy under all that makeup. That blew me away. I was only a child and couldn't even conceive of anything like that. But I looked out at the theater audience and they were going for it, applauding wildly and cheering. I'm just a little kid, standing in the wings, watching this crazy stuff.
> I was blown away.[16]

What is it that Jackson learns but doesn't name in watching this performance? Perhaps another version of what he learns by watching Jackie Wilson or James Brown in the eaves of the Apollo: that performances create a magic in excess of the bodies that perform them. Despite the hardness of a man's face, despite the oranges hidden beneath her dress, the performer has transformed both himself and the audience in the act of performing, and creating an effect that might exceed previous expectations of gender. Perhaps Jackson learned that the arithmetic of gender—these clothes plus these gestures plus this genitalia—is not constant, that all bodies exceed their own bodies, despite what he might have been told by his parents or teachers. He certainly got a peek at the underground culture hiding in plain sight—queer subcultures have existed everywhere, including on the Chitlin' Circuit. At the same time, Jackson was sampling a performative practice of gender fluidity far more boldly marked and visible than his own. Cross-dressing has been a long-standing part of vaudevillian performance and minstrel shows. He might have seen the normative response of laughter to gender shifting, but he may have also observed that gender shifting might evoke multiple responses from an audience: shock, wonder, identification, attraction, disgust. Perhaps he also learned the potential of the performance to articulate unspoken desires—to not only entertain but also create a space of freedom. The potential of performance to help one transcend one's lived experience, to create a line of flight, or to say what can't be verbalized will inform Jackson's performances again and again. Jackson's career becomes one in which we are watching his gender—and race—constantly shift, not as either/or but as "both/and." His gender, as well as his vocal and performance style, is wonderfully supplemental, in excess of historically informed codes of black masculinity (or femininity), speaking to us multidirectionally.

Soul masculinity—as exemplified by Jackie Wilson, James Brown, and Smokey Robinson—continued to be an important touchstone for Jackson throughout his career, but we must acknowledge Jackson's citation of womanly performances, too, Soul and otherwise. On his blog *Blood Beats*, Ernest Hardy points to Jackson's citation of Diana Ross in his vocal introductions, his command of glam, and his diva gaze.[17] I see Liza Minnelli in his wide kohl eyes, his sparkly jacket, the deep bow to his audience, letting his shoulders fall with his hair. Michael cites Rita Hayworth's hair flip (the *Gilda* sequence is even integrated into his performance of "Smooth Criminal" in *This Is It*), and he is very Hayworthian in his skillful command of looked-at-ness. And what about the ways that Jackson's performances, in these very citations, bring out the gender multiplicity contained within these performances: the potential femininity in Smokey's open, vulnerable falsetto, as well as his mastery of doo-wop cool in "Who's Lovin' You"; the muscularity of Rita Hayworth's shoulders and neck as she masters that flip; Liza's butchness as she commands the space of the stage, sitting wide-legged on her chair. Michael "does" wide-eyed childhood, and the wise old man in a child's body, too. And what about those other productive interactions, where Michael crosses not only gender but also the animal/human and technical divides: his soulful working of the vocoder in "P.Y.T. (Pretty Young Thing)"; the echo of Mickey Mouse's winsome knock-kneed gait in a flash of "Billie Jean"; his own lion cubbyness on the inside flap of *Thriller;* and in "We Are the World," the spirit of ET's glowing, beating heart? Jackson changes the ways that we see and hear these past performances, too. Once the performers are taken out of their context, performed by Jackson in his aesthetic and gender openness, we see the originals as denaturalized and deconstructed.

Voice and Michael Jackson's Trans-Age Performance as a Dynamic of Gender

As a child performer, Jackson developed a nuanced analysis of the ways that vocal and body performances could capture the attention of his audience in multiple ways, and "blow away" their expectations. Even as we acknowledge the ways that in this culture childlikeness is often associated with the feminine, Jackson's performances complicate what we think of as the child-and-adult voice, whether we're looking at the beginning or the end of his career. Jackson forces us to think about how voice affects the ways that we read the body, and ultimately gender, through the sometimes fluid lens of age performance. His mastery of voice has always had a strong and sometimes disconcerting effect on his audience, and still does, even in death.

In his earliest performances, Jackson's child-adult voice made him the object of fascination, desire, discomfort, and even fear. At Jackson's 2009 memorial, Smokey Robinson recalls the effect of watching young Michael performing his own song, "Who's Lovin' You," and surpassing his own performance, to great effect. Smokey recalls with loving laughter—and perhaps some lingering irritation:

> I wrote that song. I *thought* I sang it. [Pause for laughter.] I thought to myself, now they have pulled a fast one on us, because this boy

could not be ten years old. How could he possibly know these things? I quickly went over to him. I didn't believe that someone that young could have so much feeling and love and *know*. You've got to know something to sing like that.

That fateful performance of "Who's Lovin' You," on the *Ed Sullivan Show* in 1969, brings a youthful vocal openness, playfulness, and vulnerability at play against the vocal and bodily "knowing" of black male cool, drawing from the stylistics of Smokey Robinson, Jackie Wilson, Marvin Gaye, and James Brown, among others. "Who's Lovin' You" was first written and performed by the then young adult Smokey Robinson and the Miracles in 1960. It was shared between many others of the Motown family, including the Temptations and the Supremes, until it was made most famous by the Jackson 5's rerecording in 1969, and then forty years later by Kurdish Welsh child star Shaheen Jafurgholi on the TV talent show *Britain's Got Talent* (testimony to Britain's truly multicultural identity). Shaheen eventually performed the song at Jackson's memorial service at the Staples Center.

Robinson's lyrics capture the struggle for power in the face of melancholy manifest in traditional heterosexual romantic love: the speaker loves then leaves his girl, only to find himself obsessed with what he's lost. There are both regret and paranoia in that refrain, "And I wonder, who's lovin' you." The song's lyrics capture not only the masculine desire to be "on top"—to not be bested by a lover—but also the power of the imagination to move from loss to fear to obsession. It's little Michael's ability to capture the struggle for bravado, and that glimmer of darkness in between the words, that lends maturity and "knowledge" to his vocal performance.

This moment is important, as Michael Jackson burned into public consciousness (and in his immediate circle of Motown) as the "child adult." It also is important as an illustration of his potential to steal the show from his brothers, even while proving the Jackson 5 to be a viable commercial product. This is, in many ways, the dilemma of the eccentric, who wants to be noticed for his or her ability to chart his or her own course, to be recognized, even while using tactics of misrecognition, traveling to the space "past the word's or the sentence's limit," as Moten puts it.[18] In Smokey and the Miracles' version, the song is smooth, soulful, but a little formulaic in its romanticism—the already known quality of doo-wop crooning. When Michael and the Jackson 5 perform it, the song moves between formulaic and unexpected. It begins with a cute spoken opening: little Michael tells his brothers about a girl he met "at the sandbox," and a love that blossomed over milk and cookies. His outfit and those of his brothers are psychedelic–*Laugh-In* cool that will soon be fully inhabited in the kids' worlds of *Sesame Street* and *H.R. Pufnstuf*: purple vest and fuchsia porkpie hat, which pops out as if specially made for the still new color TVs that on which it might appear. His voice and gaze are steady, but he is still a precocious, if soft-spoken, little boy, telling childhood woes to his big brothers that seem a little canned. But with that opening blues chord of the electric piano, and his wringing out of that opening "Wheeeeeeeeeeeen / I met you," young Michael enters into another space. He is Soul crooner, slow, confident, telling us of the love he mistreated and lost, popping his fingers and swinging his arms in a boogaloo. Lyrically and stylistically, he captures the sense of having seen and felt things, drawing from earlier R&B performances like those of Robinson, Sam Cooke, the Platters, the Ink Spots, and the Temptations. Moving through the song with a steady bop, Jackson has mastered, for those few moments, the mask of cool, accompanied by a voice that is anything but. It is, as Smokey Robinson says, a voice of knowledge, which dips into the well of pain and living that blues singers before him have sampled—Ray Charles, Jackie Wilson, Smokey himself—and gives us a full cup. The performance warms steadily, Michael backed up efficiently by his brothers.

At the same time that Jackson performs masculine virtuosity, he also captures the breakdown of masculine control, and resulting outbursts of feeling: words that stammer with emotion, or when he confesses that he's "not, not going to make it"; moments of inarticulateness, punctuated by an "ooh" or "ah!" or maybe just "sock it to me now!" The song dramatizes the machismo struggle and then the abandonment to articulate emotion verbally, recasting and rescuing the struggle to remain unaffected by loss through the sometimes pleading falsetto of a child. It's the voice, along with the body, popping with color and a child's loose limbs, that makes such a confession plausible. Jackson's transvocalizations from childhood to adulthood allow for a deconstruction of masculine posturing in romance. Jackson's vocal movement is timely, too, in a period on the verge of reexamining traditional male and female roles. As Margo Jefferson suggests, Michael's youthful interventions in the politics of sex roles in dating—the defense of virginity and good reputation (in "The Love You Save") and schoolyard (or mock schoolyard) seduction in "ABC" ("Teacher's gonna show you / how to get an A-ay")—were gobbled up by audiences quite comfortable with the movement from pre-pubescent purity to sexual (and gender) knowledge.[19] Jackson's access to nonverbal feeling, conveyed by his cries, and shouts and exclamations of the latest cool phrase ("Sock it to me now!" spinning on the ball of one well-polished Beatles-booted foot), as well as his early skill in the phrasing and coloring of lyrics—his skills as a vocal essayist—added a transformative layer to the history of masculine cool that he's accessing. Indeed, this childlike play with masculine and feminine codes by young Michael enabled the Jackson 5 to move between racial, gender, and age niches: introducing a turned-off young audience increasingly interested in psychedelia and more politically informed protest music back to Motown; crossing over to white audiences on *The Ed Sullivan Show, American Bandstand,* and live venues in Europe and Las Vegas;[20] and even intervening in the increasingly conflicted relations between the sexes in an age of feminism, as Jefferson suggests from her own experience as a graduate student in her twenties.

> My friends and I (graduate students all) found it precious and in no way peculiar. Why would we? We were dancing and dating to his love songs. And he'd become quite a suave little crooner. In "I'll be There" the boyishness becomes a young lover's idealism. "Never Can Say Goodbye" is intense. That pure voice actually conveys emotions that smolder (anguish! Doubt!) as it leaps up a sixth for the first vehement "Don't wanna let you go" and down a fourth for the closing one. In those early years of feminism, when few grown men seemed worth trusting, little Michael was our Cupid.[21]

Relistening to the young Michael Jackson forces us to think transformatively about the impact of age on the ways that we think about gender—here socially acceptable codes of black masculinity. In "Who's Lovin' You" and elsewhere, Jackson's youth gives him a space in which to play the performance of control, loss, and paranoia latent in the love songs of the period.[22]

Queer World making and the Child Star

At the same time that Jackson complicates gender norms, his transgender and trans-age erotics of openness, emotionality, and movement might be seen as part of a larger mode of resistance, in the face of control and surveillance of the black, commercialized body, as a child star. Jackson complicates through his own example the image of the child as a (mere) projection of adult desires. In Jackson's autobiography *Moonwalk*, he compellingly conveys his awareness as a child of adult struggles for power and control over his style, his appearances, and his legal standing. If, as cultural critic Ernest Hardy suggests, later in life the adult Jackson fetishizes the notion of childhood as a place of freedom,[23] he does so in spite of (or perhaps exacerbated by) his own experiences, so convincingly recalled and analyzed here in *Moonwalk*.

> I remember lots of times when I felt the song should be sung one way and the producers felt it should be sung another way. But for a long time I was very obedient and wouldn't say anything about it. Finally it reached a point where I got fed up with being told exactly how to sing. This was in 1972 when I was fourteen years old, around the time of the song "Lookin' Through the Windows." They wanted me to sing a certain way, and I knew they were wrong. No matter what age you are, if you have it and you know it, then people should listen to you. I was furious with our producers and very upset. So I called Berry Gordy and complained. I said that they had always told me how to sing, and I had agreed all this time, but now they were getting too . . . mechanical.
>
> So he came into the studio and told them to let me do what I wanted to do. I think he told them to let me be more free or something. And after that, I started adding a lot of vocal twists that they really ended up loving. I'd do a lot of ad-libbing, like twisting words and adding some edge to them.[24]

The very aspects of what I've identified as Jackson's transgender and trans-age sound come out of this kiln of control and surveillance of freedom as a child. Despite these struggles for expressive power—ones that echo Stevie Wonder's similar struggles for creative freedom, discussed in chapter 2, one can hear in "Lookin' Through the Windows" Jackson's increasing confidence, handling with verve a sophisticated arrangement that moves from Latin to rock to jazz scat. He sings in a high, clear-as-chimes voice, enunciating the lyrics with intentionality. Jackson carries the song not only with his polychromatic twists of the melody but in his kicky riding of the modified Afro-Cuban beat, hesitating just a bit before sliding into the downbeat, punctuated by the rasp of the guiro and his brothers' rapid-fire backup. As the song opens to the chorus, Jackson's falsetto rises with the upsweep of strings, reassuring the listener with conviction, "Don't you worry, 'cause I'm gonna stay / right by your side," then settles into a relaxed scat. Jackson's rendering of "Lookin' Through the Windows," borrowing from adult contemporary and Latin Jazz stylistics, is a long way from bubblegum rock. This more sophisticated musical range on the *Looking Through Windows* album is accompanied by more restrained art direction on the album cover, featuring muted colors and fashions, and an unsmiling photo of Michael sporting a worldly cravat. Yet the song still makes use of the vocal and stylistic pliability and range of Jackson's "young" voice.

Queer World Making in the Post-Soul Era: *Killer of Sheep, Crooklyn,* "Ben"

The state of childhood is, in some ways, a state of having to be extremely aware of one's audience—this is only exacerbated in the life of a professional artist. In his own coming of age, Jackson embraces the space of art/performance as a place to resist, and to create outside of these perimeters of mimicry. Of course, the script of the child star that Michael Jackson experienced is also unlike one in any other era. In that period, from 1969, to the release of *Off the Wall* in 1980, celebrities like Jackson encountered an expanded circulation of the star text, new possibilities for synergistic multimedia advertising—including the first teen magazine marketed to young black people, Cynthia Fuchs's *Right On!*—and unprecedented possibilities of financial freedom. As someone who posted *Right On!* on her bedroom walls, I can attest to the ways that these magazines made the star in his full visual glory a part of everyday life for audiences, a part of private as well as public space, in a way that would only be pushed further with the advent of MTV and the premier of the video for "Billie Jean" there in 1983, the first song to break MTV's unofficial color barrier. This experience of the black child star was further vexed by the contradictions between a narrative of possibility and freedom and the realities of the hardscrabble life that the working-class Jacksons lived at the beginning of Michael's career, and which shaped their tough work ethic. It was also complicated by the contradictions between the discourse of "black is beautiful" and the fact that young Jackson was teased in his family for his nose and lips. In this pre-BET era, there may have been pockets where the black body beautiful was recognized and praised (those two hours on Saturday mornings with *Soul Train* and Afro-Sheen commercials), but in general, racism and colorism still commanded the airwaves, schools, neighborhoods, and families.[25]

Rather than demonstrating that childhood is supposedly free of the constraints of the body as it was particularly raced and gendered in the period, Jackson demonstrates a consciousness of the body that we might link to a Post-Soul state of black childhood. We see this awareness in one of Jackson's memories of the shift from childhood to adolescence, one particularly painful under the eye of celebrity.

> People who didn't know me would come into a room expecting to be introduced to cute little Michael Jackson and they'd walk right past me. I would say, "I'm Michael," and they would look doubtful. . . . Everyone had called me cute for a long time, but along with all the other changes, my skin broke out in a terrible case of acne. . . . I got very shy and embarrassed to meet people because my complexion was so bad. It really seemed that the more I looked in the mirror, the worse my pimples got. My appearance began to depress me. . . . The effect on me was so bad that it messed up my whole personality. I couldn't look at people when I talked to them. I'd look down, or away. I felt I didn't have anything to be proud of and I didn't even want to go out. I didn't do anything.[26]

Jackson demonstrates the ways that kids know, learn, and sometimes stretch the vocabularies of gender, sexuality, and race in performance, and he renders it to great acclaim. This ability to master these tools of communication and improvisation will ultimately provide him with a space of creation, joy, and to some extent freedom, though he acknowledges, too, that some of these lessons will come with pain—linked, in some ways, to the public experience of blackness, gender, and sexuality.

In Jackson's implicit and explicit exploration of his own very public sexualization (in his autobiography, *Moonwalk*, in interviews, and in the performances of the songs themselves), we might see a sharpened example of the potential for queer world making that we see black children practicing in this era, born out of struggle. Post-Soul has meant being caught in between, regardless of class. Post-Soul children were the canaries in the coal mine, the first generation to live out a still imperfectly integrated life, sometimes being the first black kids on their block, moving between black homes and neighborhoods to white schools, sometimes lying about one's address to be there, code switching all the way, sometimes only traveling out of the world of blackness through popular culture. And sometimes learning how to be authentically black through the messages of popular culture: *Good Times, What's Happening, Soul Train,* and later *MTV Raps.*[27] These lessons were not just for privileged kids who lived in white towns or suburbs. We all were taught and re-taught the rules of black cool through popular culture, whatever else was happening in our own neighborhoods. Members of the first generation of children after *Loving v. Virginia,* in 1968, Post-Soul kids might have integrated families, integrated friendship circles. And yet, even in these discourses of "newness," we are inheritors of older ideas of racialized, class, sexual, and gendered subjectivity.

In response, we might think of the ways that black children have found routes of escape and resistance through the bending of the rules of gender performance—through the ways they see, hear, and bodily interpret music. This is portrayed poignantly in two black-made films, Charles Burnett's *Killer of Sheep* (1977) and Spike Lee's *Crooklyn* (1994). In *Killer of Sheep,* we watch children who navigate the violent and often economically bleak world they've inherited from adults, including their parents, through music. In one scene, a little girl, listed in the credits only as "Stan's Daughter" sings along to Earth, Wind and Fire's "Reasons" as her mother prepares for her father's return from the night shift at a Los Angeles meat-packing center. The child apparently understands neither the lyrics of the song, which talk about the failure of a relationship, or her own parents' struggles. But she absorbs the heart of lessons of the circumstances around her, despite their hugeness (including poverty and marital strife). We watch Stan's Daughter sing along with the Earth, Wind and Fire album to her white doll, harnessing in her child's way Earth, Wind and Fire's soulful, emotive, sonic expressiveness but using Post-Soul's off-center strategies. She might not get all of the words—indeed, she seems to be making up her own language—but she has the rhythms, even the hand motions, and stares lovingly into the doll's face, crooning to her. The child has been left alone to play in this room, and the doll is all she's got. But somewhere in the performance, the normativity of the love song gets disrupted. The "reasons" that we're here, as the song says, are not so clear. Stan's Daughter's performance with the doll shifts from mother to lover to microphone; she holds the doll close and away, lifts her arms as the music soars in imitation of live performances of soul crooners. Stan's Daughter is caught in play where the meaning of the performance of a love song changes shape with her imagination. This small moment of lightness and feeling is a brief respite in a film where most of the characters have learned to deaden their emotions: children having a rock fight must learn to mask their pain; a father, working in a meat-processing plant, must stifle his revulsion and weariness; a mother stares at her reflection in the silver lid of a pan, longing and silent.

Likewise, we see tactics of queer world making through music in Joie Lee's semiautobiographical screenplay for *Crooklyn*, directed by her brother Spike Lee. Joie Lee explores black girlhood in the 1970s through her character, Jade. We watch Jade's tactics of childhood identity making, including imitation, obsession, reterritorializing, humor, and revenge to maintain what we might call the "queer time" of childhood, even as the meanings of the larger world threaten to encroach. Lee uses the film's soundtrack to mark moments of Jade's learning and resistance through music—here, not only as a performer but also as one who performs and understands what's otherwise unspoken through music. Through Jade's eyes, we experience the in-between state of many black middle-class people in the mid- to late 1970s. Her parents, clearly shaped by the Black Art Movement in their vocations and politics, are a schoolteacher and a musician; they struggle to maintain their own brownstone in Brooklyn, and sometimes the electricity gets turned off, or they have to resort to food stamps. As in other Spike Lee films, Jade's neighborhood includes blacks, Latinos, and ethnically marked whites, in not quite peaceful coexistence. Joie Lee also shows Jade trying to make sense of multiple versions of black femininity: her fiery, bohemian mother; the prim churchgoing aunt (who encourages wearing a bra to bed); neighbors and friends. In a household of boys, Jade watches her own body, too, at one point stuffing her shirt with tissue to fill a new bra. In one scene, Jade is at the local bodega, buying penny candy. A sight she doesn't seem to fully understand arrests her: an unusually tall, unusually glamorous woman (played by RuPaul) flirting with the store owner. The scene slows down as Jade watches RuPaul dance provocatively with the man to Joe Cuba's Soul-Latin fusion classic "El Pito – I'll Never Go Back to Georgia." Jade is wide-eyed and open-mouthed, absorbing it all: the look of pleasure on the faces of the two dancers, RuPaul's artfully gyrating hips and long arms weaving under, over, and around the man's body, two lovers, brown and black, stealing a moment of pleasure between the aisles to this song, a hybrid of African American and Afro-Cuban Soul. The adults shoo her away. But later

Jade reenacts the scene for her brothers, attempting RuPaul's gyrations and repeating the only words from the conversation that stick, "I keeps my panties clean." Jade's access to the meanings of the dance might be limited, but she gets the heart of the moment, picking up on RuPaul's rhythms, voice, and the body language—incorporating "RuPaul's" queer performance of femininity into her own roster of feminine selves.

Musical performance, then becomes a way for young black performers to flip the scripts of gender, as well as age. In his performance of "Ben," recorded at age fourteen, Michael Jackson gives a heartfelt performance of longing and empathy. The song's melancholy melody and instrumental style, arpeggio guitar, and piano chords over swelling strings, sound something like a 1950s song of star-crossed love—here, an undeniably male someone (if only a rat). And Jackson's voice, singular, unmixed, tremulous with emotion, might be drawing from the pared-down and politicized style of folk. This is a lonely song. (As if to emphasize this loneliness, on an *American Bandstand* performance of it, Jackson stands alone, suspended in space on a neon-red cube, surrounded only by starlight.) But there is danger and also defiance in a voice so willing to stand alone, wearing its heart on its sleeve. And we are reminded that this is the soundtrack to a horror film, in which the sensitive boy hero works with telepathic rats to wreak revenge on their less sensitive human counterparts. Perhaps, in that heartfelt promise that "you" will never be alone, in Michael's defense of his object of love, we might hear not only passion but protest on the behalf of forbidden friendships. As the song swells to its crescendo, and Jackson sings at full voice, "They don't see you as I do," the song moves from loneliness to rage. There is, then, perhaps, the suggestion of very barely contained revolution against the unnamed "they," the possibility of explosion. Jackson swings the 4/4 rhythm of the line, "I wish they would try to," calling out the haters, before moving to that last line, "I'm sure they'd think again / if they had a friend like Ben." Jackson caresses the words "like Ben," trading back and forth with the background voices, extending and sustaining that "n" for four more beats, until he gives one last mellismatic "like Ben"—a sigh, really, a moment of sheer beauty, a pleasure that will help us move on, leave this place, find another, better one. The song reveals and transforms the darker feelings of powerlessness and yearning into the potential for empathy, rebellion, and flight.

In "Michael," his retrospective essay on Michael Jackson, published a few weeks after Jackson's death in *New York Review of Books*, Hilton Als describes the ways that Jackson's vocal and dance performances, caught between male and female, adult and child, provided important metaphors for his audience—particularly queer audiences—for what could not be said. He includes his own childhood memory of Jackson's performance of "Ben," just a fleeting wisp of the song heard coming from the open door of a neighborhood gay bar, which become symbolic of his own yearning.

> The female elders tell us what to look out for. Staring straight ahead, they usher us past the Starlight lounge, in the Bedford-Stuyvesant section of Brooklyn, and whisk us across the street as soon as they see "one of them faggots" emerge from the neon-lit bar. This one—he's brown-skinned, like nearly every one else in that neighborhood, and skinny—has a female friend in tow, for appearances must be kept up. And as the couple run off in search of another pack of cigarettes, the bar's door closes slowly behind them, but not before we children hear, above the martini-fed laughter, a single voice, high and plaintive: Michael Jackson's.[28]

What the female elders' understood, and what Als remembers, is the power and dangerousness of Jackson's ability to make longing speak, and his ability to make it move across contexts and desires, rubbing up against constraint. Perhaps "Ben's" queer following would not have missed the fact that Michael Jackson is throwing a bit of shade in his rendering of those last lines of that song. Perhaps, too, in that last sigh, Jackson leaves open the possibility for something else—the presence of an insistent beauty—and the potential for a queer future not yet fully articulable. José Esteban Muñoz theorizes in Cruising Utopia: The Then and There of Queer Futurity, "Queerness is a longing that propels us onward, beyond romances of negative and toiling in the present. Queerness is that thing that lets us feel that this world is not enough, that indeed something is missing."[29] This sense of possibility, even in a mournful song like this one, explains why Jackson's voice could and has had such an impact on young and queer listeners, shaping memory, and importantly, leaving room for that something else on the horizon.

CODA: "Black or White"

When Michael Jackson and his brothers were made into a Saturday morning cartoon, which ran from 1971 to 1973, it was a sign of their wide appeal and success, and an early example of Jackson's ability to enter and then expand black male identity through the realm of the imagination, the gateway of childhood. Jackson says in his autobiography, *Moonwalk*, that he loved being a cartoon, and in the book's final pages we see Michael's doodles of his own face, nose and lips shrinking until he becomes an androgynous pixie. The most obvious effect of becoming a cartoon would be that you could reinvent your body: skin smoothed, noses, still wide, made piggish and impish, 'fros a simple flower of fluff, movements, always smooth—a transformation that would seem to echo some of Jackson's later real-life bodily experiments. Cartoons also put you out of the real time of the everyday and into the space of fantasy, legislated by the music itself. In *The Jackson 5* Saturday morning cartoon, even if the plots loosely followed the showtime adventures of the Jackson 5—their discovery by Berry Gordy, or their first trip to London—there was also always that moment toward the end when a song would be performed, and the bodies and voices of the group would be put into a transitional space created by the songs themselves. The song might begin onstage, with the brothers assembled with their instruments, but then there might be a psychedelic shower of flowers, or patterns of stripes and rainbows. Events from the day would be restructured to fit the rhythm of the song, following their own dreamlike logic. In the hands of producers Arthur Rankin Jr. and Jules Bass, Michael Jackson and his brothers shift and move and dance; eyes become simplified beacons of brightness. It is in the realm of make-believe—the idealized realm of childhood—that one might most easily escape, or create one's own logic of living in one's body.

It is this drama of transformation and escape that Jackson restages and relives repeatedly in his career, as an adult.[30] The possibility of escaping one's body or at least reinventing its logic through technology helps Jackson perform the yearnings that his voice has always betrayed, from those Rankin and Bass cartoons of the early 1970s to his zombification in *Thriller* to the infamous "Panther" version of "Black and White" to his own experiments of the flesh, altering skin and muscle, hair and bone. This ability to explore the desire to transform becomes heightened as Jackson reaches megastardom, and as video on TV and the Internet becomes the form of circulation of the star in the 1980s, 1990s and 2000s. Even *This Is It*, the posthumous documentary chronicling Jackson's training and production of what was meant to be his next tour, exposes the ways that technology allows Jackson to enhance, and mystify, his already overwhelming vocal and dancing talent—precisely by letting us see the seams of his stage transformations.

For example, in the 1991 video for "Black or White" Jackson embraces the transformative power of the music video, highlighting the possibilities it brings for travel and the possession of new bodies and new selves, male and female, black and white, animal and cartoon. He does so by combining rage with humor and a little braggadocio.

The extended or "Panther" version of "Black or White" is marked by the occupation of multiple worlds—a sense of geographic and technical mastery in ways that demonstrate Jackson's heightened access to an increasingly larger public through voice, dance, and Hollywood magic. It proclaims Jackson's power to inhabit the imagination of "America"—of young white boys and typical suburban homes (typified by *Cheers's* George Wendt and *Home Alone's* Macaulay Culkin). The video opens in an unnamed white suburban village. Culkin is loudly rocking out, jumping on his bed alone in his room, outfitted with Michael Jackson poster and huge speakers, while his tabloid-reading parents become increasingly angry. Wendt as the White Father is fairly inarticulate in his rage, a blustering, red-faced, cartoonish revision, perhaps, of the more daunting Joseph Jackson. He screams at his son, "You're wasting your time with this garbage!" And what "garbage" is it? The power of music, and especially musical performances that cross cultures (black and beyond black, the song wants to suggest), to break things up. The power of guitar, and one hand glove and sunglasses. The power of black style. The power of rebellion. The boy, in typical "Bart Simpson" fashion, tells his parents to "eat this"; wiping his pouty signature Culkin lips with his single leather glove, he puts on sunglasses and literally blasts his father to Africa with the power of a huge stereo speaker. Little Michael Jackson's loneliness in "Ben" becomes Culkin's rage, now transferable, now universalized. At the same time, in this ability to project his story onto one of white suburbia, the video demonstrates Michael Jackson's power to extend himself beyond safe spaces, beyond home, to be, in fact, like Eartha Kitt, placeless in his voice and movements.

This opening sequence explicitly pays homage to Michael Jackson's power as a megastar, and black music's entry into white suburban spaces with the power to transform those spaces. It continues and updates the narrative of rock and roll begun with Chuck Berry and Elvis and Little Richard and then taken up by little Michael in "Who's Lovin' You" and "ABC"—to move white bodies, to shake them into rebellion, to transform them. But in the video, Jackson is not just one of many performers; he becomes the icon of such transformation, bigger than any one individual. In the video, a name on a T-shirt and a barely glanced at poster are enough to signal his power. A quick allusion to Jackson here is imagined powerful enough to blow a hole in the wall, to expose and reverse the voodoo of a white father's secret racist thoughts: instead of sending Jackson back to Africa, the father is sent there, complete with his Archie Bunker–style easy chair.

After this opening sequence, the song "Black or White" properly begins and shifts the video from its initial story of white suburban racial transgression to an argument for color transcendence that at the same time demonstrates global and technological mastery. As the lyrics argue for not spending one's life "being a color," Jackson joins and then borrows from a variety of international and multiethnic/multiracial dancers. Each set of dancers is iconographic, but nonspecific in terms of particular performer, region, and even time. First, Jackson joins some African hunters in the bush, then a female Thai classical dancer, followed by male and female Native American hoop dancers; he meets an Indian woman dancing in the middle of a busy intersection, and then joins a line of Disneyed Russian male folk dancers. In these moments, Jackson is "himself" but also imitative, borrowing from the dancers around him. And the international dancers in turn seem to uncannily mirror Jackson's signature moves, integrating them into their own traditions' dance moves. Jackson's play with the dancers seems to offer the contradictory message of "universalism" and the transnational influence and improvisational power of black style. A Native American dancer flips his hair in a manner à la Jackson as the ghoul in "Thriller." The Indian's dancer's flirtatious neck isolations might remind us of Jackson's neck pops in "Bad." If, in "Who's Lovin' You," Jackson demonstrates his ability to become and then transform the soul man tradition, in this sequence, he moves transnationally, blurring the lines between who is imitating whom—particularly for a young generation of MTV watchers who may not have ever seen these dance styles before. Jackson attempts to both prove himself to be beyond the politics of ethnic and national authenticity—a theme that will be important to the trajectory of his music for the rest of his career—and demonstrate his own influence transculturally. Jackson's yearning to triumph over racial and gendered limits comes to a pinnacle in the ingenious morphing sequence toward the conclusion of the song (directed by Jamie Dixon of Pacific Data Images), where models morph and meld into one another, phenotypes shifting and blurring across multiracial, multigender, and amazingly wholesome and good-looking bodies: from a bouncy blonde white woman to a black man sporting well-sculpted dreadlocks.

Tonally, video then takes an abrupt shift into fierceness. The camera backs up, and we see, among the mostly white directors and technical people, among abandoned cameras and lights, a black panther. The panther escapes down the stairs with elegance and stealth, and then, in a nighttime abandoned alley, morphs into a crouching Jackson. Jackson's dancing shifts from Fred Astaire's nattiness to a sensual, seemingly abandoned improvisation, where he seems almost lost in feeling. Echoing the video's ongoing motif of freedom and constraint, color blindness and historical sensitivity, Jackson's clothing is a combination of loose and tight—the spangled glove transposed into what looks like a laced wrist guard; the pants, black stovepipes, tight with knee pads, and then loose; flowing black overshirt, which, along with his now flowing hair, gets caught in the foggy wind.

Jackson's dance heats into a frenzy of anger, fed by sensual circlings of his pelvis. This slow heat builds into the release of rage, so that he howls, and breaks windows marked with multiple racist sayings. (On the version contained on the Jackson compilation video, *HIStory*, the windows that Jackson breaks are marked with graffiti, including "Nigger Go Home" and "No Wetbacks." Notably, though, on the version of the video that aired on MTV, the video's antiracist messages were erased from the footage, so that Jackson's rebellion loses its explicitly political edge.) As the song builds, he no longer needs the trash can or other objects: his screams themselves now have the power to break things. He watches with approval, and a bit of surprise, as one howl makes a florescent hotel sign explode in beautiful sparks, like a Fourth of July display. Jackson rips his shirt, exposing delicate light brown chest and bared arms. Satisfied, Jackson returns again to the leopard body and slinks out into the night.

If a running theme of Post-Soul identity making is the negotiation of post-civil-rights integrationist politics, Jackson insists in this video that the project of assimilation and acceptance (on MTV and elsewhere) must also accommodate his rage and his insistence on being a transformational racial, gendered, and sexual subject.[31] As Jackson shifts from his message of colorblindness in the first half of the video, to animalized black masculinity, in the guise of a leopard, back to Jackson again, this time hand on crotch, his feet madly stamping out a new pattern of assertiveness, he lets out that awkward, if rough-voiced howl. While much has been made of the accelerated machismo of this video and especially of Jackson's repeated grabbing and caressing of his crotch, I have been most haunted by this cry, and what it refuses to articulate as a full explanation. This moment is an example of where Jackson moves from either/or, and both/and, to refusal. Here, he insists on the importance of the in-between as a space of creation. Here, he illustrates this space of refusal is also a space of movement made literal by morphing technology: transracial, transhistorical, transgenerational, transformational.

FIVE

"Feeling Like a Woman, Looking Like a Man, Sounding Like a No-No"

Grace Jones and the Performance of "Strangé" in the Post-Soul Moment

Every generation needs a model for how to be strange. For me, that model was Grace Jones. In my teen years, Grace Jones was the soundtrack to my first trips to Chicago's North Side by myself: to Second Hand Tunes, Wax Trax, the Silver Moon Vintage Store, and the Value Village on Kimball Avenue. In Chicago, that period between *Nightclubbing* (1981) and *Slave to the Rhythm* (1985) was simultaneous with the opening of some neighborhood boundaries—particularly those of gay and punk subcultures—and the tighter policing of others, around class and race. Which neighborhood store or club or El stop would be welcoming sometimes depended on the color of your skin, the cut of your jeans, the expense of your haircut. It might depend on whether you're perceived as cruising or just window shopping, hanging out with your friends, or congregating. But catalyzed by the election of Harold Washington, Chicago's first black mayor, in 1983, my friends and I began venturing outside of our predominantly black and brown South Side home neighborhoods, taking the Red and Brown Line to neighborhoods to the north for our fun: to the snooty stores at the Gold Coast, where we were chased out for playing in the water fountains; to the Korean barbecue shops and Middle Eastern bakeries and thrift stores in Albany Park; to the artists' spaces in Wicker Park; and to Boystown, the increasingly punk and queer spaces dotting Belmont Avenue, from Broadway to Halsted, where we'd stop in at the Dunkin' Donuts and then the Alley to shop for Doc Martins and look for old tux jackets and lace and where I found warped LPs of Eartha Kitt and Shirley Bassey. In Boystown, the early 1980s was a time of cultural and political upheaval in the face of AIDS and the continued threat of violence from the police and outsiders, but it was also a time of identity solidification, increasingly seen as Chicago's "gay village" from the outside, as well as from within. Eventually the Boystown area would become more expensive and gentrified—but at this point, it was still possible to find old diners and shoe repair shops among the newer gay clubs and bookstores, mom-and-pop video stores, and, for my family, a space where we could "move on up" from renting on the South Side. Eventually, my mother bought a condo there, not far from Augie's and C.K.'s, the lesbian bar in front of which I was once scandalized to watch two women, squatting on the sidewalk, giggling and taking a pee, right there in the open.

Boystown's thrift stores, which I rummaged with my friends Jorge and Robin, were a chance to invent and redefine a new self, to connect to other folks' pasts. (Trying on black cat's-eye frames, I suddenly became my mother caught in a snapshot, taken in her early married life.) There is in the bricolage of thrift store fashions the idea of "making do" but also a claim to the freedom of movement and access, also at the heart of the cosmopolitanism that is at the heart of Grace Jones's aesthetic. Along with this exhilaration was that joy of watching gay men—still mostly white—cruising each other on Broadway Avenue and Belmont. I loved and shared the aesthetic of camp and appreciated the open secret of yearning. But I was curious, too, about the place of black women in this world. There were the icons of style and boldness, like Donna Summer and Grace. There were the girlfriends, linked arm in arm with their boys on Saturday night. There were the kitschy greeting cards with large-breasted black women circulated for laughs in the gay-run card and gift store. And sometimes, too, there were lesbians and queer women, who seemed to take up a less visible space.

On those streets I saw shimmering in the distance the possibility to be something else, even if that shimmer was my own desire mirrored back at me. And if, perhaps, this gay male culture did not always return my interest, Grace Jones seemed to, even while she injected herself into the geometry of the desire of those men. Through reinvention and sheer demand, she kept their gaze while still remaining a mystery. There was elegance in her traditionally African beauty, and also laughter. Grace was a lesson in how to travel in multiple spaces while being resolutely herself. And this was my dream at age fifteen. This was a form of excess, made over from castaways, debris, and rejects to make new power, unaccounted-for power. It's the power of a silk blouse for only $1.25, ignoring the underarm sweat stains. Like the youthful ingenuity that invented hip-hop, hers was an art made from the unpredictable largess of her various patrons (Andy Warhol, Keith Haring, Jean-Paul Goude) but which runs away with the show.

Is Grace Jones a Hologram?

The darling of Andy Warhol and Keith Haring, Grace Jones is often associated with gay and primarily white male subculture. In Tony Kushner's *Angels in America: A Gay Fantasia on National Themes—Perestroika*, white gay male AIDS patient Prior phones his friend Belize, drag queen and nurse, about a recent dream of a woman and his unexpectedly orgasmic response.

> PRIOR: I am drenched in spooj.
> BELIZE: Spooj?
> PRIOR: Cum. Jiz. Ejaculate. I've had a wet dream.
> BELIZE: Well about time. Miss Thing has been abstemious.
>   She has stored up beaucoup de spooj.
> PRIOR: It was a woman.
> BELIZE: You turning straight on me?
> PRIOR: Not a *conventional* woman.
> BELIZE: Grace Jones?[1]

If, for Kushner's Belize, Grace Jones is a figure of desire, she is also a figure of sexual disorientation and wonder. Sociologist and Sylvester biographer Joshua Gamson describes Grace Jones's appeal as "sexy gender-fuck," a heady cocktail of glitter, camp, androgyny, and fear.[2] For white gay male subculture, I'd argue, Jones serves as an androgynous object of desire, a fitting muse for the space of the polymorphously perverse disco, and a conduit, or screen, that enables fantasies of black (and white) sexuality and subjectivity, from the dominatrix to primitive, to animal, to vampire.

In contrast to the ways that Jones circulates in mostly white gay male culture as a site of wonder and sexual disorientation, for many of her black fans, she serves as a site at which to refuse and/or dismantle essentialized notions of black subjectivity. For many of her fans of color, she might serve as what Kevin E. Quashie identifies as the "girlfriend"—a site of identity making "where the self becomes and is undone, the site where the politics of self, nation and difference are evaluated through cultural landscapes and ethical sensibilities relevant to Black women [and men], where the necessary anti-identity politics coalesce."[3] The context of black freedom struggles, her link to other black "fugitives," from the maroons to Zora Neal Hurston, gives Jones's unconventionality a context that might otherwise be missed. Gay African American artist Lyle Ashton Harris describes Grace Jones's impact on his own sense of celebrity and the feminine in the 1980's:

> I was having dinner with an artist the other day, and . . . I mentioned Grace Jones and he said that she was frightening. And I didn't say anything to him, but I just find it quite interesting. That was his nightmare. It wasn't mine. . . . To be someone who was so stunning, so androgynous, so beautiful, and just completely so self-possessed, but also just smart and sharp—it was something that was deeply inspirational. And also she was obviously a gay icon. But also I just appreciated her rudeness, her criticality. Her drama.[4]

As Harris points out, Jones's power to shake up, alienate, and speak truth to power—in admirably theatrical ways—has important implications for the ways that we think about the performance of black womanhood, and queer color sensibility, in the 1980s cultural moment. In the Paradise Garage, a disco space shaped by a primarily black and Latino gay aesthetic in the late 1970s through 1980, Jones's "Pull Up to the Bumper" and "Slave to the Rhythm" were on the Top 100 DJ list.[5] Jones's "Pull Up to the Bumper" became a bold articulation of sexual pleasure in the face of growing panic about AIDS and gay visibility. The song at once captures the exhilarating, sometimes utopic, and sometimes anonymous spirit of connection, as well as the risk that accompanies public sex in the club scenes of the 1980s and 1990s. And we can watch Jones perform these pleasures in her performance of "Pull Up to the Bumper" in her Grammy-nominated 1981 performance *One Man Show,* at one point surfing a crowd of black and white and brown dancing men, their faces kept in shadow. I read Jones's embodiment of anonymous intimacy here as an aspect of her own complicated take on the Post-Soul imperative of integration, as well as her savvy negotiation of gay male subcultures, taking up space both among and outside of the crowd.

Grace Jones, born Grace Mendoza in Spanish Town, Jamaica, in 1948, was raised along with five brothers and sisters by her grandparents, while her parents, Marjorie and Robert Jones, a clergyman and politician, lived in the United States. Contrary to her outrageous persona, church was a strong part of Jones's upbringing, and she describes herself as a child who was shy and very athletic and loved the outdoors. She and her brother Christian moved to the United States in 1965, joining her parents to live in the considerable Jamaican community in Syracuse, New York, where her father was a bishop. Both Jones and her brother clashed with her conservative family, and Jones says that she found escape in community theater and at one point a motorcycle gang.[6] Jones studied theater at Onondaga Community College and Syracuse University. She converted her skills in performance to the high-fashion world of modeling in New York and Paris, where she captured the attention of art world icon Andy Warhol, as well as photographer Jean-Paul Goude, who became her patron, collaborator, and lover. In 1977, Jones signed a contract with Island Records, with which she recorded her first dance club hits *Portfolio* (1977), *Fame* (1978), and *Muse* (1979). Jones would continue to grow as an icon of the art, dance, and music scenes, her music and live performances growing to be particularly popular in gay subcultures and in Europe in the early 1980s, and crossing over into the R&B and pop charts with *Warm Leatherette* (1980), *Nightclubbing* (1981), and *Slave to the Rhythm* (1985), said by many of her critics to be her strongest albums. With the growth in popularity of music videos, as well as her appearances in popular films like *Conan the Destroyer, A View to a Kill, Vamp,* and *Boomerang,* Jones's notoriety as beautiful, gender-bending trickster became more widespread. While the 1980s would seem to have been the pinnacle of her visibility as a performer (so far at least), she continues to perform and record in to the twenty-first century, collaborating with Luciano Pavarotti, Sly & Robbie, Lil' Kim, Brian Eno, Tricky, Wendy & Lisa, Massive Attack, and French avant-garde poet Brigitte Fontaine.

We can see the sign of Grace in the vocal stylings of Neneh Cherry in the mid- to late 1980s, in the stagecraft of Tina Turner's post-Ike renaissance, and in the sartorial and sexual outrageousness of RuPaul and perhaps even Lil' Kim and Foxy Brown in the 1990s and moving into the twenty-first century. Grace's influence is still visible on the streets, in drag queen culture, and in recent revivals of 1980s style, from flattops to Lady Gaga's surreal theatricality. And we can see Jones explicitly referenced in African American and Caribbean art that might be outside the realm of "entertainment": Lyle Ashton Harris's *Memoirs of Hadrian #17* and postmodern cubist Caribbean poet Deborah Richards's "The Halle Berry One Two," for example. Black Haitian American performance artist Dréd uses the persona of Grace Jones to open up the world of drag kings to more fluid expressions of female masculinity.[7] In Grace Jones's work and that of the other black artists influenced by her, we see the wedding of disco and punk, art and fashion, male and female, animal and human, and human and machine to create new notions of black sexuality.

Flattop, gleaming cheekbones, and muscled chest, Jones was—and is—confrontationally androgynous, and at the same time distant and sufficiently underground to seem unco-optable. (Yet my friend Jeff tells me of an urban legend that Grace Jones is actually a hologram, completely made up by Island Records.) Jones can switch from languorous, husky rap in "Walking in the Rain" and "Demolition Man" to a frisky femme alto in "Pull Up to the Bumper" and a glass-breaking screech in "She's Lost Control." Jones also uses national drag through voice, moving from Jamaican patois in "My Jamaican Guy" to middle American femme in "Man Around the House" to her mock-straight Britishisms in "I Need a Man." Jones performs multiple racialized, national, and gendered desires. In her video for "My Jamaican Guy" in her *One Man Show,* Jones romances herself, singing, snuggling up to, and kissing a male version of her "self"—and so we might add "autoeroticism" to the list of ways that Jones performs desire. Often during these same performances, Jones also performs in animal "drag." On the famous cover of his collection of works, *Jungle Fever,* Jean-Paul Goude figures Jones naked and in a cage, on all fours. At her knees is a carcass of meat (animal? human?), and around her mouth trickles blood. Her eyes are narrowed, and her teeth are exposed in a growl. Underneath the cage is a sign, "don't feed the animal." We see an apt, white audience, watching. At the beginning of *One Man Show* Jones opens in a gorilla suit *and* grass skirt playing the bongos, evoking and outsavaging Josephine Baker's banana skirt, as well as Marlene Dietrich's gorilla striptease in the film *Blonde Venus* (of 1932).

Jones's use of drag—and particularly animal drag—is an important aspect of her theatricality—one that cites previous black performances, putting her into the larger history of the ways that performers of the African diaspora use performance in complex ways to critique the dehumanization of black people. Yet Jones's use of drag and other techniques of performing identity also poses challenges of readability. She is, in many ways, a trickster figure, an androgynous Anansi, sliding out of the grasp of both her fans and her critics. Jones uses an outsized public persona (one that often risks caricature) to lobby critique and to express anger and, ultimately, agency—like three other trickster performers of color who rose to prominence during the same period of the 1980s and early 1990s: visual artist Jean-Michel Basquiat, whose works and life constantly poke fun at fears of black sexual potency; performance artist Coco Fusco, whose 1992 collaborations with Guillermo Gómez-Peña, the "Two Undiscovered Amerindians" series, document the "irony of having to demonstrate one's humanity" through over-the-top staged performances of the "savage" on display;[8] and rapper Flavor Flav, "sideman" for the group Public Enemy, whose manic comic persona, complete with gold teeth, ever present huge clock-necklace, and wacky sideways baseball cap nevertheless fueled the critical fire of many of Public Enemy's most potent political songs in 1989.

Grace Jones counters and surpasses traditional notions of gendered erotic performances—for black women in particular—by occupying and performing the image of the black female body as "strange" or "eccentric." The eccentric performance's ability to locate itself in freedom of movement in an otherwise constraining situation—in the case of Grace Jones, the constraints of a history of brittle racial and sexual stereotypes—is very important to the ways she pushes the boundaries of identity and recognition. Hers are excellent contemporary examples of Daphne A. Brooks's concept of "Afro alienation acts" discussed in her study of nineteenth-century theater, *Bodies in Dissent*. "Afro alienation," Brooks suggests, is an exploratory performative strategy meant to call attention to one's looked-at-ness as a black subject by making "strange" gender and racial categories through disruption, discomfort, and alienation of one's audience.

Just as Brecht calls for actors to adapt "socially critical" techniques in their performances so as to generate "alienation effects" and to "awaken" audiences to history, so too can we consider these historic figures as critically defamiliarizing their own bodies by way of performance in order to yield alternative racial and gender epistemologies. By using performance tactics to signify on the social, cultural, and ideological machinery that circumscribes African Americans, they intervene in the spectacular and systemic representational abjection of black peoples.[9]

This chapter considers ways that Jones creates a critical reading and disruption of these oppressive representational systems. Through the delightfully disorienting pleasures of her music and iconicity, she creates a space for pleasure and knowing for her black audiences. In their consumption of Jones's sometimes alien and alienating iconography and style, music and bodily performances, black audiences might locate a space for refashioning subjectivity. In Jones's performance of the machine or cyborg, for example, she disrupts the notion of black female sexual availability and "naturalness."[10] At the same time, she also provides a space of secrecy, of not knowing, which might also be a space of creation and pleasure for her listeners. Brooks describes those

> moments in which black cultural producers and black women in particular negotiated ways of manipulating the borders of the material and the epistemological in transatlantic performance culture. . . . We can think of their acts as opaque, as dark points of possibility that create figurative sites for the reconfiguration of black and female bodies on display. A kind of shrouding, this trope of darkness paradoxically allows for corporeal unveiling to yoke with the (re)covering and rehistoricizing of the flesh.[11]

What are the politics of occupying a position of eccentricity in the public sphere for black women? What does it mean to strategically occupy the position of gender and sometimes racial and national ambiguity—at the risk of unintelligibility? In *Undoing Gender*, Judith Butler suggests that unintelligibility might have an important role in maintaining one's humanity.

> There are advantages to remaining less than intelligible, if intelligibility is understood as that which is produced as a consequence of recognition according to prevailing social norms. Indeed, if my options are loathsome, if I have no desire to be recognized within a certain set of norms, then it follows that my sense of survival depends upon escaping the clutch of those norms by which recognition is conferred. It may well be that my sense of social belonging is impaired by the distance I take, but surely that estrangement is preferable to gaining a sense of intelligibility by virtue of norms that will only do me in from another direction.[12]

What is radical, daring and also risky about Grace Jones's work are the venues with which she explores her split selves: first in the (still white dominated) culture of the avant-garde art world of Jean-Paul Goude, Andy Warhol, and Keith Haring; and then the venue of popular, commercial culture (from Island Records to the James Bond franchise), risking misreading, reappropriation, and alienation.

Grace Jones presents a curious and challenging project of "blaxploration." Her performances are often overlooked by feminist and other critics for their political critique—I'd argue, because she is so good at what she does. Jones's theatricality: her grand gestures, the sweep of her gaze, her preference for artifice in her vocalizations in places where we expect sincerity, realness, and roughness can also be distancing. She is spectacularly successful in creating a smooth and deflecting surface, and in capturing our erotic attention through spectacle. She is so fantastic at becoming an object—animal, machine, space invader, multiplying robot, hurricane—that we might not hear her also explaining what it's like to be an object. Grace is so good at creating desire that we miss her read on where that hunger comes from, and what it costs. But it's there, in the force of her voice, in her lyrics, in the flash of her eyes. And in the highly theatrical staging of scenes of desire that occupy her work: from cage to studio to disco floor to stage. Her work is often overlooked as a project of black critique because of the contradictions she raises and refuses to resolve. Like Eartha Kitt, she is the stranger, placing herself outside of the circle of normative blackness to look back into it, and into the realm of suppressed fantasy that lies there, the space of the "no-no": dominatrix, slut, he-she, queer, black bitch. Anger incarnate in beautiful bared flesh. Crazy enough to say what you're thinking, but won't say out loud. Easier to place her somewhere else or perhaps to not place her at all.

Strange Women: Anger and the Split Self

Every generation needs a new kind of woman. For me, that woman was Grace Jones. The switching of accents. An insectlike tilt of her head. Sunglasses that block out our meeting (and reading of) her eyes. A smile that could well be a sneer. I recognized in her thrilling contrariness, her "sounding like a no-no," a female masculine home girl. When she talk-sings "You ain't gonna get it!" in "Nipple to the Bottle," or yells out

"Doesn't anyone *work* in this town?" in "The Apple Stretching," I can imagine the cutting of eyes, the sucking of teeth, the toss of hips that reveal a sensibility that I can only describe as womanish.

In contemporary entertainment culture, "strange" women might be culled from the strangers that people celebrity culture, but they may also be family, or even ourselves. In Julie Dash's groundbreaking film *Daughters of the Dust,* the story of a family of black women in the Georgia Sea Islands at the turn of the twentieth century, two sisters discuss the return of Yellow Mary, a member of the family who has gone off on her own, gone to Cuba, to work first as a servant, then wet nurse, and then prostitute. She returns to the island in style, still audaciously outspoken and providing no apology for her leaving.

> GIRL ONE: What that woman, Yellow Mary. She ain't no family woman. She a scary woman.
> GIRL TWO: She a new kind of woman.

For every generation, there is the scary woman, the woman who symbolizes the community's anger at and fear of change. Like Eartha, and like Grace, the character of Yellow Mary represents what can happen to women outside of the comfort of a small community—what can happen when one is "ruined." But Yellow Mary also represents what can happen when one survives the new challenges of the outside world. We find out that after she was brought to Cuba her employers held her captive. Yellow Mary tells us that she "fixed the tittie" to end the exploitation of her sex. She stopped the milk—the product that was paying for her room and board, as well as feeding the children of her captors—something like Lady Macbeth's unsexing of herself. In this move, she takes momentary control of her own commodification. But her next option—prostitution—is a limited one that she must also live with. The film is mysterious about just what "fixing the tittie" entails and doesn't tell us what else she has done in the process—what other changes, what other "fixing" had to occur before she made it back home. But her family and we see what she has become—beautiful, haughty, distant—a diva. She carries a big yellow parasol and brings with her a lover, a woman in yellow, another yellow woman. Over the course of the film, Yellow Mary's "Fixing the tittie" has turned out to mean a lot of things—a symbol of unknown happenings, fears of travel, fears of the body, but also the negotiation of sexuality—at once concrete and vague, suggestive.

In Toni Morrison's novel *Sula*, Nell and Sula are fighting off the white boys who bully them on their way home from school. Sula stops and pulls out a knife, and cuts herself. She makes herself bleed. She tells the boys, "If I could do that to myself, imagine what I could do to you."[13] The impulse, the act. Anger. A new self, emerging. A break in narrative, a stopping of time.

The moments when things pop out of my mouth and *I* don't know where they come from. I am followed home from school. Some boys are teasing me, calling me names, throwing rocks that barely miss my ankles. I wheel around, and I point at them. "You go straight to hell." They stop—aghast—as if I have been speaking in tongues. They laugh and frown at the same time, backing away. Perhaps—I hope—they have taken me quite literally, that I have cursed them. Maybe they assume (wrongly) that I believe in hell. But perhaps for that moment I do, because I want them to go away, and my anger is real. I want them to suffer someplace far away from me.

A different afternoon, a little later that spring, one of the same boys follows me into the lobby of my apartment building. There are three doors to get through, one locked outer and two locked inner. The boy pushes his way in after me. I make it to the second door, but he is right behind me before I can open it. I stare straight ahead, my hand in my pocket feeling for my keys. I feel him behind me, touching me, breathing Doritos breath down my neck, laughing. I jab my elbows into him, but he is pushing, and I can't get him away from me. My voice is . . . hard to find. "Stop," I say, breathless with panic. "Leave me alone." I sound too polite to my own ears, apologetic, and I wish that I didn't. My voice is betraying me. From the other side of the door, a neighbor comes down the stairs. She says, in a no-nonsense voice, "When will you kids stop?" She does not seem to see that I am pushing the boy away from me, that I am not playing. No one seems to notice that I am not playing. She opens the second door and I run in. Luckily, at the sound of the older woman's voice, the boy has disappeared. I scramble for my keys and skitter into my apartment. For the rest of that spring, I will keep seeing him around the neighborhood and at school, a beige peacoat, and when I do, my heart will leap and I will duck my head, hoping I will not be seen.

Grace Jones provides the soundtrack for my revenge. She is the voice for the things that I hold in, and that threaten to break me. She is Sula's split finger, and she is the knife. On Jones's *Slave to the Rhythm* album, her face is splintered into half a dozen refractions. Laceration. The cutting, splitting image of her face, screaming. Mouth open. Anger split and multiplied. Anger also a mirror, reflecting mine. She is acting on us, on me. She is splitting me, us. She is mirroring. Now she is opening.

In her iconography, in her music and performances, Grace Jones performs a caricature of black femininity, and then the splitting of that caricature. She is like the tall, graceful plaster Nubian statues that my great-grandmother kept in her front parlor, but it is as if they have been cracked, revealing the brittleness of their construction.

I see Jones's splitting of self in her performances as a direct response to a history of presenting the black female body as both sexually voracious and unrapeable, unable to feel pain. This split is a dominant theme in black women's feminist art of the Post-Soul era, including Toni Morrison's *Beloved*, Sapphire's *Push*, Kara Walker's heart-wrenching cutouts, Lydia Johnson's and Suzan-Lori Parks's plays about Sarah Baartman, and Julie Dash's *Daughters of the Dust*. In Yellow Mary's not quite fully revealed story of "fixing the tittie," we might think of the "culture of dissemblance" that Darlene Clark Hine discusses in her work—the culture of masking sexual experience, pain, and loss by black women, masked by an image of bravado or exposure.[14] Julie Dash discusses her own struggle with the culture of dissemblance as a central motivation in making the film.

> The stories from my own family sparked the idea of *Daughters* and formed the basis for some of the characters. But when I probed my relatives for information about the family history in South Carolina, or about our migration north to New York, they were often reluctant to discuss it. When things got too personal, too close to memories they didn't want to reveal, they would close up, push me away, tell me to go ask someone else. I knew then that the images I wanted to show, the story I wanted to tell, had to touch an audience the way it touched my family. It had to take them back, take them inside their family memories, inside our collective memories.[15]

If, as Jacqueline Bobo has documented, black female audiences had been courted and addressed through the *Daughters of the Dust*'s marketing and production, Grace Jones's black audiences, and especially her female audiences, might be seen as participating in an accidental or even eccentric form of reception. We find in Jones's songs and films less easily available narratives of black family, community, and self-actualization than what we might find in *Daughters* or *The Color Purple*—two works that critics often evoke when they theorize about black female interpretive communities and responses to popular culture in the 1980s and 1990s.[16] Yet Grace Jones's adoption of hypersexualized, animalistic, machinelike, and apparently degrading positions acts as "disidentification" with the toxic aspects of dominant ideology of black womanhood.[17] In Maria J. Guzman's insightful analysis of Jones's performances in her *One Man Show*, she points out that Jones "has been most often criticized for not addressing her audiences during the *One Man Show* period, and has been called 'Alien Grace. Detached Grace. Frozen Grace.' She is often seen as an emblem of cold steel androgyny."[18] Yet Jones's coldness might be read less as a problem than as a solution—a way to mark her refusal and spirit of critique through sound and embodiment.[19] We might then look to Jones as a way of theorizing the black female spectator's use of difficult and/or controversial figures as a means of negotiating the contradictions and complexities of race, sexuality, and pleasure, and the forging of identity within the very curtailed space of commercial entertainment culture against the grain of original intentions. In addition, as a subcultural icon, Jones forces us to think about the ways that black cultural traffic travels out from, as well as returns to, unpredictable, and unforeseen, directions.

What is additionally radical, daring, and risky about Grace Jones's work is that she explores black female anger and the split self in a popular, commercial, and often gay white male culture. In this way, we might see Grace Jones as conveying a kind of triple consciousness through the medium of celebrity; Jones gives black voice (and style) to the predominantly white-controlled text of the celebrity. But she adds to this double-voicedness a third level of critique about the space for art and critique.[20] Behind her "strange" mask, Jones presents a commentary on the condition of negotiating exploitation.

As we discuss Jones's work, and especially the extent to which we might think of her work as critique, the problem of her agency in shaping her persona emerges. Both Jan Nederveen Pieterse and Janell Hobson link Jones to the representation of the Black Venus and sexual savage. Pieterse, in *White on Black: Images of the Africa and Blacks in Western Popular Culture*, comments that Jones's image of "the construction of the exotically and erotically dangerous black woman is also an important thread running through the stage personae of a whole range of popular singers, for example, Eartha Kitt, Shirley Bassey, and Tina Turner."[21] That Jones fits into a history of commercial images of black women's bodies as animal and human sexual objects is undeniable. But what is missing here is room for the agency and complexity of a performer, or for the multiple ways that her audience might understand her.

Jones has been spokeswoman for corporate culture in the United States and elsewhere: on billboards, album covers, and advertisements. For example, her body and voice have been used to sell Honda scooters—the perfect embodiment of her sleek futurism and the mobility of identity in the 1980s. But she has also figured herself as part of the artistic avant-garde, and her carefully studied allusions reveal her understanding of an international history of the performance of "strange," from Picasso's primitives to Josephine Baker to Marlene Dietrich to the constructionists to Japanese Noh theater. In her essay "Grace Jones, Postcoloniality, and Androgyny: The Performance Art of Grace Jones," art historian Miriam Kershaw writes of Jones as a performance artist, not just as a commercial performer or representation created by others, and one who strategically intercedes in the discourse of the primitive dominant in twentieth-century modernism. Kershaw offers one of the few critical studies of Jones that credits her work as a politicized engagement with art and history, describing her work as self-referential, a "dance of sign ricochets."

> Jones' fierce stage presence destabilizes historical relations of power enacted through male/female, black/white interactions, while her commanding voice leads the viewer through a symbolic negation."[22]

Kershaw notes the importance of her experiences as a runway model, a training ground through which to think critically about body, look, and movement, as well as "rapid, multiple reinvention."[23] Other forces of influence include gay subculture and the "liminal space of the disco"—where Kershaw says Jones worked out a sense of sexual play.[24] Like Kershaw, I see Jones as consciously inhabiting and then disrupting a series of black female stereotypes, from the primitive mask to Parisian Black Venus. Indeed, Jones herself articulated her identification with Baker in her interview with Andy Warhol.[25] In her performances, Jones highlights the spectacle around gender and the theater of black identity. Her use of boxing motifs in the *One Man Show* and her other works is just one of the ways that she places herself in a tradition of the spectacle, eroticism, and violence of black bodies. To borrow Homi K. Bhabha's phrase, Jones occupies a position of "sly civility," and her artistry, in some ways, comes in her play with ambiguity.[26]

Jones's performed critique is part of its own historicizeable tradition, an engagement with cultural memory that might be accessed via her assemblage of costumes, persona, and movements (sometimes animal, sometimes machine, sometimes masculine and feminine); her gaze (aggressive, flirtatious, and sometimes shielded, a mask); her sound (use of lower, as well as high, registers, the sometimes flat boredom expressed in her voice and phrasing, her gruffness or blueing of notes, her shouts); the citationality of her performances to past performances (Eartha Kitt, Josephine Baker, minstrel shows, circuses, freak shows, and other black "displays"); and her lively engagement with countercultural audiences, especially now that her celebrity has taken on cult status. The tools of performance studies are vital in opening up Grace Jones as icon or representation to a figure of critique. By viewing Jones as a performer rather than a produced media spectacle, we are allowed to think of her as an agent always in collaboration with an audience.

In her performances, Grace Jones is something like a piece of kitschy racist memorabilia, but one that has somehow come to life, possessed and angry.[27] As she switches from automaton during "Demolition Man," to heartbroken lover in "La Vie En Rose," there is always a glimmer, a wink, and sometimes a glare, a sneer of anger, lurking just below the surface, that might well have its roots in the commercial trade of black bodies from the slave moment to the present. Jones's performances constantly call attention to her own framing, and to the expectations of her audience. She asks us to think about the "situation" of her performance, and the limits of its boundaries and the lens. This not only gets us to think further about the artificiality of her performance of identity: black, woman, and Jamaican. It also invites the audience to consider their participation as audience/consumer.

Grace Jones's attention to the framing and sale of her sexuality, as well as her disruption of easy categorization and harnessing of sexual power and control, is informed, I'd argue, by a history of resistance of Caribbean slave women, and in particular, the voice of disdain and anger that can be located in Caribbean oral culture. Jones may transmogrify this

Caribbean tradition into a patois informed by bodily, as well as vocal, manipulations of punk and performance art, but the spirit is still shared.

For example, in Carolyn Cooper's landmark *Noises in the Blood: Orality, Gender, and the "Vulgar" Body of Jamaican Popular Culture,* she traces the image of the transgressive black female woman in Jamaican culture who uses both her body and her speech as a means of resistance. Cooper begins with the figure of Nanny, the maroon leader who, according to legend, raised her skirts and mooned British soldiers, and in the process deflected their bullets. Cooper traces the centrality of the bottom in dance hall culture as going back to this first "potent female bottom."[28]

From Nanny on, sexual transgression, as well as theatrical self-presentation, becomes a means of critical commentary in Jamaican folk culture. Cooper points to the song "Me Know No Law, Me Know No Sin" as an example of where the transgressive black woman declares her strategic use of her master's economic interest in her sexuality, her ownership of her own sexuality, and her refusal of moral responsibility.

> Altho' a slave me is born and bred,
> My skin is black, not yellow;
> I often sold my maiden head
> To many a handsom fellow. . . .
>
> Me know no law, me know no sin,
> Me is just what ebba them make me;
> This is the way dem bring me in;
> So God nor devil take me.

Cooper suggests that this song gives us a female character who declares her freedom as she

> flaunts her cunning ability to capitalize on her body—selling her "maiden head" several times over "[t]o many a handsome fellow." The qualifying "'[al]tho' a slave me is born and bred" declares her refusal to be commodified by anybody but herself. She may be a legal "slave" but she is free nevertheless to exploit her status as a commodity in the sexual marketplace. She is able to seduce gullible men into purchasing a non-existent product, not her body, but the illusion of virginity and first conquest of undiscovered territory; the imperial myth (dis)embodied.[29]

At the same time, by claiming ignorance of the transaction at hand (through the play of "no/know") the speaker claims the right to innocence, placing herself outside the boundaries of the social. In this way, Cooper suggests, she claims her right to humanity.[30]

I see in Grace Jones's covers of Bill Withers's "Use Me" and Johnny Cash's "Ring of Fire," a similar presentation of self as sexual trickster, at once offering herself as an accessible source of and product of consuming sexual desire, and, at the same time, in her aggressive and sometimes surreal performance style, mocking the idea that she might not have the upper hand.

In Jones's collaborations with her former husband, Jean-Paul Goude, we see a similar tug-of-war of representational and, in the end, sexual control, and ultimately, the emergence of Jones as trickster. Goude says that he first met Jones, artist, model, and then an emerging disco singer, after seeing some of her "outrageous" performance art in Paris and New York.[31] Jones becomes the subject of a series of photographic art, collage, and drawings. The content, as well as the strategy, of Jean-Paul Goude's work reveals a fascination with the black female body, as well as with technology. He combines both to denaturalize and sometimes at the same time exploit stereotypes about black female bodies as primitive, excessive, and accessible. His photographic technique includes supplementation of fetishized body parts like the buttocks (as in his photographs of black model and former Robert De Niro inamorata Toukie Smith, in "Carolina" [1978]), and the elongation of neck, legs, and torso, as in the 1978 photo collage created of Grace Jones, which Jones jokingly called his "Nigger Arabesque." Goude, in fact, appropriates this title as a caption in his book *Jungle Fever* without scare quotes, undercutting Jones's critical response. Goude describes his pre-Photoshop process of altering the figure in *Jungle Fever*.

> First I photographed her in different positions—to get all my references—, which I combined, as you can see, in the cut-up version of the picture. I cut her legs apart, lengthened them, turned her body completely to face the audience like an Egyptian painting, and of course, once I was all done, I had a print made which I used as my preliminary drawing. Then I started painting, joining all those pieces to give the illusion that Grace Jones actually posed for the photograph and that only she was capable of assuming such a position.[32]

Here, as well as in other work, Goude would seem to demonstrate an obsessive desire to control and reshape both Jones's image and her history.[33] In a photo entitled "Grace at seven, imagined. Spanishtown, Jamaica. 1979," he reimagines Jones's childhood, and perhaps her sexual coming of age, figuring her as a girl in pigtails and without panties, raising her dress to the camera. In "Grace and twin, imagined. Paris, 1979," Goude reconceives Jones's relationship with her real-life twin brother, creating an incestuous family drama by replicating Jones's face and putting it on a nude male body, the two spooning on a yellow satin loveseat. By including the word *imagined*, Goude both marks his shaping hand as the artist and erases Jones's participation in either her life or this new conception. *He*, it is assumed, is the imaginer. This passion for orchestration comes out even stronger in his description of his work with Grace in their performance piece *One Man Show*. He writes, "Grace let me make her over completely, use any effect I could find to turn her into what I want her to be."[34]

Yet it is in the moments of performance during *One Man Show* that Goude's control slips, which he himself acknowledges. He describes here one of the sequences where Grace confronts a tiger.

> Grace, dressed as a tiger herself, sings to the beast. They hiss and snarl at each other. She opens the door of the cage and, suddenly, all the lights go off. The music stops. It is pitch black! Then this loud tape comes on of two tigers roaring as though in a fight to the death. Ten scary seconds go by. Then the lights and the music come back on, the tiger has disappeared and in its place, Grace is singing and chewing on a big piece of meat.
>
> To tell you the truth, I couldn't see where all this stuff was leading. It was certainly fun, but also very tiring and very difficult to control. So I decided to go back to my still pictures where I was the undisputed boss.[35]

As it turned out, the tour of the show became a place where the professional and personal collaboration between Goude and Jones broke down. He ends his chapter on Grace bitterly.

> My masterpiece was a vision entirely my own of what was essentially a simple, naïve person, holding back to what she had always been. Trouble. By the time "One Man Show" reached the U.S., I

knew I had lost her. The "party nigger" had gone back to what she knew best, and I would have to find a new vehicle.[36]

Goude's version of the production of the performance reveals a sinister implication of the title *One Man Show*—with Goude's vision as the true subject and Grace as the vehicle of that vision. But the subversive spirit suggested by Goude's phrase "party nigger" is impossible for me to ignore. Jones's performances create a production that is greater than the sum of its parts.

The video production of *One Man Show* (1982), culled from performances in New York and London, provides a rich locus of analysis because it combines a filmed live performance of one of Jones's concerts with video art that is "canned." We are forced to think about the ways that Jones's performances are mediated by the hand of Goude, underlined by the video's use of stop action, speed, color, and other forms of distortion. Indeed, one might say that the show as a whole is about mediation— about the experience of being shaped and altered by an outside, a "slave to the rhythm," as the opening song suggests. Yet the performance also forces us to interrogate our assumptions about live performance as the most authentic. As Philip Auslander has discussed, some studies of performance participate in a bifurcated and reductive binary opposition between the live and the mediated, where "the common assumption is that the live event is 'real' and that mediatized events are secondary and somehow artificial reproductions of the real."[37] There are many ways, indeed, that the nonlive aspects of *One Man Show* convey important problems and issues of Jones's identity and agency in her performances. Jones's lyrics, facial expressions, voice, and other embodied performances add commentary to Goude's editing and other artistic choices.

The sequence for "Living My Life," for example, calls on the visual vocabularies of minstrel shows, Dada, and punk. Jones wears several cone-shaped appendages over her head, nose, and eyes, which are pulled by a white hand from her chin, breast, and forehead, extended from her chin and her breast, announcing the artificiality of that body under the constraint of fame and "art," and less explicitly, the dynamics of race and power in these worlds of performance, art, and music. A pulsing heartbeat of a synthesizer creates suspense as Jones brings a gun to her head. The gun goes off with a comic shot, while the cone hat goes flying into space, and Jones is left standing. The action then speeds up to match the speed of the synthesizer, which is beginning to sound like an aerobics lesson. Jones swims in her stiff cone of a skirt. Multiple white ballet dancers dressed like Jones but wearing gorilla masks race across the screen. Jones's movements capture the hopped up, surreal, and often comic aesthetic of punk—one that, according to Dick Hebdige, feeds on discomfort about and even alienation from the body, a mechanized and therefore dehumanized relationship to natural processes, and an interest in the debris of society, sometimes putting such debris on the same level as "highbrow" culture.[38] Cast-away sources of past racial shame—the gorilla mask, the blackface of the minstrel show—are put into collaboration with the highbrow movements of ballet, ballet's classic graceful beauty also made more grotesque by Jones's pained expressions and movements, as well as by being sped up.[39] "Living My Life," penned by Jones herself, might be the most explicitly angry song:"You choke me for living my life . . . you brainwash me for living my life . . . You can't stand me for living my life." Yet the imagery is surreal, and her gestures of anger are comically melodramatic, flinging her arms in frustration or clutching her head, filmed in off-center close-up. In *One Man Show,* then, we see Jones negotiating the flotsam and jetsam of racist traditions of representation, working within and standing outside of them, always still asking us to notice their frame.

Conclusion: Grace Jones as Corporate Cannibal

By 1998, with several hits, as well as film roles, behind her (including in *A View to a Kill* and *Boomerang*), Grace Jones was a known quantity of strangeness, packaged, in some ways, to create an experience of risk, particularly for her straight and white gay audiences. This is reflected in Brian Chin's comments in his liner notes to Jones's *Private Life: The Compass Point Sessions* (1998) that "In a recent poll by *Men's Health Magazine,* the male readership named Grace Jones (along with Hilary Clinton, RuPaul and, of course, 'my mother') among the women who scared them the most."

To what extent can this strangeness be domesticated? With each public appearance, Jones changes the nuance of her performance. Her audience never quite knows which Grace they'll see, and if in fact they will become a part of the act. Perhaps this wily reinvention is part of the "scariness" that the men surveyed in *Men's Health* zero in on. (Or it could be her muscles.) But this unpredictability risks being packaged as

exoticism or shtick, as Jay Hedblade suggests in a review of a Jones performance at Chicago's House of Blues.

> Roughly half way through her set Sunday night, Grace Jones was
> chanting the word "strange" while staring down the front row with
> steely eyes and baring her chest for all to see. It was perfectly fit-
> ting, and anyone at the House of Blues who wasn't expecting Ms.
> Jones to challenge the limits of decorum had certainly stumbled in
> without knowing the evening's main attraction.[40]

As an artist who is also a commercial commodity, Jones's continual re-
generation is a necessary means for keeping a place in the public memory.[41]

The tension is perfectly captured in Jones's role as Strangé in Regi-
nald Hudlin's 1992 film *Boomerang*. In the film, which centers on the
comeuppance of Marcus, played by Eddie Murphy, a "player who gets
played," Grace Jones plays a wild diva whose outrageousness is eagerly
sought after to energize a flagging cosmetics line, but who threatens to
steal the show.

Boomerang is a Post-Soul time capsule from the appearances of black
1990s comic men: Murphy, David Allen Grier, Martin Lawrence, and
Chris Rock. It features Robin Givens, bad girl still in the midst of her
public romance and struggles with Mike Tyson, and a pre–*Monster's Ball*
and pre-*Catwoman* Halle Berry. Along with Grace Jones, it features celebrity eccentrics of a past generation: Geoffrey Holder and Eartha Kitt,
figures known, like Jones, as cosmopolitan and sometimes "exotic." The
film presents an idealized version of black life in the early 1990s. The
characters inhabit incredibly swanky New York corporate and domestic spaces. In the office, black and brown faces of many shades are everywhere, on every level—from the secretarial pool to art direction to
middle management to the CEOs. Yet the film is also conversant with
a multicultural world. They are served by white waiters and buy from
white-run clothing stores, and Marcus and Halle Berry's character, Angela, fall in love while bonding over *Star Trek*.

The interiors of the office are hip, masculine: brown gleaming marble
pillars, black leather chairs, and chrome. The geometric angles of the flattop dominate. The office is a space of New Jack freedom, the aesthetic
and space clearly African American, hip, and male. (In fact, the film
opens with a riff from "Atomic Dog," George Clinton's call of the black

masculine wild.) The life of the corporation, a beauty company, seems to provide ample food for sexual appetites—whether it's the lineup of honeys waiting to be cast for the next commercial spot or the art director's playfully erotic commercials. The chase of women (and men) is presented as compatible with corporate competition. Getting freaky is okay as long as it can be shaped for profit.

Strangé's explicit sexuality, sartorial splendor, and showwomanship are an updating of the sly, if more genteel, Catwoman charms of Eartha Kitt, the aging but still voracious former owner and spokeswoman of the cosmetics line in the film. In other words, Jones plays herself—and the film places her as a generational bridge in a cultural history of outrageous and "strange" black women of the twentieth century. We see the corporation continually scheming to track and sell Strangé's outrageousness. In one fantastic sequence, Strangé bursts from a helicopter-delivered crate on a carriage drawn by leather-harnessed, bare-chested, beefy white men. This display is used to open a swanky corporate dinner and inaugurate a new perfume line. The admen and adwomen struggle to accommodate Strangé's eccentricity. All are shocked when she removes her panties in the boardroom to demonstrate what the "essence of sex" smells like. As she calls out possible names for the fragrance ("Afterbirth," "Love Puss," "Steel Vagina"), pacing the floor in fishnets, blond fall, and whip, she threatens to steal the scene. An alarmed Jacqueline (Givens) warns Marcus (Murphy), "You do realize that you're never going to be able to control her." But Marcus answers with confidence, "I don't want to control Strangé. Just let her do what she does and we'll get more coverage that way. Strangé is buck wild." In other words, Strangé's wildness will help them get the publicity they need to make the perfume a success. Marcus calls out to her, "You go, girl!"

Strangé disciplines Marcus, however, in the next scene. At a chichi restaurant meeting, Strangé grabs his hand and pulls it to her crotch under the table, demanding (rather than questioning), "You don't want some of this?" When Marcus demurely turns her down, telling her that "it's not that kind of a dinner," Strangé chases Marcus from the crowded restaurant, shouting "Pussy, Pussy, Pussy!" to Murphy's rising embarrassment. It is only Jacqueline's threat to sue Strangé that calms her down (an allusion to Jones's occasional offscreen legal troubles, perhaps). While the film argues that the "essence of sex" is business, Strangé's outrageousness keeps her patrons guessing.

Jones's 2008 song "Corporate Cannibal," from her CD *Hurricane,* aptly captures the ambiguity of her work. Jones is both the icon of the savage, sold and traded by corporations like Island Records, and the force that threatens to destabilize the economy that trades in her—ingesting it and spitting out the bones, always altering the venues in which she travels. In Michel de Montaigne's essay "On the Cannibals" (1580), written in response to early European fascination with the peoples of Brazil and the Caribbean, he corrects the misconception that cannibals eat their enemies because they are uncivilized. Cannibalism, he argues, is a stylized act of revenge, which gives recognition to the fortitude of the enemy.[42] As a "corporate cannibal," Jones gives testimony to the ravaging hunger of the marketplace, as well as her own ability to stay one step ahead of it. In this way, Jones is part of the ongoing dynamic of black cultural traffic, initiated by the mid-Atlantic slave trade, which continues into the current moment—where black performers negotiate the pressure to be "authentically," recognizably "black" and always cutting edge. As Tricia Rose writes in her foreword to the collection *Black Cultural Traffic* (2005):

> Racial ideologies undergirding the historical trade of bodies on which black cultural traffics are based have ensnared interpreters of black cultures in an endless paradox: black culture has been both an enduring symbol of unchanging purity, in full and complete opposition to white, western normalcy and yet a highly celebrated example of cutting-edge change, dynamism and innovation. Forever "new," "exotic," and yet "always black," black culture must always be recognized as black for its daily bread (as in familiar in its blackness) and yet must also be newly black (as in pure and untainted by "outside forces" for the same ration.[43]

A complicating factor of Jones's art has always been its collaboration with commercialism, even as it comments on that process. Black artists in the 1980s and 1990s enjoyed a new kind of corporate recognition and movement/trade, and we can see this in the arc of the film and television career that accompanied Jones's musical successes, as Bond villain May Day in *A View to a Kill* or working the talk show circuit, chatting up Merv Griffin, shocking Regis and Kathy Lee, competing with Joan Rivers to see who can be the most campy and outrageous on the *Tonight Show*. Given this, one might be tempted to read Jones's appropriation of corporate gray flannel and (military?) flattop less as a queering of corporate power than a commandeering of it.

Yet Jones's presence refuses complete assimilation. A figure of excess, Jones moves between the known and unknowable. In Deborah Richards's poem" The Halle Berry One Two," her Grace Jones persona says, "I am not natural. I'm not super heroine. I dabble with the organic yet I am not vegetable matter."[44] At times she is a Jamaican home girl, at other times a Parisian diva on a catwalk. In *Boomerang*, Grace is Strangé, a more fabulous and amplified Cleopatra; at other times, she seems to be a work out of science fiction. Yet there is still a way that her critical spirit is also grounded in a shared history, from Nanny to Josephine Baker. Jones brings together the strange with a historically rooted sexual subjectivity. She is the "three-line whip," a "walking disaster," as she sings in "Demolition Man." But she is also the sister outsider of "Walking in the Rain"—performed in a her trademark flattened key, one note blued.

Feeling like a woman,
Looking like a man
Sounding like a no-no
Making when I can.

SIX

Funking toward the Future in Meshell Ndegeocello's *The world has made me the man of my dreams*

As I listen to Meshell Ndegeocello's sonic dreamscape, *The world has made me the man of my dreams* (2007), I think of the work of changing structures to create new futures, as well as the necessity of dream. It's 2012. The State of Illinois has legalized civil unions for six months now. Gay and lesbian parents can adopt, though some organizations, like Catholic Charities, refuse to serve us. This year, at ages fifty-five and forty-five, my partner Annie and I are preparing to adopt a child. We've just moved into a neighborhood of small bungalows all built in 1910s, and this house will become the place where we'll forge this new life. A dream, an experiment, an investment in the future, though making a household is also something so ordinary at the same time. We are inventing family and home, but we are also shaped by the history of this particular city and neighborhood: Chicago, Illinois, North Side, Rogers Park. Redlining, neighborhood covenants, riots, foreclosures. We're two women, one black, one white, with hopes of raising a black child. Right now, as we walk through the neighborhood together, some might see us as lovers, but others might dismiss us as "just friends," walking buddies, coworkers, even relatives. But with our child walking between us, the stakes are raised. We will redefine family just by being together, by demanding to be seen by our neighbors. What will our future bring? How will our community receive our child, queer by association? What will be awakened by broken rock, the pressure of elements accidental and purposeful? In her final song on the album, "Soul Spaceship," Ndegeocello imagines the possibility of laughter, connection, communion, but only after cataclysmic change—and "episodic memory"—that is, a knowledge of history: "We were once earth / We were once flowers / Soon to be one made of light."

In Meshell Ndegeocello's seventh studio album, *The world has made me the man of my dreams,* she performs visionary, highly collaborative, and often unclassifiable sound, lyrics, and performance. How, in particular in her models for collaboration, might we think of this album as a kind of "archive" for a black and queer future for the Post-Soul generation and those who come after it?

Feminist, futurist Funkateer and "Mack Diva" Meshell Ndegeocello was born Michelle Lynn Johnson in Berlin to an army lieutenant father and a health care worker mother in 1968. Ndegeocello's chosen stage name reveals her commitment to freedom and reinvention, as well as to rootedness, Ndegeocello meaning "Free as a bird" in Swahili. Ndegeocello spent much of her childhood in Washington, DC, soaking up emerging hip-hop and go-go, and attended the Duke Ellington School of the Arts, one of DC's public schools. Among her influences and collaborators, Ndegeocello cites Prince, Raz of the Wu-Tang Clan, Jimi Hendrix, Miles Davis, Joni Mitchell, Fiona Apple, Bob Dylan, and Jaco Pastorius.

Harnessing the powers of butch and femme, cosmopolitan and DC go-go, funk, and jazz (and hip-hop and Soul, as well as classical and techno), her albums present a blueprint for sonic, sexual, political, and imaginative freedom, backed up by the insistent throb of her own electric bass. She is also a sought-after producer and arranger for others, and her own albums reflect the Post-Soul, postintegrationist spirit of collaboration in their wealth of influences and borrowed, remade sound. The themes tackled in her lyrics are similarly expansive, as well as challenging: from homophobia in the black community to violence and terror on a global scale to the politics of bisexuality to music as a form of space travel. Her compositions are embodied and earthy, "sounding out" a received history of homophobia, sexism, and racism, but at the same time promising a line of flight through reinvention.

Queering Afrofuturism in *The world has made me the man of my dreams*

The world has made me the man of my dreams, at times danceable, at times challenging, or even obscure, moves between spaces of fantasy and futurism and immediate social realities. Here Ndegeocello's sound and performance—intimate, exploratory, emotive—is erotic in its willing push toward the unknown and ambiguous. In the short film for "The Sloganeer: Paradise," the first single from *The world has made me the man of my dreams,* videographer Jason Orr captures in visuals the feeling of frenetic energy, loneliness, and dislocation that we also hear in Ndegeocello's sound in this song. Night shots of a sped-up ride down an anonymous highway, streetlights and stoplights streaming as if on Ecstasy. Colors: the washed out green/grays of urban nighttime, suddenly submerging into the black of a tunnel. The driver's-seat view twists and turns according to its own map, moves from highway to empty city streets, travel that seems to be driven by yearning. These scenes are intercut with shots of Ndegeocello pogoing and jacking her body to the muscular beats with the rest of her all-male band. Here Ndegeocello is almost anonymous, too, in stretched-out white T-shirt, a *boi* among boys, playing in what seems to be a suburban basement or garage nowhere in particular. Her face, however, is the film's main locus, its only point of distinction: caught in close-up, her eyes remain closed, as if watching this inner landscape of travel and speed, a tattooed star at the corner of her eye replacing a tear, a pledge to the future.

Ndegeocello's voice moves from her trademark deep talk-whisper to high soprano to whine, belying the distinctly masculine dress and dance style. We also see her listening, head cocked, responding to her drummer, the ghost of a smile crossing her lips. She is modeling the power of both listening *and* performing, and the potential of both of these collaborative acts to transport us, to lend us the possibility of travel through sound.

This short film highlights the Afrofuturist impulse behind Ndegeocello's music, in the ways that the yearning for imaginative freedom is dramatized as a negotiation between individual desire and collaboration, becoming and being, speed and friction, the traditions of the past, promise of a future, and the critique of a very present now. In this search for freedom, voice, along with instrument, video and filmic technologies, cars, and other machines are all fair game in this search.

In Mark Dery's influential essay, "Black to the Future: Afro-futurism 1.0," he describes Afrofuturism as the self-conscious appropriation of technology in black popular culture in order think out the problems of imaginative freedom in the past, present, and future. He asks, "Can a community whose past has been deliberately rubbed out, and whose energies have subsequently been consumed by the search for legible traces of its history, imagine possible futures?"[1] Recent Afrocentric thought and creative production have explored, for example, relationships between new technologies of science and old technologies of bodily control and exploitation that began in slavery. How, for example, as Steven Shaviro has asked, have hip-hop divas Lil' Kim and Missy Elliott explored their own embodiment as black women through video and sonic technologies that critically "make strange" their already highly visible, highly known images, especially as they've been shaped by past histories of commodification? Shaviro suggests that in their videos for "The Rain (Supa Dupa Fly)" and "How Many Licks" Missy Elliott and Lil' Kim "raise questions about identity and otherness, and about power and control. They ask us to think about how we are being transformed as a result of our encounters with new and digital technologies . . . as beings whose very embodiment is tied up with technological change, as well as with ascriptions of race and gender."[2] Lil' Kim's and Missy Elliott's harnessing of video technologies and high-tech mise-en-scènes in their videos reflects an Afrocentric impulse that counters the idea that black people are aliened from technology as a means of creative expansion. Indeed, as Alondra Nelson suggests, the history of black creativity and innovation forces us to challenge the idea of technological futurism as inherently "new."[3] How might such creative strategies be part of a larger continuum of black creativity that spans the desires of the past and present and desires that have not yet been formed? In his 1995 film *The Last Angel of History,* John Akomfrah credits the drum as the first Afrofuturistic technology, in its ability to communicate both across the African diaspora and across time.

If Afrofuturism takes African American culture's already improvisational nature—making a way out of no way—and applies it to the project of imagining a new future, for Ndegeocello, this is a project that is by necessity genderqueer. It is a space of healing, critique, and artistic and political engagement. Ndegeocello's synthesized aesthetics is committed to a playful relationship to past black music and technology, while also always foregrounding both the sensuality of an openly queer aesthetics and the material conditions of an unjust political and economic world, highlighting the queerness of her own body and voice and the potential queerness of all bodies as they are effected, changed, and reorganized through sound.

From the otherworld visions of Sun Ra to the healing powers of the Mothership Connection, the sexy, space-funky gospel of Labelle, and DJ Spooky's new mutations of hip-hop and electronica, Afrofuturistic sound exemplifies and continues this history of black technological ingenuity, signifying on mainstream science fiction's fascination with technology and speed to rethink and expand the already innovative creative space of Soul, funk, blues, and beyond. In her music, Meshell Ndegeocello uses

Afrofuturism to put to question not only how the black imagination has been commodified but also how we love and how we are in community have been limited by means of war, greed, racism, and homophobia. In *The world has made me the man of my dreams,* future community can include our lovers, male and female, our children, and those we don't know, beyond boundaries of nation and time. Ndegeocello's is an Afrofuturism that foregrounds the escape from and return to the black body that we also hear in Sun Ra's work, as well as in George Clinton's, as I discussed in chapter three. Ndegeocello draws from Sun Ra in her expansion of gender and sexual codes,[4] as well in her expansive artistic, national, and planetary loyalties, and does so informed by an updated politics of gender performance that includes transgender identity. Sun Ra's own eccentric queerness is a fascinating subject in its own right, though I don't have room to give it full justice here. His sexuality has been variously described in obituaries and jazz retrospectives as "asexual" and "unconfirmed" and occasionally as "homosexual." John Gill embraces Sun Ra's image as both performatively queer and a gay man closeted by the jazz world,[5] but in many ways who Sun Ra did and didn't sleep with isn't the point. Certainly, Sun Ra's campy, outlandish, and often gender-bending stage aesthetic, combining futurism, Egyptology, and Afroglam (pharaonic headpieces, glittery turbans, scarves, jewels, and African bubas and wraps), as well as his relationship to space and time (he believed he was an angel from Saturn) could be read as queer, as could his reconfiguration of family among his circle of musicians, where, according to journalist Val Wilmer, "he was regarded as figure embodying the qualities of both mother and father."[6] In his 1993 obituary of Sun Ra, John F. Szwed effectively captures his theatrical and often excessive performance style.

[I]n the 1970's his six-hour multimedia barrages could be genuinely frightening experiences. The music moved from stasis to chaos and back again, with shrieks and howls pouring out of an Arkestra dressed like the Archers of Arboria; dancers swirled through the audience ("butterflies of the night," a French critic called them); fire-eaters, gilded muscle-men, and midgets paraded in front of masks, shadow puppets, and films of the pyramids. Performance rules were being broken one-a-minute.[7]

Most significantly, Sun Ra's sound, discombobulating, charismatic, otherworldly, visionary, and transformative, is closely aligned with the eccentric performances studied here, including Ndegeocello's.

Ndegeocello's sound, voice and bass, sometimes assisted by technology, sometimes through the manipulation of her own breath, or throat or hands, explores and complicates the ways that gender is coded in music, drawing from and then departing from traditional forms of funk, Soul, jazz, and rock. Breath, pitch, texture, and also emotive distance all contribute to the ways that she performs, as well as "hears," gender, and so, too, does her voice's collaboration with other voices. This includes calls-and-responses, supplementations, and harmonies that speak to the differentials of top and bottom, power and control. This is Ndegeocello's intervention in Afrocentric discourse: her space of creativity centers an open and formative notion of gender that tarries with the past, as well as sets up possibilities for the future. Her vocal and otherwise performative gender play is one of the many ways that she opens up and intervenes in the project of redefining blackness.

The man of my dreams: Ndegeocello's Gender Fluidity

The very title *The world has made me the man of my dreams*—which could be read as a transgender manifesto, a Disneyed romantic yearning, or a not-quite-sexist-language-free declaration of imaginative freedom—suggests a kind of slipperiness and play with identity that has become a trademark for Ndegeocello. Ndegeocello has described herself in fluid gender and sexual terms, as bisexual, as lesbian, and as "a femme in a butch body," for example, and, in *The world has made me the man of my dreams,* I'd suggest, as transgendered. Indeed, Ndegeocello's career spans a period of incredible flux, invention, and new visibility in terms of the performance of specifically genderqueer identities for black women in everyday life—particularly young people, including the emergence of "aggressive," "lesbian stud," "femme aggressive," and transgendered—and sometimes all of these at once—as documented in Daniel Peddle's 2005 film *The Aggressives.* Although she's never used the term *queer* to describe herself in print (as far as I know), she has publicly critiqued the term *gay* as centering a white male aesthetic.[8]

Within the narrative structures of her songs, as well as through sound, Ndegeocello embodies several points of view, reaching across gender and sexuality to create new, collaborative structures. For example, in the song "Solomon," featured on *The world has made me the man of my dreams,* Ndegeocello sings an ode to her son, performing a gender-fluid conception of parenthood. The song opens with a spoken-word introduction by performance artist Jack Bean about fatherhood. The song then segues into Ndegeocello's sung voice, which remains in its lowest register. She thanks the creator for her son, "All that I am / flesh and blood." She never names her role as mother, but instead performs an open-gendered conception of parenthood, providing multiple points of entrance and identification for her listeners. In this way, the song departs from distinctly feminine-centered odes to motherhood like Lauryn Hill's "To Zion" or Madonna's "Little Star."

Ndegeocello stretches the collaborative lines of gender by courting "misrecognition" and what I like to think of as deliberate "mistakes" in gender interpretation that allow her to subvert traditional relationships. A telling moment in Andreana Clay's recent article on Ndegeocello, "Like an Old Soul Record: Black Feminism, Queer Sexuality, and the Hip-Hop Generation," is when Clay identifies a "mistake" in her listening to Ndegeocello's song "Leviticus: Faggot," from the 1996 album *Peace Beyond Passion*. Clay confesses that when first listening to the line "Stop acting like a bitch / that's all he sees / ain't that what faggot means," she thought that Ndegeocello was saying "Ain't that Faggot me?"[9] I think that Clay's mishearing of the lyrics was no mere mistake. In her exposure of homophobic violence in the song, Ndegeocello is not only expressing allegiance to gay men but also identification with them. In many of her songs, Ndegeocello deliberately performs cross-gender identification, sometimes with and at other times against the grain of her lyrics.

In her earliest music video performances, we can see how Ndegeocello's gender-fluid and sexually ambiguous performances might be a strategy of subversion for offering queer comment within mainstream venues. In the video for "Dred Loc," her debut on BET, from the 1993 release *Plantation Lullabies,* Ndegeocello stages a genderqueer seduction between Ndegeocello and an unnamed lover. In contrast to Ndegeocello's strong, more dominant masculine presence, including a shaved head, her lover is presented as the more passive object of desire, with beautiful, gender-ambiguous dreads that reach below the shoulder. Although the song opens with the line "How I love a black man," the visual story departs from traditional narratives of romance to explore the performance of gender at the heart of black hair politics. Hair, freed from traditional gender role-playing, becomes a place in which to explore gender-fluid, problack sensuality. The video begins with Ndegeocello watching herself in the mirror, surrounded by a tableau of women's hair care products, including pink foam curlers and hot irons. Ndegeocello strokes her own closely shaven head, and smiles at herself in approval. Is she, in fact, the black man that she loves? The video promises a departure from the traditional politics of black beauty that dominate the hip-hop and other videos that most frequently air on BET. Next we see a blurred close-up of another face through a curtain of long dreadlocks. We watch Ndegeocello twisting, then tenderly running her fingers through the other's hair. They are clearly lovers. We watch then as Ndegeocello and the other begin to make love, the dreadlocked head now moving erotically between Ndegeocello's legs. At this point, it's not clear if we're watching two women, two men, or a woman and a man. Just as the passion of the scene heats up, the video delivers its first full body shot of the lover, now visibly marked as masculine, with a lightly muscular chest, slim torso, and a very slight beard and mustache. At the same time, the song picks up tempo, and shifts from Ndegeocello's languid, breathy, higher singing voice to a husky rap. The rap presents an Edenic vision of procreative heterosexual love, while inverting or blurring expectations of masculine and feminine roles. Her description of her male lover echoes the ways that women are often described in Afrocentric discourse as beautiful, "One with nature with his head held high," but also silent and obeying.

> He never questions why
> Together we make the fruit of life
> So I love and treat him right.

Even after "revealing" the presumable "fact" of her lover's masculinity through facial hair and bared masculine torso and chest, the video continues to shoot both Ndegeocello and the lover in ways that leave room for us to change our minds about their gender. We watch the lover tenderly shaving Ndegeocello's bald head in the middle of a forest, both now wearing flowing, feminine clothing. In this song, as well as in others on this early album, Ndegeocello performs gender fluidity in a way that is consummately soulful.

Ndegeocello's ability to move across different positionalities of identity is linked to her performance of the bass and the sometimes-eccentric space that the bass creates in music. The makers of funk have most visibly been men—especially those associated with the popping bass, the driving spirit of The One (Bootsy Collins, James Brown, the Brothers Johnson, Prince). As a purveyor of funk through the bass, in past works as well as in *The world has made me the man of my dreams*, Ndegeocello commandeers male funk practice to explore key and often overdetermined sounds, as well as issues shaping black humanity and black life, including parenthood (in the song "Solomon"), cultural change, and romantic love (in "Elliptical"), and the violence of corporate capitalism on the agency and freedom of black bodies (in "Article 3" and "Relief: A Stripper Classic").

Cultural critic L. H. Stallings sees Ndegeocello as a sexual and spiritual trickster figure, one who is empowered by the open status of bisexuality to blur the lines between sacred and secular. Stallings suggests that the bass functions in Ndegeocello's music as a kind of lesbian phallus, a site of desire that decodes the symbolic order of the phallus, a tongue "capable of pressure, penetration, fluidity and hardness."[10] Stallings quotes a revealing (and titillating!) interview between Ndegeocello and Allison Powell on fan behavior and the new centrality Ndegeocello provides for the bass as object of desire.

> MN: I mean, you could be ugly, but as long as you play the guitar or something . . . guitar players and sax players really do O.K.
> AP: But the bass is sexy, right?
> MN: I don't know. I just think because I'm up front I get a little bit more . . . I get more attention. [laughs]
> AP: Well, the bass is sexy. It's so pelvic and deep.
> MN: Yea, in fact, the uterus is very responsive to bass tones. It's the low frequencies. Go to a party or to big shows and watch how girls love to sit on the woofers.[11]

Whereas in traditional rock and other live band structures, the guitar or sax plays romantic lead, here the bass gets new attention. Moreover, Ndegeocello configures her female fans as those who seek out their own pleasure, rather than as passive participants in the music. We can also see this decoding of the phallic in Ndegeocello's reworking of the bass's rhythmic function. For one thing, the bass often operates without one central point of contact, especially within polyrhythmic music.[12] Meshell's bass is the heartbeat of music. But it can also play against other rhythms as counterpoint. It is the pulse from below, the bottom guiding the top, a secret pact. But the bass can also open up new space in a song, make you pay attention to the silences. As a philosophy of the future, her bass is the guarantee of funkiness, as well as a shape giver to what might otherwise seem random. The bass is the pulse of history, a chronology, and a dateline. It is tradition and freedom at once, the timekeeper and the space for play. It can be technology, as well as hands, the reassurance of knowledge of the body and of craft in an age of colonized space and time. Through her play with the "bottom" position as well as the "top" of bass guitar and voice, Ndegeocello is able to highlight gaps in our conceptions of the funk genre, as well as in discourses about gender and sexuality.

At the same time, Ndegeocello explores the potential of technology, space, and a place for spiritual renewal and humanism, the stuff of an often male-dominated space of Afrofuturist music. Technology becomes the mechanism for desire—and we might think of this as sexual desire, as well as the desire for spiritual transcendence. She does so by worrying the lines between body, voice, and identity. We hear, for example, in the song "Elliptical" on *The world has made me the man of my dreams*, backup singer Sy Smith's human female voice in call-and-response with Ndegeocello's, transformed by a deep vocoder synthesizer. In this same song, the swell of an (acoustic?) coronet wraps itself around the rhythm of a drum machine. I'd argue that these juxtapositions of human and machine are queered, both in the ways that they play with and alter lines of masculine and feminine, human and nonhuman, and in the larger sense that sociologists Eva Illouz and Steven Seidman use them when they use queering as "a deconstructive and discursive strategy involving the displacement of foundational assumptions (e.g. about the subject, knowledge, society and history) for the purpose of opening up critical social analysis and political practice."[13] As I'll discuss further, Ndegeocello's intertwining of machine and "human" becomes the soundtrack for the desire for political and spiritual freedom and transcendence.

"Elliptical" is a romantic slow groove, creating a lush orchestra of synthesized and nonsynthesized sound: the acoustic sounds of coronet, cowbells, and high-hat meeting with synthesized vocals, electric bass thumps, computerized guitar arpeggios, all meshing in a landscape of human and posthuman interaction. Ndegeocello's vocoder-altered voice, in its flattened range and coldly technical timbre, is nevertheless human in its inflection and read of words, and in its complementarity with the sweetness of Sy Smith's very human sounding soprano. The song thus demonstrates the ability of the synthesized voice to seduce and capture. The play of Ndegeocello's electric bass beats both perform and induce heart and blood beat; the texture and rhythm of fingers on flesh. Synthesized swoops of a theram mimic the rise and fall of the stomach anticipating making love. The sound and lyrics evoke Philip K. Dick's *Do*

Androids Dream of Electric Sheep?, exploring the possibility of machines to give shape to our deepest desires. Sy Smith's human voice sings to her cyborg lover: "I've tasted to your grace / and felt it diffuse all around me." Meshell answers in cyborg voice: "With the sweetest hope of love everlasting." Departing from Dick's dystopic vision (later cinematized) in *Blade Runner* (1982), the song itself demonstrates the viability of this vision, the possibility of full melding: "Shall we remove these veils / So you can fully experience me?"

The structure, instrumentation, and gender performance of voice in "Elliptical" all explore the vision of a boundaryless and yet still totally soulful future, one that takes its cues from the silky, bluesy seductions of quiet storm jazz and bass-loving funk to explore issues sexual, political, musical, and spiritual. The song troubles the "proper" hierarchies of human over machine, masculine over feminine, even "live" song over programmed. All of this is done in the context of a love song sung, almost as an afterthought, between two "women." The song's final declaration, "Love is God's creation," claims the holiness of these categories of so-called unholy love: android and queer. Here Ndegeocello tarries with the negative of the *post*—postmodern, Post-Black, posthuman, Post-Soul—to ask us to think about this *post* not so much as a space of negation as a space of becoming.[14]

Ndegeocello's rethinking of the black body and black voice as complexly and fluidly gendered opens up the possibilities for collaboration with others in unprecedented ways. Indeed, collaboration is the spiritual and political payoff of Ndegeocello's gender play, and her offering to a black community in search of a future. *The world has made me the man of my dreams* imagines a new black self that is deeply and intimately connected to others, one for whom the relationship with others is able to survive because it shifts and moves and flows. Ultimately, Ndegeocello's conceptualization of a radical black future is one that must also reimagine blackness as transnational and collaborative in character, linked to the larger struggles of war, survival, and change. At stake is a larger humanity that is diasporic, all riding a "soul spaceship" to an unknown but shared future.

Blaxploration: Transnational and Transgender Alliance

Meshell Ndegeocello's *The world has made me the man of my dreams* points to the work still to be done with the Post-Soul project of

"Blaxploration"—by reimagining black futures that foreground transnational diasporic alliance, as well as gender adaptability. In addition to its radical exploration of gender, this is a post-9/11 album about global existential crisis, which necessarily casts a black future as part of a larger social stage. In a 2003 interview with Mark Anthony Neal, Ndgeocello describes a feeling of urgency after September 11, 2001, that first led to the production of her 2003 album *Comfort Woman.* "After September 11th," she admits, "I would just sit at home and play music." She adds, "*Comfort Woman* is just to say, after Sept 11th, I was like thoughts are the architecture of the mind. I wanted to put out something, like God-forbid, something happens to me."[15] *The world has made me the man of my dreams,* continues the sense of creative urgency in *Comfort Woman.* Moving from the architecture of thought to a kind of architecture of relation, *The world has made me the man of my dreams* is propelled by a spirit of collaboration as a resource for Afrofuturist community building. Here Ndgeocello queers Post-Soul struggles for community in the context of the "precariousness" of life in a time of recurring war and state-sponsored terror. Ndegeocello's transgendered transnationalism pushes the boundaries of previous Post-Soul projects to link the struggle for Post-Soul blackness to transracial, transgender, global, and collective struggle.

Signifying on the more visible term *blaxploitation,* cultural theorist Bertram Ashe coined *blaxploration* as one of the key components of a Post-Soul aesthetic among black writers, artists, and musicians born and producing after the civil rights era.

> These artists and texts trouble blackness. They worry blackness; they stir it up, touch it, feel it out, and hold it up for examination in ways that depart significantly from previous—and necessary—preoccupations with struggling for political freedom, or with an attempt to establish and sustain a coherent black identity.[16]

This self-conscious, denaturalizing rumination, this opening up and re-mixing of blackness, as an identity, aesthetic, and defense of the human, has often emphasized the individual journey, the untapped and quirky departures from an agreed-upon black collectivity—in other words, eccentricity, in the popular sense. But in Ndegeocello's work, she moves from the individualistic exploration that we might associate with the traditional notion of eccentricity to an investment in collective change across boundaries of nation, and religion, as well as race. In this way,

Ndegeocello follows the lead of many Afrofuturist predecessors, like Sun Ra and George Clinton, and the creative forces of P-Funk in their yearning for a collective journey to new spaces, new architectures of thought to lead us to new notions of blackness. At the same time, Ndegeocello takes up the fight for peace and a global unity in the struggle for black freedom found in the work of Soul forebears like Aretha Franklin, Stevie Wonder, Marvin Gaye, and Bob Marley. Ndegeocello's explicit foregrounding of queer gender and queer desire in her blaxplorations, I'd argue, set her apart.

Through a transnational and even intergalactic exploration of vulnerability, desire, and empathy in a post-9/11 moment of violence, terror, surveillance, and the destruction of communities, Ndegeocello widens the quest for freedom implicit in the Post-Soul project. Beginning in the middle of the experience of change and loss, *The world has made me the man of my dreams* performs the positive effects of dislocation: the realization of a shared despair. The album, in its timeliness, is linked globally to war, and to the ability of music, here Post-Soul music, to capture the experience of dislocation and despair, as well as an undying investment in the possibilities of a collaborative and collective future.

This sense that—especially at this important historical moment—poets (and musicians) have important, world-saving work to do is captured in Palestinian American poet Lisa Suhair Majaj's poem, "Arguments."

> Consider the infinite fragility of an infant's skull
> How the bones lie soft and open
> Only time knitting them shut
>   . . .
>
> Consider a delicate porcelain bowl
> How it crushes under a single blow—
> In one moment whole years disappear
>   . . .
>
> Consider your own sky on fire
> Your name erased
> Your children's lives "a price worth paying"
>   . . .

How in these lines
The world
Cracks open.[17]

Like Majaj, Ndegeocello explores the ways that music, like poetry, can dissolve the boundaries between genders, between races and between performer and listener. Music can crack our worlds open, and can help us understand our shared stakes in the human. In the song "The Sloganeer: Paradise," for example, we hear the rolling drums as a collection of miniature explosions, contained (for now) between earphones. Are the drums the fire of synapses in our brains, each explosion cracking our worlds open? Are they gunfire? Or are they the culmination of a history of explosions, the way, if we could open ourselves somehow, we'd hear a world, a history of homes, bodies, skies cracked open and burning? The history of women, brown and black, displaced women of war? The history of the world as a theater of war, the stage crowded with voices, with bodies? Can you hear them now? And what happens when you listen? This is life during wartime.

In *Precarious Life: The Powers of Mourning and Violence,* Judith Butler considers the combined state of vulnerability and aggression in a post-9/11 world, where we are forced to recognize our interdependence on others that we may never see or meet. In this state, we are all vulnerable to violence, but some of us might be more vulnerable than others, determined by our relative degrees of privilege as national and global actors. Butler asks us to reconsider the politics of "First World privilege," which masks this state of vulnerability. We might instead build on an ethics that recognizes a fundamental lack of control over world events, and that acknowledgment might in turn commit us to act as part of a larger global community, says Butler.[18] Through the dislocating musical strategies of funk, hip-hop, jazz, and noise, here Ndegeocello reminds us of this dislocated and vulnerable state, weighing the privilege of First World objectivity against her complex positionality as black and queer.

In *The world has made me the man of my dreams,* Ndegeocello revisits the issues of political disenfranchisement and spiritual loss explored in her earlier albums. In her second album, *Peace Beyond Passion,* for example, she explores the interconnections of spirituality and politics, in which she uses the language of the Bible to frame stories of queer desire and also homophobia in black Christian communities. (See especially her songs "Mary Magdalene" and "Leviticus: Faggot" in *Peace Beyond Passion*.)[19] Invested in a fluidly comparative spirituality, she is both deeply curious and critical about the politics of organized religion. In a 1996 interview, Ndegeocello says:

> For me, God is probably the source of my every breath. So I don't throw away religion because of the people. That's why I want to be able to eventually study all [religions]. But just as Hindus believe you find an inner self when you release the worldly self, I'm starting to wonder if religion might not be just a remnant of the world, too. I want to get to the point where I'm so one with God and so peaceful that religion is obsolete.[20]

In *The world has made me the man of my dreams*, Ndegeocello, once a practicing Buddhist raised Baptist, and recently converted to Islam, returns to religion as a means of exploring the politics of imagining the future. Here religion is a point of inquiry rather than a solace or solution.

In the album's exploration of spirituality, violence, and existential crisis, Ndegeocello considers the space of chaos as a potential locus of spiritual possibility. The opening song, "Haditha," a one-minute, thirty-one-second sampled opening from a lecture on apocalypse, sets the tone for the album's engagement in social transformation, violence, and the pursuit of freedom. "Haditha" loops spacey, twanging guitars and reverberating feedback around the voice of Muslim teacher and Islamic scholar Sheik Hamza Yusuf Hanson. Hanson describes what he calls the "intensification" of events in the Muslim world that seem to bear out the prophet Muhammad's predictions for the future and the end of time, which we are told include the increased ingestion of intoxicants, nakedness, public sexuality, speed in travel, and the ability to move great distances in a short period of time. At the same time, the prophet Muhammad describes this moment as ecstatic and intensely musical: "Dancing will be everywhere. . . . Music will be everywhere . . . even with people wearing music on their heads." In this short sequence, Ndegeocello is illustrating the ways that hip-hop uses sampling to create political and spiritual, as well as artistic, conversations—with the potential to widen community. Spoken over a hip-hop beat and redub, the predictions take on an additional seductive and immediate power. Ndegeocello makes a similar move in her previous album, *Cookie: The Anthropological Mixtape*, by sampling another prophet—here Angela Davis—from one of her speeches on the prison industrial complex, to frame and give political seriousness and weight to the album.

"Haditha" refers directly to the 2005 massacre of unarmed noncombatant Iraqi men, women, and children by the US military in the city of Haditha. Ndegeocello perhaps has chosen this context because of the ways that the war in Iraq has intensified US fears of Islam for some while signifying a crisis about the justice of the War on Terror for other Americans. More specifically, the civilian casualties at Haditha—and the military's efforts to cover up those deaths—became a watershed moment in terms of shifting US citizen support of the war, bringing to light questionable ethical behavior, uneven reporting, and lack of accountability of the US military. Ndegeocello's use of these contexts to advance her own "blaxploration" shows an engagement with the world, and with social justice, a particularly post-9/11 version of the "cultural mulattoism" that is one of the qualities of Post-Soul blaxploration.

The song that follows, "The Sloganeer: Paradise," continues the thematic struggle of "Haditha" between secular and human desire. It opens with the uncomfortable question, "If you're the chosen, why / Don't you kill yourself now?" The previous allusion to "Haditha" makes way for a reading of lyrics from "The Sloganeer" that refer to the existential dilemma of a potential suicide bomber. The song explores a variety of persuasive voices—spiritual, commercial, interpersonal—and the larger question of living for a future on Earth. Ndegeocello engages these contexts to frame an analysis of crises in national and religious identity, and desire, ultimately revealing the false dichotomy between sexual and spiritual yearning.

"The Sloganeer: Paradise" shifts from personal angst to the politicized image of the suicide bomber to the spiritual idea of paradise to the commercial hawking of female bodies to the use of sex as a form of escape to the reembrace of the female body as a form of pleasure. Ndegeocello uses gender fluidity to launch new thinking about spiritual and political commitments. She gives her own queered and eccentric reading of the desire for spiritual answers by assuaging spiritual angst with the solace of the body, and particularly the feminine body: "Open up your legs /The waves and swells soothe my dissatisfaction."

The soothing "waves and swells" are the place where one seeks solace in the midst of existential confusion. This is a particularly pointed choice in "Haditha" in light of its declaration that the end of the world is predictable because of appearance, the visibility of women's bodies, sexuality, and nakedness. But in the end, even sexual solace is incomplete. The song ends on a note of loss and yearning: "Can you imagine utter nothingness? / Give me a sign."

Sonically, "The Sloganeer: Paradise" is a techno song that is post-techno, dance music postdisco, driven by the rolling drums and bass of drum 'n' bass. The song takes jazz elements of compositional freedom—for example, the space where the solo opens up the song, or the spontaneous shifting of riffs—but presents them in cramped, claustrophobic ways. The song has a danceable beat but seems to be troubling that desire for escape that disco and psychedelically enhanced rave offer. We hear whispers of doubt and seduction. The twanging space sounds of the synthesizer that dot the drum and bass lines are not yet the space sounds of a utopic elsewhere, because we haven't yet escaped our fears. The crowded soundscape relays a sense of cramped and overdetermined choices, as well as the pressure to push past those boundaries of confinement. The increasing shakiness and fragility of Ndegeocello's strangled voice—her theatrical British accent evoking *The Cure,* suggest the looming threat of psychic breakdown. This song captures the moment of "not yet" that precedes improvisation, that haunts and chases the spaceship on its way to the future.

At the same time, "The Sloganeer: Paradise" is anticonfessional, the voice distanced from the audience, the occasion obscured, distanced from a clear time and place, and certainly from the everyday specifics of black life explored in her previous CD, *Cookie.* Ndegeocello takes us into a post-9/11 dystopia of troubled bodies and sounds that counter the natural, playing with distance and speed, and with what we might think of as a traditionally styled "black" voice. Rather than opening to us, seducing us with melisma, the song sits back, draws us into its vortex. Her performance is not black female "Soul," in the traditional sense. Like her Post-Soul companions Earth Kitt and Grace Jones, Ndegeocello is contending with and transforming traditional black female Soul performance—in this case, the confessional R&B style of sexual wanting and need—which is typically conveyed stylistically by an open voice, sincerity, and heat.[21] Nor is it a performance meant to comfort and ground a white listener. (Think of all of the ways that the black female body, sometimes singing, has been used to ground the white body as it runs and pursues its future. In Baz Luhrmann's film *Romeo + Juliet,* a black torch singer sings the blues while the young lovers in angel and intergalactic knight costumes kiss and pursue flight on an elevator, up and up and up, soaring with the power borrowed from that black voice.) Instead, Nde-geocello evades the responsibility of the black Soul voice to guide others. She seeks instead something more risky, which makes the black Soul voice the site of her own exploration, as it is linked to others. Here she has a lot in common with the female narrators in Octavia Butler's novels, each guiding us through a position of unresolved extreme dislocation.[22]

In "The Sloganeer: Paradise," Ndegeocello is exploring the potential of music to capture a state of grief while complicating the black Soul aesthetic of open feeling and emotion. While the traditions of Soul might be an obvious space in which to perform a state of grief and vulnerability, Ndegeocello chooses an alternative vocal strategy of distance and dislocation often avoided in black Soul performance. Her music offers a place to acknowledge loss and feel it "in the flesh," creating music that reproduces the feeling of loss and grief viscerally in its listeners. Ultimately Ndegeocello's performance of dislocation is a form of dissent in a national climate where the acknowledgment of political dissent and grief shared with our so-called enemies is a sign of being "against us" rather than "with us."[23]

The world has made me the man of my dreams continues to explore these themes of spiritual and social crisis, yearning and transcendence. If the opening songs cast the problem of spiritual crisis globally in a post-9/11 context of violence, religious suspicion, and the melding of corporate and military power, the songs that follow explore the desire for (and perhaps the inevitability of) the destruction of the material world, and the possibility for new creation. In "Evolution," for example, Ndegeocello reimagines the ultimate in global warming, where beneath a burning sun we're given a chance to be freed from the constraints of our flawed bodies and human relationships: "No more tears to cry / No tongue to hurt you."

Scenarios of interplanetary transition become the backdrop for a reconsideration of change in human relationships, in songs that also wrestle with power and distrust in love and sexual relationships (in "Shirk" and "Michelle Johnson"), but even these songs might be read, alternately, as an interrogation of corporate or national regimes of power. "Shirk," lyrics, sung by Ndegeocello and Oumou Sangare, ends with the lines "I'm sorry I left you no home / But your words shattered my bones"—a line which could speak of both a struggle for power in a personal relationship and the struggle of a refugee to find home and nation. A ballad that is both plaintive and rocking, "Shirk" features wicked Mali-style finger work on the guitars by Pat Metheny and Herve Sambe.

The final song, "Soul Spaceship," is an Afrofuturist vision of imaginative and spiritual freedom, healing the pain of past memory through the future's "supreme technology," with the help of a stomping bass line. Ndegeocello sings of the ultimate ride—or is it jam?—with the power to "Transport myself into your dreams."

A bonus track, this song stands as the capstone—a seductive promise of music to take us to new places sexually, religiously, and musically. This song recruits the listener to enlist in Ndegeocello's imagined community, to come along for the ride. We might foreground this move with that of other thinkers about a queer black future in black science fiction writers Octavia E. Butler and Samuel Delany, who are also conceptualizing a black future as an inherently queer one. Like Ndegeocello, Butler and Delaney ground their rethinking of gender boundaries and desires for the future in the soul death of a slavery past, as well as homophobia and sexual oppression of the present. These works have been asking for the past few decades how we imagine ourselves beyond the state of death. In *The world has made me the man of my dreams*, Ndegeocello continues this question, asking: What does that still-absent future feel and sound like? What is its beat?[24]

Conclusion: Ndegeocello's Third World Feminist Practice and Future World Dreams

In *The world has made me the man of my dreams*, Ndegeocello is sounding out the relationship between queer gender and the ways that we define and delimit the human, within a frame of black, transnational, and distinctly feminist practice. While it is forward looking, I also link this album to Third World feminist work of the 1980s and 1990s like Cherríe Moraga and Gloria Anzaldúa's "theory in the flesh" and its interest in the ways that the body yields knowing and a "politics of necessity,"[25] Audre Lorde's conception of the erotic and the deep knowledge and ethics yielded by intentional desire,[26] and Chela Sandoval's "differential consciousness" and its deep and hopeful investment in community and collaboration—a "hermeneutics of love."[27] Like Anzaldua and Moraga, Ndegeocello uses her queerly gendered body and voice as media for critical and creative inquiry. Following Lorde, Ndegeocello's performance of desire and shared vulnerability become starting points for widening community and spiritual connection. And like Sandoval, Ndegeocello's exploration of sometimes nonverbalizeable dislocation, vulnerability, and loss are all lit with the fire of hope, and a sense of possibility. Through her musical explorations of desire, as well as the political and social precariousness of life, Ndegeocello helps us to better understand the relationships between the body and ways of knowing. Ultimately, in *The world has made me the man of my dreams,* Ndegeocello seeks to open up black aesthetics to make connections so that black sound is also global and even interplanetary, black feminism is about more than black women, and blaxploration yields insight and connection to all people. She examines the problematics of black embodiment through music to convey the relevance of fluidity and vulnerability as key to the projects of spirit, love, and healing—all important aspects of a free queer future.

Epilogue

Janelle Monáe's Collective Vision

In many of the everyday images of eccentricity that populate our collective consciousness, we see the confirmation of the stereotype of the eccentric as isolated, and even sociopathically single-minded: the slippers-in-the-snow distracted genius of Facebook's founder Mark Zuckerberg, as played by Jesse Eisenberg in the film *The Social Network* (2010); or Natalie Portman, possessed by the human-animal erotic in *Black Swan* (2010). Among Post-Soul protagonists, we might consider the socially isolated Birdie, passing and on the run, in Danzy Senna's *Caucasia,* or the caustic observer Gunnar Kaufman, one in a long line of caustic observers biding their time and on the lookout for opportunity, in Paul Beatty's *The White Boy Shuffle.*

Despite the common image of the eccentric as antisocial outsider, the eccentrics I've explored here are sharp of mind, fierce in spirit, and infectiously interested in other people, and ultimately in something bigger than all of us: imaginative freedom. In the music of P-Funk, there has always been an interest in an us, freeing our minds, so that our asses can follow. Despite his sometimes crippling shyness and odd behavior, Michael always wanted to rock with us. Stevie wants to share his inner visions, Meshell invites us on her Soul spaceship. Prince, George Clinton, and Meshell Ndegeocello are leaders of bands, as well as individual performers. Their invitation is, despite the resistance of previously limiting narratives of nation, family and racial belonging. Counter to the idea of eccentrics as isolated in their own off-centered galaxy of one, these eccentric musicians are deeply interested in inciting collective freedom through grooving collaboration.

And as the twenty-first century enters its double digits, Post-Soul eccentricity has an impassioned representative in Janelle Monáe. We can see the spirits of crunk collectivity and Afropunk in Monáe's work. In the fever dreams and science fictions of Monáe, she rallies for imaginative freedom and shared struggle by extraordinary and truly strange means. She has created the character Cindi Mayweather, sometimes androgynous android heroine and muse at the center of her concept EP *Metropo-*

lis, Suite I: The Chase (2007) and her full album *ArchAndroid* (2010), to argue for the rights of the marginal. Monáe tells the *Guardian,* "The android represents the minority, whether it's a black person, an immigrant, or coming from another country."[1] She does so, though, with a palate of songs and styles and samples that are extraordinarily polychromatic and quirky. From the new wave love song "Cold War" to the folksy-dreamy "Oh, Maker" to the tight James Brown funk of "Tightrope," Monáe is hard to pin down sonically. Her voice can move from sweet, belting, rocking, and funky to deadpan. Monáe is also hard to classify by her critics, and for once this seems to suit them just fine. Already with a strong alternative hip-hop, funk, and Soul following in the United States, Monáe made her first tour in the United Kingdom in the summer of 2010, taking it by storm, with sold-out seats and five-star reviews. The London *Times* says that she's like "the biggest pop star from a planet you've never heard of."[2] The London *Observer* calls her an "extraordinary cyber diva with a mission," "Dizzying," and a "Supernova."[3] And (happily for me), the *Guardian* calls her "POP MUSIC's HOTTEST NEW ECCENTRIC."[4]

The success of Janelle Monáe takes us to a new expansiveness, embodying the best memories of the last fifty years of black musical performance, along with a commitment to invention and intergalactic freedom. In the highly theatrical, self-consciously citational performance strategy of many of the performers discussed in this book, Monáe moves from David Bowie's high-concept theatrics to Prince's loose-spined, funky splits and squeals to Missy Elliott's rolling b-girl worm to Grace Jones's coolly imperious robot, crossing lines of race and gender, as well as genre, in her allusions and appropriations. She might break into a Temptations snap-tight bop, and then break out into a Bad Brains burst of manic energy, stage diving, her quiff coming undone, working up a sweat. Her winsome, too-long-to-be-real (I-think) eyelashes also take us back to an earlier era; they can be lowered into a Marilyn Monroe smolder, broken only by goggle-eyed David Byrne goofiness. She has an androgynous, high-style sense of fashion, including asymmetrically striped oxford shoes, uniforms, and tuxedos—all always in black and white, "a hint of Grace Jones . . . minus all the flesh," says critic Kitty Empire.[5] Monáe's style, as well as her musical content, does stretch the physical and artistic territory that many women in Soul, funk, and R&B have been allowed by this still male-driven industry. She is not afraid to sweat, or let her hair come undone, dancing with a manic energy that signals both pleasure and purpose.

For Monáe, eccentricity is both an aesthetic and a tactic. Indeed, she has circumvented many of the constraints of the business through her collective vision and creativity. After studying musical theater in New York at the American Musical and Dramatic Academy, she went to Atlanta, attracted to it by Outkast's artistic circle. There, she helped form her Afrofuturist collective, the Wondaland Arts Society, whose manifesto declares, "We believe truth can be broken down with the following formula: Thought = Love + Imagination. We believe songs are spaceships. We believe music is the weapon of the future. We believe books are stars."[6] She and the other members of Wondaland call themselves "thrivals": "individuals who won't allow race or gender to be a barrier to reaching their goals."[7] To get her music heard, she's used multiple tactics: distributing her first EP from the trunk of her car and using social networking spaces like MySpace to gain a following. And she has found alliances and mentors in some of the most productive folks in the music industry: Sean "Puffy" Combs, Big Boi, Prince, and Erykah Badu. Yet she insists on her own artistic independence, and stays connected to her collective. Together with Wondaland, she creates the concepts for her own videos, and is at work on a Broadway musical and graphic novel based on her android muse, Cindi Mayweather.

Despite her commitment to the fantastic, Monáe is unafraid to take on explicitly political positions. She says that she wears uniforms onstage to avoid the pressures of gender conformity, and as a salute to the working class: "My mother was a janitor, my father drove trash trucks, my stepfather works at the post office. . . . I worked at Blockbuster. I was a maid, so I connect with those who every day are struggling."[8] In 2008, she filmed a Rock the Vote video for Bad Boy Records, naming health care and education as the most important aspects of the campaign, and she speaks out in her interviews against sexism and homophobia. In the song "Many Moons," she salutes a wide-ranging list of outcasts, drug addicts, and other outsiders, some reflecting the everyday hatred of internalized racism: "Black girl, bad hair / Broad nose, cold stare."

Her video for "Tightrope" is set in the Palace of the Dogs, a fictional (?) asylum that she insists is in fact a real place that has imprisoned Jimi Hendrix, Charlie Chaplin, and also herself. Monáe leads a band of tuxedoed "patients" in a funky tightrope shimmy through its gray concrete halls, an androgynous James Brown, complete with horn section and pompadour. Their grooving survival seems to be despite the surveillance of two hooded, video-faced ghouls and a Soul Nurse Ratched, who is prone to slipping into a little bit of tightroping herself, when no one is looking. The video is a little bit *Cuckoo's Nest,* a little bit *Rocky Horror,* a little bit of *Night at the Apollo* and might very well capture what it's like to be black and creative and queer in the twenty-first century, where freedom is still a tightrope walk. If the exuberant group dance scenes are a sign, freedom is clearly the magic of making music together, in the celebration of a lively horn section, in Big Boi's solo, in the shaking and slipping of wigs, and an impromptu electric slide. Kanye might have been a little lost in his own "Dark Fantasy" in 2010, but Janelle Monáe imagines the possibility for liberation as a collective vision.

Within the video, Monáe interrogates the strange familiarity of prisons and asylums—both far away and very much a part of our lives. The plot of escape is featured in countless films, television shows, and music videos—from *One Flew over the Cuckoo's Nest* to *Frances* to *Alias* and *Lost.* Yet everyday culture distances prisons and prisoners from our everyday experience. As Angela Davis points out, we are asked to forget about prisons and not imagine ourselves or the ones we love there—even if our loved ones *are* there, and even if we ourselves have been there.[9] At the same time, the prison and asylum, in their shared history, have become the mechanism for self-surveillance and control in the larger social sphere.[10] In this cultural moment, when incarcerations of black and brown folks are at epidemic levels, all of our own imaginations are at stake. As Monáe sings, "You've got to dance up on them haters / keep getting funky on the scene."

In "Tightrope," Monáe reminds us of the many ways the prison industrial complex infiltrates our lives by means of surveillance and the heightened fear of black bodies in motion. We watch as Monáe and her band of tightropers stop and pose as the nurse and faceless guards pass by. To an onlooker, they are wasting time gossiping and posing. But we know that this pose is a tactic, the mask of the trickster. The dancing is smooth, light, and infectious, that gospel-inflected lyric "Whether you're high or you're low" punctuated by the gesture of a bird taking flight, at once comic and graceful—a little bit of Man Tan, a little bit of P-Funk, flying out of the underpass. "Tightrope" celebrates the power of creative rebellion in the music itself. Dance and music are both metaphors for creative freedom to be protected, and the tools to protect creative freedom. Monáe is the ringleader in the highly theatrical spirit of George

Clinton, yet she also acknowledges the trickiness of rebellion in the public eye, and in this way is profoundly feminist in her exposure of the pressures to be heard, and the psychic costs of vulnerability.

Monáe's creation, the android Cindi Mayweather is another eccentric tactic used to address issues of power specific to the music industry: the dehumanization of the commercial marketing of black performance, the ways that capitalism manages to appropriate the underground, and the always present push back of that underground to keep creating. Set in the year 2719, *Metropolis, Suite I: The Chase* is located in a moment of war and capitalism gone wild, "partying robo-zillionares," and "riotous ethnic, race and class conflicts and petty holocaust," according to the liner notes. Cindi is the only android among the pack whose programming includes "a rock-star proficiency package and a working soul." Cindi must use her extraordinary skills of rock and soul to escape and locate freedom. In the video for "Many Moons," a song from *Metropolis* that features Cindi, Monáe imagines a catwalk of androids (all played by Monáe herself). The androids strike various poses of black style: sultry, haughty, cool, funky. The androids seem to be modeled on past black performances: a chorus of identical Cindis echo Grace Jones's use of an army of selves in her *One Man Show*. Another android shakily prepares herself for the stage, combing her long back wig, a visual echo of Tina Turner in "What's Love Got to Do with It?" We watch as the androids are all to be sold to the highest bidder by their "madam," herself an android, played by Monáe. The auction is the site of multiple exchanges of power and desire, and we watch while the androids are traded between men and women competing for power and visibility. In the background, providing the soundtrack and entertainment for the android auction, is a live band, also played by Monáe and her band. But this rocking Cindi, sampling inspiration from black performance mavericks Prince, Little Richard, and Michael Jackson, has the power, with the help of her audience, of interrupting the auction. As she breaks into an M.J. moonwalk, the musician Cindi brings an audience of screaming female fans to such a fever pitch that she interrupts the auction, taking the attention of the bidders away from the sale, until this final rocking Cindi explodes in a lightning bolt of energy.

"Many Moons" captures the rebellious energy of black quare musical performance, but it also speaks to the power of black performance to meet and produce the demands of pleasure seekers, sometimes to the point of their own destruction. Indeed, in the video productions, co-

conceived by Monáe and her Wondaland collective, she explores both the radical energy of performance and the psychic costs of fame. In the video for "Cold War," a diva (Cindi? Monáe herself?) breaks down in the course of singing, the camera still whirring, taking in her tears. (As we watch the singer's increasing psychic distress, I'm reminded of Yoko Ono's performance art piece *Cut Up*, as audiences participate in cutting apart the black knit dress of a passive Ono, leaving her exposed as a camera takes it all in.) In her rendition of "Smile," performed on *Billboard*'s "Mashup" series, Monáe's performance evokes the earnestness of Michael Jackson's ballad singing style on "Ben," and the raw emotionalism of Judy Garland's own version of "Smile," reminding us of the vulnerability of the performer. She lampoons the larger-than-life hysteria of the performer who knows that she has the audience in her pocket, and who just might be going a little too far, in her performance of "Let's Go Crazy" at the 2010 BET Awards—performing her parody of Prince right in front of the Purple One himself, to his amusement. In this performance she is both Prince, successfully quare performer, and his persona, *Purple Rain*'s The Kid, isolated and a little lost to himself, but still capable of explosive performance.

Monáe brings her funky, energized, and citational approach to the ongoing questions posed by Post-Soul eccentricity. How do we negotiate the tightrope of black authenticity to create original art? How do we keep creating a future that includes all of us, when the crises of the present and past have the power to stop us in our tracks? How do we deploy our bodies, in their quareness, to create positive change? Monáe continues the forward and backward thinking of the eccentrics before her while keeping in mind the shared humanity of all of us.

Notes

Introduction

1. Alvin Poissant, "An Analytical Look at the Prince Phenomenon," *Ebony,* June 1985, 170.

2. Nelson George, quoted in Lynn Norment, "Prince: What's the Secret of His Amazing Success?," *Ebony,* June 1985, 162.

3. In a *Jet* retrospective of Prince's career, journalist Rashod Ollison, in "Prince and His Evolution" (*Jet,* July 5, 2010), quotes Mark Anthony Neal, who suggests that Prince capitalized on the trends of androgyny in rock, especially glam rock, while also opening up spaces for new black performances of masculinity.

> "It's always important to put Black male performers of that generation into a certain context. . . . Prince is doing his gender-bending thing. Rick James has the braids and glitter and Michael Jackson has the androgynous thing going. And they're all trying to cross over to what is White rock at the time, which is heavily pushing androgyny. So it made sense that all of them tried to push the envelope in that regard. What is interesting about Prince is that there was not a lot of feedback about some of his gender-bending. But I don't think anybody saw Prince's androgyny in the way they saw Michael's, because Prince was always clear about his heterosexuality."

> As hip-hop pushed its way into the mainstream in the late '80s, just as Prince's reign in pop was beginning to wane, a decidedly more thuggish image of Black masculinity became the norm. But the influence of Prince, his synthesis of Little Richard's flamboyant theatricality and James Brown's sweaty funk, was still strong. As Neal says, Prince proved that "we didn't have to have these two positions: the soft R&B balladeer versus the hard-core hip-hop thug. In other words, he's saying there is no actual script for Black masculinity except whatever you choose to perform. You don't have to choose between being Chuck D or Luther Vandross." (28)

4. See Daphne A. Brooks, *Jeff Buckley's Grace* (New York: Continuum Books, 2005); and her discussion in "Journey: 'Lights,'" in "Critical Karaoke," by Joshua Cone, Ange Milinko, Greil Marcus, Ann Powers, and Daphne A. Brooks, *Popular Music* 24, no. 3 (2005): 423–27. See also Michael C. Ladd, "Hard Core Jollies in the Himalayas, Staring at the Cosmic Slop: The Mothership Connection between Triple and Qua-

druple Consciousness," in *Rip It Up: The Black Experience in Rock 'n' Roll*, edited by Kandia Crazy Horse (New York: Palgrave Macmillan, 2004).

5. See Maureen Mahon's excellent ethnographic study of Black Rock Coalition members, *The Right to Rock: The Black Rock Coalition and the Cultural Politics of Race* (Durham: Duke University Press, 2004).

6. Stuart Hall, "What Is This 'Black' in Black Popular Culture?," in *Black Popular Culture*, edited by Gina Dent (Seattle: Bay Press, 1992), 22.

7. Bertram Ashe, "Theorizing the Post-Soul Aesthetic: An Introduction," *African American Review* 41, no. 4 (Winter 2007): 609–23, especially 611–15.

8. Trey Ellis, "The New Black Aesthetic," *Callaloo* 12, no. 1 (1989): 233–43.

9. See Mark Anthony Neal, *Soul Babies: Black Popular Culture and the Post-Soul Aesthetic* (New York: Routledge, 2002).

10. George Lipsitz, *Footsteps in the Dark: The Hidden Histories of Popular Music* (Minneapolis: University of Minnesota Press, 2007), iv.

11. Ibid., xiv–xv.

12. On the importance of irony as an aspect of Post-Soul aesthetics in particular, see Richard Schur's "Post-Soul Aesthetics in Contemporary African American Art," *African American Review* 41, no. 4 (2007): 641–54.

13. Monique Guillory and Richard C. Green, "By Way of Introduction," in *Soul: Black Power, Politics, and Pleasure*, edited by Monique Guillory and Richard C. Greene. (New York: New York University Press, 1998), 1.

14. Ann Cvetkovich, *An Archive of Feelings: Trauma, Sexuality, and Lesbian Public Cultures* (Durham: Duke University Press, 2003), 1.

15. For conversations on the black fugitive impulse, see Nathaniel Mackey, "Other: From Noun to Verb," *Representations* 39 (Summer 1992): 51–70; Nathaniel Mackey, "Cante Moro," in *Disembodied Poetics: Annals of the Jack Kerouac School*, edited by Anne Waldman and Andrew Schelling (Albuquerque: University of New Mexico Press, 1994), 71–93; Fred Moten, "'Words Don't Go There': An Interview with Fred Moten by Charles Henry Rowell," *Callaloo* 27, no. 4 (2004): 953–66; Fred Moten, *In the Break: The Aesthetics of the Black Radical Tradition* (Minneapolis: University of Minnesota Press, 2003); and the first chapter of Daphne A. Brooks, *Bodies in Dissent: Spectacular Performances of Race and Freedom, 1850–1910* (Durham: Duke University Press, 2006).

16. Mackey, "Other," 52–56.

17. Brooks, *Bodies in Dissent*, 4–5.

18. Moten, "Words Don't Go There," 959.

19. García Lorca, quoted in Mackey, "Cante Moro," 74.

20. Moten, *In the Break*.

21. Quoted in Margena A. Christian, "Prince Continues His Purple Reign at 50," *Jet*, July 23, 2008, 58.

22. Cynthia Fuchs, writing at the moment when the conflict with Warner was still unresolved, suggests that "The uncertainty of [the glyph], as a marker for a post-Prince identity, extends and complicates what was already visible in then-Prince's performances, his differences from a variety of bodies, selves, and identities, including male and female, black and white, queer and straight. Unfixed over time, at each moment determined in relation to another performance, [the glyph] marks (and unmarks) an

identity which is at once full and void of meaning. He/it challenges the representational system where bodies are visible indices of 'identities' which exist prior to acts, insisting on the simultaneity of signs, selves, and fantasies." Cynthia Fuchs, "'I wanna be your fantasy': Sex, Death, and the Artist Formerly Known as Prince," *Women and Performance: A Journal of Feminist Theory* 8, no. 2 (1996): 140.

23. See Harvey Young, *Embodying Black Experience: Stillness, Critical Memory, and the Black Body* (Ann Arbor: University of Michigan Press, 2010), 6. Young complicates the ways that we might read such acts of reclaiming of the black body by insisting on the simultaneous experience of present and pastness in these acts: "Re-claiming does not require that we erase the past and script a new one. The prefix tells us this. To reclaim is to take something back. It is to possess something in the present while knowing that it has only recently been back in your possession. It is to remain aware of the previous 'claims' even as you articulate your own. It is to know the past in the present as you work toward creating a future" (135).

24. Jason Draper, *Prince: Chaos, Disorder, and Revolution* (New York: Hal Leonard, 2011), 168–69.

25. I fear that as "Post-Soul" has circulated, there has been a kind of reduction of the potential of the moment, and of its politics, by those who chart it primarily as identified with the consumption of hip-hop. In *Buppies, B-Boys, and Bohos: Notes on Post-Soul Black Culture* (New York: Harper Collins, 1992), Nelson George embraces the rise of renegade filmmaker Melvin Van Peebles as the prototype of the most innovative aspects of the Post-Soul moment in its early days, which then was carried through to a fuller extent even in early hip-hop: "homegrown heroes with larger-than-life personas" like Grandmaster Flash, Afrika Bambaataa, and Kurtis Blow. The problem here is that Nelson limits his view of Post-Soul's most transformative spirit as one that is also traditionally macho and relatively limited in its scope of racial, gender, or sexual reinvention. Van Peebles might well be seen as the reembrace of patriarchy for black manhood through his *Sweetback*, but he does not characterize what to me might be some of the most imaginative and even fierce aspects of Post-Soul culture—the edge of the edge. Instead, the book presents as the heart (and heat) of Post-Soul rebellion and critique a particular and more traditional model of masculinity.

While Nelson George includes in his Post-Soul taxonomy the Boho, the bohemian figure of black intellectualism, experimentation, and exploration that might open up a discussion of more eccentric performances, his discussions of this figure are limited. Indeed, George's Bohos are characterized as flaky and politically ineffective, and more often than not they are fictional constructions: the figure of gentle derision in sitcoms such as Cree in *A Different World* or Lisa Bonet's Denise in *The Cosby Show*. The Boho in George's taxonomy is vague and ineffective: "relatively color blind children" of a "race-neutral environment" (7) rather than engagingly experimental.

26. Ellis, "The New Black Aesthetic," 235.

27. E. Patrick Johnson, "'Quare' Studies, or (Almost) Everything I Know about Queer Studies I Learned from My Grandmother," in *Black Queer Studies: A Critical Anthology*, edited by E. Patrick Johnson and Mae G. Henderson (Durham: Duke University Press, 2005), 125.

28. Carla Peterson, "Foreword: Eccentric Bodies," in *Recovering the Black Female Body: Self-Representations by African American Women*, edited by Michael Bennett

and Vanessa D. Dickerson (New Brunswick, NJ: Rutgers University Press, 2001), xii.

29. Ibid., xii.

30. E. Patrick Johnson, *Appropriating Blackness: Performance and the Politics of Authenticity* (Durham, NC: Duke University Press, 2003), 3–4.

31. As Alexander G. Weheliye has pointed out quite brilliantly, in *Phonographies: Grooves in Sonic Afro-Modernity* (Durham: Duke University Press, 2005), tensions between technology and authentic black sound—particularly oral culture—have been a part of discussions of modern blackness since the first recorded sounds of black voices (6–7).

32. Paul Gilroy, *The Black Atlantic: Modernity and Double Consciousness* (Cambridge, MA: Harvard University Press, 1993), 97.

33. Hall, "What Is This 'Black' in Black Popular Culture?," 21–33.

34. Quoted in Gilroy, *The Black Atlantic*, 98.

35. For example, see Barbara Smith's critiques of homophobia and black respectability in her essay "Home," Cheryl Clarke's essay "The Failure to Transform: Homophobia in the Black Community," and Pat Parker's Poem "Where Will You Be?," all included in the 1983 anthology *Home Girls: A Black Feminist Anthology*, edited by Barbara Smith (New York: Kitchen Table–Women of Color Press, 1983).

36. In *In a Queer Time and Place: Transgender Bodies, Subcultural Lives* (New York: New York University Press, 2005), Judith Halberstam defines "queer time" as those ways that queer relationships and living necessitate a logic of being in the world outside of the constraints to heteronormative time, birth, marriage, reproduction, and death. She uses it to think about community and bonds, subcultural lives, and an "epistemology of youth." Queer temporality is a way of thinking about ways of living and connecting within queer subcultures that "disrupt conventional accounts of youth culture, adulthood, and maturity" (2).

37. For a discussion of "post-liberation" identity, see Greg Tate's "Cult-Nats Meet Freaky-Deke," in *Flyboy in the Buttermilk: Essays on Contemporary America* (New York: Simon and Schuster, 1992), 198–209. Like *Post-Soul*, *post-liberation* suggests that the life-and-death struggles for freedom and civil rights have already been won. I'm arguing here, though, that the quaring of this moment repoliticizes it.

38. For example, despite years performing an outrageous persona that was markedly queer in his own neighborhood and underground spaces in Georgia, once Little Richard gained his first hits with "Tutti Frutti," "Long Tall Sally," and "Rip It Up," he describes a careful and strategic reframing of his eccentricity.

> We were breaking through the racial barrier. The white kids had to hide my records 'cos they daren't let their parents know they had them in the house. We decided that my image should be crazy and way-out so that the adults would think I was harmless. I'd appear in one show dressed as the Queen of England and in the next as the pope. (Charles White, *The Life and Times of Little Richard: The Authorized Biography* ([London: Omnibus Press, 1984]), 66).

As Little Richard moves into the larger public sphere, his unpredictable oddness at best gets shaped into more recognizable and perhaps containable codes of outrageousness, at worst is censored and erased. Despite his profound influence on the music of the time, from Pat Boone to the Beatles to James Brown, Little Richard's career went dormant until the 1980s, when he found some space in which to reclaim his role as one of rock and roll's chief architects and outrageous cultural icons, suddenly appearing in commercials for margarine, and in cameo roles in *Down and Out in Beverly Hills* (1986), *The Pickle* (1993), and *Mystery, Alaska* (1999).

39. Here, I'm calling on Gramsci's idea of the organic intellectual as a scholar whose work is connected to everyday struggles of the people and their experiences, which he details in his essay "Hegemony, Intellectuals, and the State" in his *Prison Notebooks* (Antonio Gramsci, *Selections from the Prison Notebooks,* translated by Geoffrey N. Smith and Quintin Hoare [New York: International Publishers Company Inc., 1971], 10). While recent scholars of black culture have used the term *organic intellectual* to describe some hip-hop artists, I haven't seen this term applied to Michael Jackson, Grace Jones, or the other pop artists discussed here—perhaps because of the ways that their performances and lyrics often move away from realism or the explicitly political. But we might indeed think of these artists' embodied exploration of identity as having an overlooked political dimension. On hip-hop artists as organic intellectuals, see Robin D. G. Kelley's characterization of gangsta rap in "Kickin' Reality, Kickin' Ballistics: Gangsta Rap and Postindustrial Los Angeles," in *Droppin' Science: Critical Essays on Rap Music and Hip-Hop Culture,* edited by William Eric Perkins (Philadelphia: Temple University Press, 1996), 121; and Jeffrey Louis Decker, "The State of Rap: Time and Place in Hip-Hop Nationalism," *Social Text* 34 (1993): 53–84.

40. See Mahon, *The Right to Rock,* especially the chapter "The Post-Liberated Generation" (33–58).

41. Cultural historian Todd Boyd writes that *Soul Train,* the longest-running syndicated show on television, "showed a generation what it meant to be cool. There's something about it that suggested hipness. And if you wanted to be hip, you watched 'Soul Train.' . . . In the '70's, there was no other place to see this in the mainstream" (quoted in Christine Acham, *Revolution Televised: Prime Time and the Struggle for Black Power* [Minneapolis: University of Minnesota Press, 2004]). As both Christine Acham and Christopher Lehman point out, *Soul Train* gave visibility to black artists, black dance moves, and styles that had important commercial as well as political ramifications, creating a black cultural space and also capturing the imagination of the mainstream public (54–66; Christopher P. Lehman, *A Critical History of Soul Train on Television* [Jefferson, NC: McFarland Publishers, 2008], especially 79–105). Lehman points to the influential premier of Michael Jackson's dance, the Robot, during a 1973 performance of "Dancing Machine" on the show as an example of *Soul Train's* nationwide, and even global, influence as a cultural phenomenon. And he points to *Don Kirshner's Rock Concert's* second season premier, which featured only black artists, as evidence of the influence of Don Cornelius and *Soul Train* (104). Significantly, just about every artist that I discuss in this study, from the most visible Michael Jackson to the less infamous Meshell Ndegeocello, has performed on *Soul Train,* which ran from 1970 to 2006.

42. In his discussion of post-Soul intellectual debates, and particularly Trey Ellis's "New Black Aesthetic," Mark Anthony rightly traces the NBA movement to the oppositional writings of previous and contemporary queer and feminist black intellectuals not mentioned by Ellis, including Anna Julia Cooper, Bayard Rustin, Audre Lorde and James Baldwin: "Cooper Rustin and Lorde in particular have been instrumental

in rearticulating notions of blackness along an axis of gender and sexual preference—constructions that remain at odds with dominant representations of blackness and challenge popular motions that increasingly posit patriarchy and heterosexuality as the foundations for acceptable social constructions of blackness" (Neal, *Soul Babies,* 114).

43. Chela Sandoval, *Methodology of the Oppressed: Theory Out of Bounds* (Minneapolis: University of Minnesota Press, 2000). As I'll discuss further below, the third space is also an important concept in José Esteban Muñoz's framework of" disidentification."

44. Essex Hemphill, "Heavy Breathing," *Ceremonies: Prose and Poetry* (San Francisco: Cleis Press, 1992), 6.

45. José Esteban Muñoz, *Disidentifications: Queers of Color and the Performance of Politics* (Minneapolis: University of Minnesota Press, 1999), 4.

46. Ibid., 7.

47. Muñoz notes:

> Disidentification is the third mode of dealing with dominant ideology, one that neither opts to assimilate with such a structure nor strictly opposes it; rather disidentification is a strategy that works on and against dominant ideology. Instead of buckling under the pressures of dominant ideology (identification, assimilation) or attempting to break free of its inescapable sphere (counteridentification, utopianism), this "working on and against" is a strategy that tries to transform a cultural logic from within, always laboring to enact permanent structural change while at the same time valuing the importance of local or everyday struggles of resistance. (Ibid., 12)

48. Joshua Gamson, *The Fabulous Sylvester: The Legend, the Music, the Seventies in San Francisco* (New York: Henry Holt, 2005), 149.

49. Sylvester's challenge reminds me, too, of the life and death of Jean-Michel Basquiat, who challenged notions of black identity while at the same time keeping the community itself at a studied distance, even in death. Note Greg Tate's confession after Basquiat's death: "'I remember myself and Vernon Reid being invited to Jean-Michel Basquiat's loft for a party in 1984, and not even wanting to meet the man, because he was surrounded by white people.'" Greg Tate, "He Is Truly Free Who Is Free from the Need to Be Free: A Survey and Consideration of Black Male Genius," in *Black Male: Representations of Masculinity in Contemporary American Art,* edited by Thelma Golden (New York: Whitney Museum of Art, 1994), 117–18.

50. Judith Butler, *Bodies That Matter: On the Discursive Limits of "Sex"* (New York: Routledge, 1993), 187.

51. Ibid., 221–22.

52. For an extended discussion of becoming and the reanimation of desire, see my *Becoming Cleopatra: The Shifting Image of an Icon* (New York: Palgrave Macmillan, 2003).

53. LaShonda Katrice Barnett, *I've Got Thunder: Black Women Songwriters on Their Craft* (New York: Thunder's Mouth Press, 2007), 31.

54. Moten, *In the Break,* 1.

55. Ibid., 26.

56. A brilliant example of Moten's uncovering of political passion underneath the grain of the voice is this reading of Billie Holiday's recording *Lady in Satin.*

> The lady in satin uses the crack in the voice, extremity of the instrument, willingness to fail reconfigured as a willingness to go past, through the achievement or arrival at the object is neither undermined by partiality or incompleteness nor burdened by the soft, heavy romance of a simple fullness. The crack in the voice is an abundant loss, the strings of a romance with what she don't need and already has. The crack is like the laugh in the voice of "My Man"—trace of some impossible initial version or inaugurative incident and effect of the resistance and excess of every intervening narrative and interpretation. Those last records, when leaned into, into the depth of the grain, grain become crack or cut (you can lay your pen in there; upon what is this writing before writing inscribed? What temple?), undermine any narrative of life and art that would smoothly move from a light business (busyness) to spare tragedy. Willingness to fail goes past; new coefficients of freedom. (Ibid., 107–8)

57. I find it noteworthy that at least three of the performers discussed in this book—Eartha Kitt, Grace Jones, and Janelle Monáe—all studied theater on either the high school or college level, and this speaks to their interest in theatricality and their ability to effectively create character in their voices, movements, and personae.

58. Simon Frith, *Performing Rites: On the Value of Popular Music* (Cambridge, MA: Harvard University Press, 1996), 214.

59. In her description of virtuosity, Jones continues, "The vocalizations, the gestures, the thinking, and the beauty are honed through repeated experiences that support solo gifts and the development of a personal voice." Such development of personal voice is intimately connected to embodiment, where "cellular thinking is linked to emotional and intellectual learning" and "experience is passed on, person to person." Omi Osun Joni L. Jones, "Making Space: Producing the Austin Project," in *Experiments in a Jazz Aesthetic: Art, Activism, Academia, and the Austin Project,* edited by Omi Osun Joni L. Jones, Lisa L. Moore, and Sharon Bridgforth (Austin: University of Texas Press, 2010), 6.

60. Moten, *In the Break,* 39.

61. While I am certainly interested in self-consciously queered spaces of interpretation and community, much can be learned from L. H. Stalling's inclusion of multiple arenas in black culture under the umbrella of "queer," from black femininity in general (in its inability to never quite or at least conditionally achieve the state of ideal black womanhood) to the space of the Chitlin' Circuit (here a specifically classed notion of sexuality where hidden truths of black life could/can be voiced boldly through the comedy of Lawanda Page and others) to black folktales of Brer Rabbit and Sister Goose. Stalling's use of *queer* is not just a blanket statement but rightly argues for the bridges always present between so-called straight black and gay cultures. See L. H. Stallings, *Mutha' Is Half a Word: Intersections of Folklore, Vernacular, Myth, and Queerness in Black Female Culture* (Columbus: Ohio State University Press, 2007).

62. Rachel Devitt "Girl on Girl: Fat Femmes, Bio-queens, and Redefining Drag,"

in *Queering the Popular Pitch,* edited by Sheila Whiteley and Jennifer Rycenga (New York: Routledge, 2006), 28.

63. Sheila Whiteley and Jennifer Rycenga, "Introduction," in *Queering the Popular Pitch,* edited by Sheila Whiteley and Jennifer Rycenga (New York: Routledge, 2006), xiv.

64. Munoz, *Disidentifications,* 146.

Chapter 1

1. Farrah Jasmine Griffin, *"Who Set You Flowin'"? The African-American Migration Narrative* (New York: Oxford University Press, 1996), 6–7.

2. For example, when Kitt performed "I Want to Be Evil" and "Santa Baby" for the Greek king and queen in 1953, Los Angeles mayor Norris Poulson called the songs "risqué, filthy and off-color," though reportedly the king and queen said that they enjoyed the songs very much. "Eartha's 'Evil' Song Causes Row," *Chicago Defender,* November 28, 1953, 1.

3. When dating Loew's Theater heir Arthur Loew, *Confidential* magazine snarkily suggested that "When Eartha comes to Hollywood, she and Arthur Loew Junior set up white and tan housekeeping," quoted in Eartha Kitt, *Still Here: Confessions of a Sex Kitten* (New York: Barricade Books, 1991), 138.

4. "Readers, 'Fans' Join Pro and Con Predictions on Eartha Kitt Style," *Chicago Defender* (national ed.), May 15, 1954, 19.

5. White and black press sources debated her manners, the acuity of her analysis, and the sincerity of her motives (some in the black press speculating that this was a self-serving publicity stunt.) The *Chicago Defender* printed Martin Luther King Jr.'s praise of her actions, though a later story suggests that her "emotional outburst" was not only "a shocking exhibition of bad manners, it was obviously a raw, naked quest for publicity." "Eartha Kitt's Outburst," *Chicago Defender,* January 23, 1968, 13. *New York Amsterdam News* wrote with a hint of admiration that she "got her claws in the Whitehouse." Cathy Aldrige, "The Ladies and Eartha: Pro-Con," *New York Amsterdam News,* January 27, 1968, 1.

6. Kwakiutl Dreher, in *Dancing on the White Page: Black Women Entertainers Writing Autobiography* (New York: State University of New York Press, 2008), gives a fantastic analysis of how Kitt embodies her critique of the Vietnam War as well. She suggests that Kitt not only gives the lie to the White House's euphemistic descriptions of war deaths as casualties, but she does so using the authority of her own body as a woman and mother, and in language that directly confronts the propriety of the white southern womanhood of Lady Bird Johnson.

> As a privileged guest of the First Lady, Kitt's candor sullies Lady Bird's invitation. A veritable changeling, appearing as a well-behaved guest then transforming into a serious sociopolitical critic—Kitt essentially spills the dirt on the White House carpet. This dirt, or a black woman's daring to convey her awareness of sociopolitical cruel realities, disorders Lady Bird's universe. (113)

7. Organizing committees like the Committee of Concerned Blacks, headed by novelist Louise Meriwether, called her out specifically, urging her not to travel to South Africa. Louise Meriwether, "Blacks to South Africa: Progress or Sellout?" *New York Amsterdam News*, May 25, 1972, A5. The white press used her travel as a site of speculation for US policy and to what extent the South African state should be economically supported. See Robert Rotberg, "Apartheid: Changes Are at the Surface," *Washington Post*, May 14, 1972, B5.

8. Thomas Postlewait and Tracy C. Davis suggest that "Melodramatic drama and performance are faulted not only for the surplus of emotionalism and spectacular dramatic action but also for the lack of truth representation. And yet this surplus may be precisely what makes theatre (or opera and dance) gripping, providing the thrill of difficult accomplishment and uncommon talent that catapults a viewer into pleasures that derive from the abandonment of certain restraints." Tracy C. Davis and Thomas Postlewait, eds., *Theatricality* (Cambridge: Cambridge University Press, 2004), 21.

9. Shane Vogel provides a powerful reading of Lena Horne's aloof style of cabaret performance as a means of negotiating the pressures of black respectability in his chapter "Lena Horne's Impersona" in his book *The Scene of the Harlem Cabaret: Race, Sexuality, Performance* (Chicago: University of Chicago Press, 2009), 167–93. In his study, Vogel characterizes Horne's performed elegance as one that often tips into coldness: "She offered not love but hostility, not warmth but aloofness, not presence but absence, not immediacy but hesitation, not touch but distance, not an old friend, but a stranger" (167). Indeed, within the strictures of the cabaret space, Horne's performances might share much with Kitt's contrariness that I discuss here. Vogel historicizes the Harlem cabaret space as an intimate space of racial crossing, and as a space in which black performers could both expand and constrict subjectivity.

10. For a powerful discussion of Eartha Kitt's cosmopolitanism as critical feminist practice, see Daphne A. Brooks, "Planet Earth(a): Sonic Cosmopolitanism and Black Feminist Theory," in *"Cornbread and Cuchifritos," Ethnic Identity Politics, Transnationalization, and Transculturation in American Urban Popular Music*, edited by Wilfred Raussert and Michelle Habell-Pallán (Tempe, AZ: Bilingual Review Press, 2011, 111–26).

11. Anne Anlin Cheng, *The Melancholy of Race: Psychoanalysis, Assimilation, and Hidden Grief* (New York: Oxford University Press, 2001), xi.

12. Ibid., x.

13. Here, my thinking is informed by Daphne A. Brooks's persuasive analysis of Nina Simone's performances, and the importance of Simone's memoir, *I Put a Spell on You*, as a form of theorization in line with her performances. Brooks says in a note in this essay that in this formulation she is following the lead of the work of Shane Vogel and Thomas Postlewait by "reading Simone's autobiography as a 'document' not of performance history but of 'performance theory' in which we can hear and see her making sense of a complex web of racially, gendered, class, and sexually charged politics that made her career." Daphne A. Brooks, "Nina Simone's Triple Play" *Callaloo* 34, no. 1 (Winter 2011): 194, n. 4.

14. Cheng, *The Melancholy of Race*, x.

15. Dreher, *Dancing on the White Page*, 110.

16. Eartha Kitt, *Thursday's Child* (London: Cassell, 1957), 3.

17. Ibid., 17.

18. Eartha Kitt, *Alone with Me: A New Autobiography* (New York: H. Regnery, 1976), 22.

19. Kitt, *Still Here*, 10.

20. Kitt, *Alone with Me*, 257.

21. Ibid., ix.

22. Ibid., 28.

23. Kitt, *Still Here*, 112.

24. Ibid., 14.

25. Ibid., 243.

26. Ibid., 13.

27. Ibid., 123.

28. The "Freestyle" exhibit, curated by Thelma Golden, ushered in the discourse of Post-Black among artists and critics. See Thelma Golden, *Freestyle: The Studio Museum in Harlem* (New York: Studio Museum in Harlem, 2001). Along with Post-Race, Post-Black has taken on a more widespread usage with the election of Barack Obama. See Carly Fraser, "Race, Post-Black Politics, and the Presidential Candidacy of Barack Obama," *Souls* 11, no. 1 (January 2009): 17–40. On Post-Black as an emerging identity, see Ytasha Womack, *Post-Black: How a New Generation Is Changing African American Identity* (New York: Lawrence Books, 2010) and Touré, *Who's Afraid of Post-Blackness? What It Means to Be Black Now* (New York: Free Press, 2011). In a review of Colson Whitehead's memoir *Sag Harbor* in the *New York Times Book Review* (May 3, 2009), Touré suggests that the ushering in of Obama has produced a new visibility for Post-Black identity.

> Now that we've got a post-black president, all the rest of the post-blacks can be unapologetic as we reshape the iconography of blackness. For so long, the definition of blackness was dominated by the '60's street-fighting militancy of the Jesses and the irreverent one-foot-out-the-ghetto angry brilliance of the Pryors and the nihilistic, unrepentantly ghetto, new-age thuggishness of the 50 Cents. A decade ago they called post-blacks Oreos because we didn't think blackness equaled ghetto, didn't mind having white influencers, didn't seem full of anger about the past. We were comfortable employing blackness as a grace note rather than as our primary sound. Post-blackness sees blackness not as a dogmatic code worshiping at the altar of the hood and the struggle but as an open-source document, a trope with infinite uses. (1)

If, as Touré suggests, we are in the age of Post-Blackness without shame, Kitt embraced a Post-Blackness that centered that feeling of discord and contradiction. Hers was a Post-Blackness with critical purpose.

29. Kitt defends herself against the accusation that she is only interested in dating nonblack men in *Alone with Me*.

> Over the years, I have been asked thinly veiled questions about the loves of my life, with an emphasis on color and the implication that, perhaps (amateur psychologists all), I was searching for my lost white-father figure. In truth, on society's skin-color scale, my relationships would reg-

ister about fifty-fifty, or at least sixty-forty. And considering the ratio of white to black in the west, it's a wonder that I haven't registered a ninety-ten. But I haven't. Some of you will understand when I say that I don't see people as white or nonwhite. I see them as human beings, male or female, friendly or hostile, and so on. . . . I'm a human being with a full complement of needs and desires and drives. And needs and drives are colorless. (216–17)

30. Kitt, *Still Here,* 57.

31. Griffin, *"Who Set You Flowin'"?,* xx.

32. Kitt, *Alone with Me,* 4.

33. Dennis Hunt, "Kitt: The Tip of a Persona," *Los Angeles Times,* July 28, 1977, G13.

34. John L. Scott, "Eartha Kitt Opens Century City Stint," *Los Angeles Times,* December 11, 1969, H19.

35. Kitt, *Alone with Me,* 50.

36. Brenda Dixon Gottschild, *Digging the Africanist in American Performance: Dance and Other Contexts* (New York: Praeger, 1998), 13.

37. Michael Hanchard, "Cultural Politics and Black Public Intellectuals," *Social Text* 14, no. 3 (Fall 1996): 95.

38. Shane Vogel discusses New York cabarets and the space of white gay drag in his essay "Where Are We Now? Queer World Making and Cabaret Performance," *GLQ: A Journal of Lesbian and Gay Studies* 6, no. 1 (2000): 29–60.

Chapter 2

1. Wonder is quoted in Crescent Dragonwagon, *Stevie Wonder* (New York: Putnam Publishing Group, 1977), 68–69.

2. Rosemarie Garland-Thomson, "The Politics of Staring: Visual Rhetorics of Disability in Popular Photography," in *Disability Studies: Enabling the Humanities,* edited by Sharon L. Snyder, Brenda Jo Brueggemann, and Rosemarie Garland-Thomson (New York: Modern Language Association of America, 2002), 56.

3. Michel Foucault, "Nietzsche, Genealogy, History," in *Language, Counter memory, Practice,* edited by D. F. Boucherd (Ithaca, NY: Cornell University Press, 1977), 153.

4. Alexander Weheliye, *Phonographies: Grooves in Sonic Afro-Modernity* (Durham, NC: Duke University Press, 2005), 110.

5. Quoted in ibid.

6. I think it's noteworthy that Wonder's own view of his "blindisms" has been good-natured acceptance. Indeed, as Terry Rowden points out, while Wonder had been pressured by Motown early in his career to stop his swaying movements because they were feared to be too conspicuous or "odd," they have instead become a trademark of his persona, especially as television appearances became an increasing way for Americans to get to know African American performers. Terry Rowden, *The Songs of Blind Folk: African American Musicians and the Cultures of Blindness* (Ann Arbor: University of Michigan Press, 2009), 114–15.

7. Greil Marcus, "Speaker to Speaker," *Artforum,* March 1987, 11.

8. Kodowo Eshun, "FUTURYTHMACHINE," in *The Popular Music Studies Reader*, edited by Andy Bennett, Barry Shank, and Jason Toynbee (London: Routledge, 2006), 294.

9. E. Patrick Johnson, "'Quare' Studies, or (Almost) Everything I Know about Queer Studies I Learned from my Grandmother," in *Black Queer Studies: A Critical Anthology*, edited by E. Patrick Johnson and Mae G. Henderson (Durham, NC: Duke University Press, 2005), 125.

10. Werner writes. "Where Aretha and Curtis kept their best music firmly grounded in the African American church, Stevie Wonder lit out joyously for territories usually associated with 'white' music. That's not to say he wasn't 'black enough.' His early hits 'Fingertips, Part 2' and 'I was Made to Love Her' infused Motown with pure gospel fervor at a time when the label was aggressively pushing a pop crossover strategy. It's just that Wonder's idea of blackness was as comfortable with the Beatles and New Age mysticism as it was with Duke Ellington and Detroit's Whitestone Baptist Church, where he sang in the choir. By the time he embarked on his beautifully baffling *Journey through the Secret Life of Plants* at the end of the Seventies, he'd made it clear that he was a true American original. Stevie took America at its word, and like Walt Whitman, set about remaking it in his own quirky and charismatic image." Craig Werner, *Higher Ground: Stevie Wonder, Aretha Franklin, Curtis Mayfield, and the Rise and Fall of American Soul* (New York: Crown Publishers, 2004), 6.

11. Ibid., 8.

12. Ibid., 6.

13. The revenge of the black nerd has been caught on film recently, as in the film *Drum Line*, in which a bookish band professor blows his improvisational street drummer student out of the water with old school rescorings of Wonder's "As If" and Earth Wind and Fire's "Getaway." And if we scoff at Urkel, the fictional preteen nerd on ABC's black family sitcom "Family Matters," we must in some ways acknowledge and perhaps fear the savvy rise to power of supernerd Condoleeza Rice, concert pianist and Russia wonk, who might represent another revenge of the black nerd. (On the often unexamined cultural construction of nerds as white, see Benjamin Nugent, "Who's a Nerd Anyway?," *New York Times Magazine*, July 29, 2007, 15.) Nugent suggests that while the nerd is the object of derision he or she is, at the same time, an important part of the narrative of the insistence and naturalization of white intellectual superiority. I would like to suggest that Wonder claims the space of nerdiness for black and brown people, something that has been furthered recently by Junot Díaz in *The Brief Wondrous Life of Oscar Wao* (New York: Riverhead Books, 2007).

14. Quoted in Sharon Davis, *Stevie Wonder: Rhythms of Wonder* (London: Robson Books, 2003), 131.

15. Stephen Holden, "The Last Flower Child," *Village Voice*, December 3, 1979, 53.

16. Davis, *Stevie Wonder*, 127.

17. Jeffrey Peisch, *Stevie Wonder* (New York: Ballantine Books, 1984), 121.

18. Rod Michalko, *The Mystery of the Eye and the Shadow of Blindness* (Toronto: University of Toronto Press, 1998).

19. Quoted in Davis, *Stevie Wonder*, 33.

20. Garland-Thomson, "The Politics of Staring."

21. Douglas C. Baynton's "Disability and the Justification of Inequality in American

History," in *The New Disability History: American Perspectives* (New York: New York University Press, 2001), 33–57, links disability and justification of inequality in the big citizenship debates of the nineteenth and early twentieth centuries: women's suffrage, African American freedom and civil rights, and the restriction of immigration. "When categories of citizenship were questioned, challenged, and disrupted, disability was called on to clarify and define who deserved, and who was deservedly excluded from, citizenship" (33). Illustrative is Edmund Burke's attack on the French Revolution rhetoric that contrasts the natural constitution of the body politic and the monstrosity caused by the revolution in ways that are both gendered (as Joan Scott has argued) and reliant on notions of disability. See for example, the repeated use of blindness to evoke the ignorance of the people: "'blind prejudice,' actions taken 'blindly,' 'blind followers,' and 'blind obedience'" (35). While blind schools, organizations, and institutions emerged in the twentieth century to help train blind people to be functional citizens, they were often discouraged from marriage and independent living.

Developing evolutionary discourse, and its emerging standardizations of "normal" and "abnormal" bodies, became a regular tool of racism, in which blacks and other nonwhites were often linked to people with disabilities as "evolutionary laggards and throwbacks" (3). Baynton points to prominent doctors, as well as politicians, who used the language of disability in the defense of slavery. John C. Calhoun, a senator from South Carolina, for example, "thought it a powerful argument in defense of slavery that the 'number of deaf and dumb, blind, idiots, and insane, of the negroes in the States that have changed the ancient relation between the races' was seven times higher than in the slave states" (37–38). In the international eugenics movement of the early twentieth, racial and bodily deviances were often conflated, resulting in theories and policies to classify disabled bodies and restrict their access to public institutions and privileges like marriage, reproduction, jobs, immigration, and the right to live in unsegregated communities. Susan L. Snyder and David T. Mitchell, *Cultural Locations of Disability* (Chicago: University of Chicago Press, 2006), 113. Films like *The Black Stork* (1917) warned early cinema audiences of the moral dangers of attempting to save the lives of "defective" babies, including crippled black children. One such baby in the film was the product of a hereditary disease passed along in a white family line by a grandfather's liaison with a "vile filthy slave." See Martin S. Pernick's study of this film and its context, *The Black Stork: Eugenics and the Death of "Defective" Babies in American Medicine and Motion Pictures since 1915* (New York: Oxford University Press, 1996), 144. Pernick points out that in its 1927 release, the "filthy black slave" is replaced with an "unclean white servant girl" (144). Likewise, Garland-Thomson suggests, "[J]ust as the dominant culture's ideal self requires ideological figures of the woman to confirm its masculinity and of the black to assure its whiteness, the figure of the disabled body becomes an important definitive tool for white, normative sexual citizens, from The Venus Hottentot to Captain Ahab: The freak, the cripple, the invalid, the disabled— like the quadroon and the homosexual—are representational, taxonomical products that naturalize a norm comprised of accepted bodily traits and behaviors registering social power and status." Rosemarie Garland-Thomson, *Extraordinary Bodies: Figuring Physical Disability in American Culture and Literature* (New York: Columbia University Press, 1997), 44.

22. Davis, *Stevie Wonder,* 46.

23. On Wonder's "declaration of independence from Motown, see Nelson George's *Where Did Our Love Go: The Rise and Fall of the Motown Sound* (London: Omnibus Press, 1986), 178–83. For a detailed analysis of the new contract's impact on his creative direction afterward, see Joel Selvin, "Stevie Wonder: Mojo," in *Da Capo Best Music Writing, 2004,* edited by Mickey Hart and Paul Bresnick (Cambridge, MA: Da Capo Press, 2004).

24. See the descriptions of the lesbian bar scene in Greenwich Village in the 1950s in Audre Lorde, *Zami: A New Spelling of My Name—a Biomythography* (Freedom, CA: Crossing Press, 1982); and Ray Charles's joyful description of "pumping the prime" in Ray Charles and David Ritz, *Brother Ray: Ray Charles' Own Story* (Cambridge, MA: Da Capo Press, [1978] 2004), 54.

25. Dragonwagon, *Stevie Wonder,* 72.

26. Kobena Mercer, "Monster Metaphors: Notes on Michael Jackson's *Thriller,*" in *Welcome to the Jungle: New Positions in Black Cultural Studies* (New York: Routledge, 1994).

27. Jason King, "Toni Braxton, Disney, and Thermodynamics," *TDR: The Drama Review* 46, no. 3 (Fall 2002), 54–81; see especially 55–58.

28. In their recent study of Miles Davis and John Coltrane, *Clawing at the Limits of Cool* (New York: St. Martin's Press, 2008), Farah Jasmine Griffin and Salim Washington compare the two musician's contrasting responses to the persona of cool in their performance styles and philosophical and spiritual trajectories.

29. In Brenda Dixon Gottschild's, *Digging the Africanist Presence in American Performance: Dance and Other Contexts.* New York: Praeger, 1998, she differentiates between a European aesthetic of cool aloofness and detachment and a specifically Africanist aesthetic that I also see in the work of Davis and Glover: "It is seen in the asymmetrical walk of African American males, which shows an attitude of carelessness cultivated with a calculated aesthetic clarity. It resides in the disinterested (in the philosophical sense, as opposed to the uninterested), detached, mask-like face of the drummer or dancer whose body and energy may be working fast, hard, and hot, but whose face remains cool. Conversely, it may be expressed as a brilliant smile, a laugh, a grimace, a verbal expression that seems to come out of nowhere to break, intercept, or punctuate the established mood by momentarily displaying its opposite and, thus, mediating a balance. It is through such oppositions, asymmetries, and radical juxtapositions that the cool aesthetic manifests luminosity or brilliance" (17).

30. Audre Lorde, "The Uses of the Erotic: The Erotic as Power," in *Sister Outsider: Essays and Speeches* (Freedom, CA Crossing Press, 1984), 53–59.

31. Indeed, Terry Rowden points out that Eddie Murphy was even considered for a starring role in a biopic about Wonder, reflecting the degree to which Wonder's iconography has become entangled with Murphy's. The film has not yet come to fruition, a possible reflection, Rowden suggests, of "Murphy's and his consultants' realization of the potential for embarrassment and critical backlash that a feature-length extension of Murphy's controversial impersonation of the singer might have caused. The project's failure may also have been influenced by the growing power of the disability rights community to bring negative attention to such cavalier disregard of their sensibili-

ties and concerns as Murphy's performances seemed to reveal" (Rowden, *The Songs of Blind Folk,* 115).

32. Robert McRuer, *Crip Theory: Cultural Signs of Queerness and Disability* (New York: New York University Press, 2006), 2.

33. Robert F. Reid-Pharr, *Black Gay Man: Essays* (New York: New York University Press, 2001), 103.

34. Garland-Thomson, *The Politics of Staring,* 57.

35. Martin Welton , "Seeing Nothing: Now Hear This . . . ," in *The Senses in Performance,* edited by Sally Banes and Andrew Lepecki (New York: Routledge, 2007), 151.

36. Carla Hall, "In the Key of Green: Stevie Wonder Plants New Seed of Melody," *Washington Post,* December 5, 1979, B6.

37. Peter Tompkins and Christopher Bird, *The Secret Life of Plants* (New York: Harper & Row, 1973), 8.

38. Richard Doyle, "Finding Animals with Plant Intelligence: Attention, Doctores, Mysteries." Box.net. July 31, 2009. Web. (April 12, 2010), 9.

39. If in traditional views of film soundtracks and scores the music is a modifier of the image, music scholar Royal S. Brown has pointed out that postmodern theory has challenged the patriarchal hierarchy of signifier over signified. Brown suggests a shift in the 1960s of the relationship between film image and preexisting music on a non-diegetic music track. Brown considers the use of classical music scores in post-1960 films like Ingmar Bergman's *Through a Glass Darkly* (1961, Bach's *Solo Cello Suite No. 2*) or Stanley Kubrick's *2001: A Space Odyssey* (1969, diverse works) where the scores "no longer function purely as backing for key emotional situations, but rather exist as a kind of parallel emotional/aesthetic universe." Royal S. Brown, *Overtones and Undertones: Reading Film Music* (Berkeley: University of California Press, 1994), 239–40. Reconsidering the relation between soundtrack and image is especially pertinent to *Journey to the Secret Life of Plants* given the unavailability of the film to most audiences after its initial limited release.

40. Rickey Vincent, *Funk: The Music, the People, and the Rhythm of the One* (New York: St. Martin's Press, 1996), 4.

41. See of course, Orlando Patterson's *Slavery and Social Death: A Comparative Study* (Cambridge, MA: Harvard University Press, 1992), for the definitive discussion of social death in slavery; and Sharon Patricia Holland's *Raising the Dead: Readings of Death and (Black) Subjectivity* (Durham, NC: Duke University Press, 2000), for a discussion of its continued and often generative relevance in black culture.

42. Tricia Rose, *Black Noise: Rap Music and Black Culture in Contemporary America* (Hanover, NH: Wesleyan University Press, 1994), 21. See Rose's chapter "'All Aboard the Night Train': Flow, Layer, and Rupture in Post-industrial New York" for an expansive discussion of the links between style and socioeconomic contexts of early hip-hop culture (21–61).

43. Greg Tate, "He Is Truly Free Who Is Free from the Need to Be Free: A Survey and Consideration of Black Male Genius," in *Black Male: Representations of Masculinity in American Art,* edited by Thelma Golden (New York: Whitney Museum of Art, 1995), 118–19.

44. Greg Tate, "Cult Nats Meets Freaky-Deke," first published in the *Village Voice* in

1992 and collected in his *Flyboy in the Buttermilk: Essays on Contemporary America* (New York: Simon and Schuster, 1992), 198–220.

45. She stakes Billie Holiday's place in the pantheon of black, mostly jazz geniuses in Farah Jasmine Griffin, *In Search of Billie Holiday: If You Can't Be Free, Be a Mystery* (New York: Ballantine Books, 2001), 1–2.

46. Quoted in Stanley Crouch, *Considering Genius: Writings on Jazz* (New York: Basic Civitas Books, 2006), 47.

47. For a discussion of the powerful grip of destruction in the lives of black male geniuses, see Tate, "He Is Truly Free"; and Sharon Patricia Holland, "Bill T. Jones, Tupac Shakur, and the (Queer) Art of Death," *Callaloo* 23, no. 1 (Winter 2000): 384–93.

48. Quoted in Tate, "He Is Truly Free," 111.

49. Crouch, *Considering Genius,* 5.

50. Rowden, *The Songs of Blind Folk,* 86.

51. Steve Waksman, "Black Sound, Black Body: Jimi Hendrix, the Electric Guitar, and the Meanings of Blackness," in *The Popular Music Studies Reader,* edited by Andy Bennett, Barry Shank, and Jason Toynbee (London: Routledge, 2006), 64.

52. Wonder's use of ARP, Moog, and other synthesizers to expand his sound is documented in Trevor Pinch and Frank Trocco's cultural history of the synthesizer, *Analog Days* (Cambridge, MA: Harvard University Press, 2002), esp. 182–86. Wonder was even featured in an advertisement for the ARP 2600 in the early 1970s, along with rocker Peter Townshend (267).

53. In a Post-Soul, "cultural mulatto" move, Wonder cites the Beatles' *Sergeant Pepper's Lonely Hearts Club Band* and Marvin Gaye's "What's Going On" as two of his most important inspirations for expanding his sound and structure in his 1970s work. Of the Beatles, Wonder writes, "I just dug the effects they got, like echoes and the voice things, the writing, like 'for the benefit of Mr. Kite.' I just said, why can't I? I wanted to do something else, go other places" (quoted in Werner, *Higher Ground,* 148).

54. Waksman, "Black Sound, Black Body," 70.

55. Wonder worked with film producer Michael Braun for three years on the creation of the score. Wonder would sit at a piano or synthesizer with a pair of headphones. In one ear, Braun would explain the film sequences in meticulous detail. In the other ear, an engineer would count down the time for each scene. At the same time, Wonder would play his musical ideas, taping them as he went (Peisch, *Stevie Wonder,* 120–21). Once the film was edited, Wonder himself remixed the soundtrack, adding an additional layer of ambient sounds from nature. Since Wonder lost his sight at birth, he was creating a soundtrack for plants and other creatures that he had never seen. But this freed him from a more literal interpretation. Michael Braun comments that this score would be an especially challenging process for any musician because it deals with things rarely seen onscreen: "[T]here are no standard ways of composing music for those things, like seeds sprouting or the Venus flytrap catching a bug. I bet a lot of veteran composers wouldn't know what to do with those sequences—except in the most mundane, literalistic way. But Stevie did. He's uncanny" (Davis, *Stevie Wonder,* 128).

56. E. Patrick Johnson points to the risks involved in Riggs's inclusion of his nakedness in *Black Is, Black Ain't* and ways that Riggs's nakedness is open to the dangers of misreading as "hypermasculine," on the one hand, and fragile and the site of (AIDS)

trauma, on the other. At the same time Riggs's performance insists on reminding the film's viewers of his fleshiness, his status as a site of being as well as becoming (Johnson, "'Quare' Studies," 145–46).

Chapter 3

1. I see in this film a yearning for freedom in public space that was becoming increasingly rare in cities like New York in the Post-Soul era. Robin D. G. Kelley, in *Yo' Mama's Disfunktional! Fighting the Culture Wars in Urban America* (Boston: Beacon Press, 1997), points to the ways that budget cuts in the post-civil-rights era, as well as as "the militarization of urban life," have shrunk such spaces for free play in parks, schoolyards, and other spaces.

> Beginning in the 1970's, a wave of public recreational service employees were either furloughed, discharged, or allowed to retire without replacement; the service and maintenance of parks and playgrounds was cut back substantially; many facilities were eliminated or simply deteriorated; and the hours of operation were drastically reduced. During the mid-1970's, for instance, Cleveland's recreation department had to close down almost $50 million dollars worth of facilities. In New York City, municipal appropriations for parks dropped by more than $40 million between 1974 and 1980—a sixty-percent cut in real dollars. Staff cutbacks were even more drastic: between the late 1960's and 1979, the number of park employees dropped from almost 6,100 to 2,600. To make matters worse, a growing number of public schoolyards in inner city communities have become inaccessible during after-school hours. (50–51)

2. "The One," coined by James Brown, is one of THE central musical aspects of funk: the use of the downbeat at the beginning of every bar. But as Arthur Kempton points out, its meaning acquired wider symbolic meaning over time: "By the late 1970's, 'on the one' was a descriptor as well—applied to a good meal, a favorable outcome, a beat, a timely insight, an admired performance, or life in a balanced state." Arthur Kempton, *Boogaloo: The Quintessence of American Popular Music* (New York: Pantheon Books, 2003), 394.

3. P-Funk's often futuristic theatricality and gender-bending aesthetics could quite possibly have been influenced by the simultaneous emergence of glam rock in the late 1960s and early 1970s, though I haven't found any writings or interviews explicitly making the connection. On glam's theatrical spirit and gender contrariety, see Philip Auslander's *Performing Glam Rock: Gender and Theatricality in Popular Music* (Ann Arbor: University of Michigan Press, 2006). George Clinton includes punk and sometimes glam rocker Iggy Pop as a friend and collaborator in P-Funk's early days, and for a time they shared a manager. Iggy and Clinton even joked about staging a marriage between the two of them for publicity, but the story was never picked up by the media. See Dave Marsh, *For the Record: George Clinton and P-Funk, An Oral History* (New York: Avon Books, 1998), 38.

4. George Clinton, quoted in Marsh, *For the Record*, 8.

5. In the music of Outkast, we see the strong influence of Parliament/Funkadelic in the band's use of psychedelic and rock, as well as funk, in their carnivalesque stage performances and sexually playful lyrics. André 3000 has cited Funkadelic's "Maggot Brain" as one of his biggest musical influences. He has even been spotted wearing a diaper onstage, like Gary Shider. But I'd argue that while the members of Outkast have the sartorial and musical playfulness of George Clinton, they differ in their business sense, and in their commitment to the truly funky, found/dirty/grimy fashion of the earlier group. In many ways, I see P-Funk as courting a kind of improvisational style—a bit of "country" that is not afraid to show its seams. (Here I'm thinking of a parallel to José Muñoz's discussion of Vaginal Cream Davis's embrace of "country" in *Disidentification*.) André 3000, on the other hand, openly embraces a slicker entrepreneurial spirit—see, for example, his luxury clothing line, Benjamin Bixby. Thanks to Deborah Whaley for her suggestions on the Outkast/P-Funk connection.

6. According to Dean Rudland's liner notes to the 2005 reissue of *Cosmic Slop*, for many in the band, including lead singer Gary Shider, *Cosmic Slop* attempted a more commercial departure from the earlier *Maggot Brain* and *America Eats Its Young*. Shider recalls that the song "Cosmic Slop" was a big hit in Washington, DC, and that there was even a dance to it, though the single released as a 45, never made the charts.

7. Funk scholar Amy Nathan Wright notes the centrality of identification with working-class blackness in P-Funk's music in her essay "A Philosophy of Funk: The Politics and Pleasure of a Parliamentfunkadelicment Thang!," in *The Funk Era and Beyond: New Perspectives on Black Popular Culture*, edited by Tony Bolden (New York: Palgrave Macmillan, 2008), 33–50. Wright argues that P-Funk's vision of "individual and collective freedom and equality" linked spirituality, sci-fi images, and psychedelia to a worldview privileging black working-class experiences. She points to the song "What Is Soul," which she says "celebrates images typically associated with poor blacks, defining soul as 'a hamhock in your Cornflakes,' 'rusty ankles and ashy kneecaps,' 'chitlins foo yung,' and finally, 'you baby.'" The band's message of black working-class pride, challenged government officials and social scientists such as Patrick Moynihan, "who had deemed blacks a 'pathological' 'underclass' trapped in a 'cycle of poverty' that resulted from this population's values and behaviors" (38).

8. Ronald "Stozo" Edwards, quoted in Marsh, *For the Record*, 73.

9. Sidney Barnes, quoted in ibid., 40.

10. Haki R. Madhubuti, quoted in Phillip Brian Harper, *Are We Not Men? Masculine Anxiety and the Problem of African American Identity* (New York: Oxford University Press, 1996), 197.

11. We might note that Haki R. Madhubuti's thinking about black LGBTQ politics has evolved and opened over the course of recent years. In his 2009 poem "Liberation Narratives," Madhubuti writes against the closeting of same-sex desiring men and women within the black community, concluding, "They were born that way, / enough said." Haki R. Madhubuti, *Liberation Narratives: New and Collected Poems, 1966–2009* (Chicago: Third World Press, 2009), 25.

12. In his essay "Tearing the Goat's Flesh," Robert F. Reid-Pharr speaks to the terror for Cleaver and others represented by the black gay male subject, in his ability to give voice to the larger idea that black masculinity is conceptually queer, writing that "black gay men represent in modern American literature the reality that there is

no normal blackness, no normal masculinity to which the black subject, American or otherwise, might refer. Indeed, Orlando Patterson, Henry Louis Gates, and Paul Gilroy, among others, have argued that the black has been conceptualized in modern (slave) culture as an inchoate, irrational nonsubject, as the chaos that both defines and threatens the borders of logic, individuality, basic subjectivity. In that schema, all blacks become interchangeable, creating among the population a sort of continual restlessness, a terror." Robert F. Reid-Pharr, *Black Gay Man: Essays* (New York: New York University Press, 2001), 103. I'd argue that P-Funk's play with gender norms takes this moment of inchoateness and runs with it, pushes it forward as a space of imaginative freedom.

13. Barbara Smith, ed., *Home Girls: A Black Feminist Anthology* (New York: Kitchen Table: A Women of Color Press, 1983), xl.

14. Harold Cruse, *The Crisis of the Negro Intellectual: A Historical Analysis of the Failure of Black Leadership* (New York: Quill, [1967] 1984), 33.

15. Ibid., 196.

16. Ibid., 298.

17. Ibid., 297.

18. DeWayne "Blackbyrd" McKnight, quoted in Marsh, *For the Record*, 45.

19. George Clinton, quoted in ibid., 23–24.

20. See Sue-Ellen Case's discussion of gender masquerade in "Toward a Butch-Femme Aesthetic," in *Making a Spectacle*, edited by Lynda Hart (Ann Arbor: University of Michigan Press, 1989), 291.

21. See Patricia Williams, "Meditations on Masculinities," *Callaloo* 19, no. 4 (Fall 1996): 814–22. Williams meditates on journalist Brent Staples's description in his memoir *Parallel Time* of his coping strategy of "Scattering the Pigeons"—watching and laughing as fearful white couples scatter to opposite parts of the sidewalk when he fails to cross the street or step aside. Williams laments, "The gentle journalist who stands on the street corner and howls. What upside down craziness, this paradoxical logic of having to debase oneself in order to retrieve one's sanity in this remaindered marketplace" (816). This "Scattering the Pigeons" game becomes a touchstone for queer black male critic E. Patrick Johnson as well, in his stage show *Strange Fruit*. See E. Patrick Johnson, "Strange Fruit: A Performance about Identity Politics," *TDR: The Drama Review* 47, no. 2 (Summer 2003): 88–116.

22. Kathryn Bond Stockton, *Beautiful Bottom, Beautiful Shame: Where "Black" Meets "Queer"* (Durham, NC: Duke University Press, 2006), 24.

23. See John Corbett's comparative analysis of Clinton, Sun Ra, and Perry and their strategic embrace of "disorientation" in his chapter "Brother from Another Planet: The Space Madness of Lee 'Scratch' Perry, Sun Ra, and George Clinton," in *Extended Play: Sounding Off from John Cate to Dr. Funkenstein* (Durham, NC: Duke University Press, 1994), 7–25. Corbett says that all three share an iconography built on an image of disorientation, which then becomes a space to critique social marginalization: "Staking their claim on this ec-centric margin—a place that simultaneously eludes and frightens the oppressive, centered subjectivity—the three of them reconstitute it as a space of creation" (18).

24. George Clinton once said, "Soul is from Church. But funk came from the people who didn't have enough money to buy shoes to go to church, and had to work on Sun-

day." Quoted in Tony Green, "Tracing Funk's Sources," *St. Petersburg Times,* November 27, 1994, 1F.

25. These references are deep within the DNA of P-funk's music, but George Clinton explicitly references the importance of recognizing funk's deep roots in black culture in the face of the pressures of crossover on his 1986 satiric solo album *R & B Skeletons in the Closet.* When interviewed about the album, Clinton comments, "In order to have that crossover appeal, the companies tell the artists to use less bass or don't say the word "funk" or something like that. So you can get played on pop radio. Once you do that to sell all those records you start gearing your music for that market. Before you know it, all the R & B that you had in you is completely hidden." Quoted in a review by Robert Palmer, "The Pop Life: Clinton's Satire Has a Bite," *New York Times,* May 7, 1986, C26.

26. Eve Zibat, "A Summer Day of Chocolate Jam," *Washington Post,* July 3, 1978, B1.

27. P-Funk's melding of funk and psychedelia could also have a disquieting effect on normative notions of black nationhood. In *Turn on Your Mind,* Jim Derogatis characterizes psychedelic sound as including often ambivalent, playful lyrics and a sound that brings "a loss of ego or depersonalization and sense of physical connection to everything one sears or hears." Jim Derogatis, *Turn on Your Mind: Four Decades of Great Psychedelic Rock* (New York: Hal Leonard, 2003), 11.

28. According to Robin D. G. Kelley, "Throughout the seventies and eighties, the black male prison population increased threefold." Robin D. G. Kelley, "Into the Fire: 1970 to the Present," in *To Make Our World Anew: A History of African Americans,* edited by Robin D. G. Kelley and Earl Lewis (Oxford: Oxford University Press, 2000), 284. For more on the continuing spiral of deindustrialization, community dismantling, and growth in prisons since 1982, as well as grassroots resistance, see Ruth Wilson Gilmore, *Golden Gulag: Prisons, Surplus, Crisis, and Opposition in Globalizing California* (Berkeley: University of California Press, 2007).

29. For a cogent analyses of black manhood, gender, and heterosexuality, see Mark Anthony Neal, *New Black Man* (New York: Routledge, 2006); Athena Mutua's collection *Progressive Black Masculinities* (New York: Routledge, 2006); Rudolph P. Byrd and Beverly Guy Sheftall, *Traps: African American Men on Gender and Sexuality* (Bloomington: Indiana University Press, 2001); and Harper, *Are We Not Men?*

30. George Clinton, quoted in Marsh, *For the Record, 10.*

31. See Phillip Brian Harper, "The Evidence of Felt Intuition: Minority Experience, Everyday Life, and Critical Speculative Knowledge," in *Queer Black Studies: A Critical Anthology,* edited by E. Patrick Johnson and Mae G. Henderson (Durham, NC: Duke University Press, 2005), 106–23.

32. I hear echoes in Clinton's fantasy of aquaboogieing and Luce Irigaray's description of women's diffuse sexual pleasure and logics in *This Sex Which Is Not One* (Ithaca, NY: Cornell University Press, 1985): "She experiences pleasure almost everywhere . . . [and] the geography of her pleasure is much more diversified, more multiple in its differences, more complex, more subtle." Quoted in Ann Rosalind Jones, "Writing the Body: Toward an Understanding of l'Ecriture Feminine," in *Feminisms: An Anthology of Literary Theory and Criticism,* edited by Robyn R. Warhol and Diane Price Herndl (New Brunswick, NJ: Rutgers University Press, 1997), 372.

33. I owe much inspiration from Kodowo Eshun's writing on P-Funk's instrumen-

tality and the music's effects on our relationship to our bodies in *More Brilliant Than the Sun: Adventures in Sonic Fiction* (London: Quartet Books, 1998). Eshun captures the erotics of abduction in P-Funk's *Clones of Dr. Funkenstein,* stating that "P-Funk compels you to succumb to the inhuman, to be abducted and love it. Funk gets drawn out of the body, an entelechy harvested by an alien force. . . . P-Funk is the gladallover suffusion of Funkentelechy, the enjoyment of mutation. Instead of resisting alien extraction, dancing turns it into a gift, turns into the joy of being abducted" (14). Ricky Vincent's definitive chapter on the P-Funk empire in *Funk: The Music, the People, and the Rhythm of the One* (New York: St. Martin's Press, 1996) takes some time to note the disconcerting sexiness of Bootsy Collins's music, as an important contribution to the band. He calls the period that Bootsy and Rubber Band joined the P-Funk empire "the nastayest and most liberated form of P-Funk, symbolically the exposed genitals of the P-Funk vibe." In Vincent's description, in songs like "Munchies for Your Love," Collins combines "a giddy, childlike geepiness" with the "orgiastic bass effects" of "an erotic troubadour"—certainly an eccentric combination (243). Ann Danielsen's *Presence and Pleasure: The Funk Grooves of James Brown and Parliament* (Middletown, CT: Wesleyan University Press, 2006) takes an ethnomusicological approach to beats, time, and pleasure in P-Funk's music. In "A Philosophy of Funk: The Politics and Pleasure of a Parliafunkadelicment Thang!" in *The Funk Era and Beyond: New Perspectives on Black Popular Culture,* edited by Tony Bolden (New York: Palgrave Macmillan, 2008), Amy Nathan Wright discusses the band's sexual politics postsexual revolution. But these writers don't discuss the implications of P-Funk's experiments with gender for their constructions of pleasure.

34. On Parliament/Funkadelic's Afrofuturism, and the politics of black utopia or dystopia in the music, see Eshun, *More Brilliant Than the Sun,* especially 53–54; Kodowo Eshun, "Further Considerations of Afrofuturism," *CR: The New Centennial Review.* 3, no. 2 (2003): 287–402; Corbett, *Extended Play,* 7–24; Paul Gilroy's brief discussion in *The Black Atlantic: Modernity and Double-Consciousness* (Cambridge, MA: Harvard University Press, 1993), 202–3; Mark Anthony Neal, *What the Music Said: Black Popular Music and Black Public Culture* (New York: Routledge, 1999), 102–3; Michael C. Ladd, "Hard Core Jollies in the Himalayas, Staring at the Cosmic Slop: The Mothership Connection between Triple and Quadruple Consciousness," in *Rip It Up: Black Experience in Rock 'n' Roll,* edited by Kandia Crazy Horse (New York: Palgrave Macmillan, 2004), 71–84.

35. On P-Funk, techno, and automation, see George Lipsitz, *Footsteps on the Dark: The Hidden Histories of Popular Music* (Minneapolis: University of Minnesota Press, 2007), 240–45; Andrew Bartlett, "Airshafts, Loudspeakers, and the Hip-Hop Sample: Context and African American Musical Aesthetics," *That's the Joint! The Hip-Hop Studies Reader,* edited by Murray Forman and Mark Anthony Neal (New York: Routledge, 2004), 399; and Arthur Kempton, *Boogaloo: The Quintessence of American Popular Music* (New York: Pantheon Books, 2003), 382–414. Clinton's legal cases against copyright violations and sampling have been profiled in the recent documentary *Copyright Criminals* (2008), directed by Benjamin Franzen.

36. Indeed, later in "Confessions of a Nice Negro," Kelley glances at but doesn't fully engage the sometime gender incongruity of black gangster style: "Some of the hardest brothas on my block in West Pasadena kept their perms in pink rollers and hairnets. It

was not unusual to see young black men in public with curlers, tank-top undershirts, sweatpants, black mid-calf dress socks, and Stacey Adams shoes, hanging out on the corner or on the basketball court. And we all knew that these brothas were not to be messed with. (The rest of the world probably knows it by now, too, since black males in curlers are occasionally featured on 'Cops' and 'America's Most Wanted' as notorious drug dealers or heartless pimps.)" (15).

37. Ultimately, I'm thinking of Cathy Cohen's directive to reexamine queerness through the lens of nonnormative black heterosexuality in order "to think about how we might construct a new political identity that is truly liberating, transformative, and inclusive of all those who stand on the outside of the dominant constructed norm of state-sanctioned white middle-and-upper-class heterosexuality." Cathy Cohen, "Punks, Bulldaggers, and Welfare Queens: The Radical Potential of Queer Politics?," in *Black Queer Studies: A Critical Anthology,* edited by E. Patrick Johnson and Mae G. Henderson (Durham, NC: Duke University Press, 2005), 25.

38. See Danielsen's analysis of "Give Up the Funk," in *Presence and Pleasure,*122. While she doesn't offer a specifically gendered reading of funk performance, Danielson usefully suggests that funk has been read uncritically as a "primativist" sound, or "body music," affirming a notion of a "pure blackness" that nonetheless overlooks the rhythmic complexities of the style. Such readings confirm the idea of black music as "unmediated bodily expression" and reduce the black body as merely sexual (20–28).

39. On the gendered dynamics of local funk scenes, see Scot Brown, "A Land of Funk: Dayton Ohio," in *The Funk Era and Beyond: New Perspectives on Black Popular Culture,* edited by Tony Bolden (New York: Palgrave MacMillan, 2008), 82. On women navigating the sexist and often homophobic worlds of funk, see Carmen Phelps, "Living the Funk: Lifestyle, Lyricism, and Lessons in Modern and Contemporary Art of Black Women," in *The Funk Era and Beyond: New Perspectives on Black Popular Culture,* edited by Tony Bolden (New York: Palgrave MacMillan, 2008), 187–91; and my own chapter on Meshell Ndegeocello in this book.

40. George Clinton, quoted in Wright, "A Philosophy of Funk," 3.

41. Rinaldo Walcott, "Reconstructing Manhood, or the Drag of Black Masculinity," *Small Ax* 13, no. 1 (2009): 75.

42. Ladd, "Hard Core Jollies in the Himalayas," 74.

43. Tony Bolden, "Theorizing the Funk: An Introduction" *The Funk Era and Beyond: New Perspectives on Black Popular Culture,* edited by Tony Bolden (New York: Palgrave Macmillan, 2008), 13–29, especially 15–17; Cheryl Keyes, "Funkin' with Bach: The Impact of Professor Longhair on Rock 'n' Roll," in *The Funk Era and Beyond: New Perspectives on Black Popular Culture,* edited by Tony Bolden (New York: Palgrave Macmillan, 2008), 213–26, especially 222–23.

44. See, for example, Gil Scott Heron's "Comment #1," on his first album, *Small Talk at 125 and Lenox* (1970): "America was a bastard the illegitimate daughter of the / mother country whose legs were then spread around the / world and a rapist known as freedom—free doom." Heron's "Comment #1" was recently sampled in Kanye West's "Who Will Survive in America" on *My Beautiful Dark Twisted Fantasy.*

45. Still, I suspect that any confessional aspect of the song is overshadowed by its sheer, lusty coolness. The song's hip rhythmic panting, deep-voiced "Dawg," and "bow

wow wow yippee yay" have been sampled by an amazing number of artists, most nota- bly Snoop Dogg in "Who Am I." In fact, this song has been sampled in over fifty songs and was subject of a 2007 copyright lawsuit between Clinton and his former produc- ers, Bridgeport (formally Westbound Records).

46. In his essay on quadruple consciousness and Funkadelic's *Cosmic Slop* in the context of US imperialism, "Hard Core Jollies in the Himalayas," Michael C. Ladd writes:

> It can be argued that black Americans are the only four-dimensional peo- ple on the planet. Double-consciousness is whipped up and beat down in every essay; I maintain that triple consciousness is the view that black American has of him-or-herself in a neocolonial context. One examines one's self as an oppressed person of color who, in a "third world" context shares an imperialist position with whites of the United States. Ugly but true. A fourth consciousness, however, allows the black American to re- invent him-/herself from space and therefore rearrange her/his gaze to that of the ultimate outsider and simultaneously insider. A fourth con- sciousness allows one to bypass the other three. . . . Fourth consciousness view exposes the absurdity of race and simultaneously continues to focus on the Diaspora. It runs the risk of slipping into universalism—"space people universal lover"—but the tradition is deeply connected to home and the soul. (79)

47. *Guardian* critic Tom Cox wrote in 2000, "Clinton has probably never written a boy-meets-girl song in his life. Boy-meets-girl-and-offers-her-some-intergalactic- urine, maybe, but not boy-meets-girl." Tom Cox, "Funkenstein Lives: George Clinton is 60, but He's as Barmy as Ever," *Guardian* (London), July 21, 2000, 14.

48. Corbett, *Extended Play*, 147.

49. Original Funkadelic bassist William "Billy Bass" Nelson and George Clinton recall a particular moment of revenge on Berry Gordy and Motown, while Clinton was apparently on LSD.

> BILLY BASS: "We found out that everybody from Motown was at that gig [at the Twenty Grand in Detroit one Christmas]. Berry Gordy's whole family had the front row. Well, nobody told George not to trip, 'cause we had a green light to do whatever we wanted to do in the Twenty Grand. He took off his clothes and jumped right down on Berry Gordy's table, and Berry Gordy's wife was there, and his mother and father. And told Berry to kiss his ass. 'You didn't sign me before, now kiss my ass!'"
>
> GEORGE: "No, hell naw. . . . Naw, I ain't do no 'kiss my ass'. Everbody tells those lies. . . . I was naked, probably. And I probably poured some wine over my head, then it dripped all down my dick, and as I run across all the tables in there—I don't know if Berry was there, but I know the fam- ily was there—I would run up and down the table, up the bar, and wine would drip down so everybody say it looked like I peed in everybody's drink. But I was too out of it to even know if I did it or not." (Marsh, *For the Record*, 62–63)

50. See Shane White and Graham White, *Stylin': African American Expressive Culture from Its Beginnings to the Zoot Suit* (Ithaca, NY: Cornell University Press, 1998); as well as Monica L. Miller, *Slaves to Fashion: Black Dandyism and the Styling of Black Diasporic Identity* (Durham, NC: Duke University Press, 2009).

51. Glenda R. Carpio, *Laughing Fit to Kill: Black Humor in the Fictions of Slavery* (New York: Oxford University Press, 2008). Carpio suggests that

> Through various modes of "conjuring," through gothic, grotesque, and absurdist comedies of the body, through stinging, satirical narrative defamiliarization, through hyperbole, burlesque and perhaps most important, through what Hortense Spillers might call the "cultural vestibularity" of racial stereotype itself, these black humorists have enacted oral, discursive, and corporeal rituals of redress with respect to the breach of slavery. (11–12)

52. Corbett, *Extended Play,* 13.

53. Bob DeDeckere, quoted in Marsh, *For the Record,* 109. At the same time, in songs like "U.S. Custom Coast Guard Dope Dog" and others, Clinton offers an explicit and heated critique of institutional powers of policing and commerce, suing and countersuing Warner Brothers to have control over the masters of his music, and at several points forming his own label to have more economic and creative control over his music. Clinton comments on his own, sometimes indirect strategies of critique.

> I keep it tongue in check, 'cause I ain't into preachin' and anything people got to get they got to be able to get it and able to think about it, they can't get it, jump up and do nothin' about it other than think, 'cause the minute you start to go crazy, they prepared to tear this country up. They don't care nothing 'bout this country. The people that's in charge is a very small number of bankers, federal reserve, secret organizations and shit like that. They don't care which country stand and which country go. They could care the fuck less about that. Matter of fact there's more money, 'cause they usually have a bank financin' both sides of any war. That's all it is. So it's a waste of hip-hop or rap or kids' energy to be pissed at a cop. Cop is a broke motherfucker! My thang is, I ain't gonna be mad at no mother broke as me. . . . There's always somebody pullin' strings in black and white situation. (Corbett, *Extended Play,* 283–84)

54. Quoted in David Gonzalez, "Is There Life after Jimi?," *Newsweek,* April 30, 1990, 68.

55. William Nelson, quoted in Marsh, *For the Record,* 32.

56. Anthropologist Aimee Cox, in her study of gender and the sexuality of black women and girls, notes the use of the phrase "turned out" to mean opening oneself up to the possibilities of a fluid sexuality in her essay "Thugs, Black Divas, and Gendered Aspirations," *Souls* 11, no. 2 (2009): 113–14. She writes, "Getting turned out does not necessarily mean that a young woman has taken on a new sexual identity but that she has . . . become open to the possibilities" (132).

57. See Eric Lott's classic *Love and Theft: Blackface Minstrelsy and the American Working Class* (New York: Oxford University Press, 1995), on white fetishization and

desire for blackness through minstrelsy, as well as Glenda R. Carpio's cogent analysis of resistant redress of such thievery in *Laughing Fit to Kill*, especially 24–25, on minstrelsy and black humor in particular.

58. Billy Bass Nelson describes in more detail this experience of being altered by listening to and playing with white rockers Vanilla Fudge (great name!) in an interview with Dave Marsh.

> We were playing at Sacred Heart College in Connecticut, and something happened that our equipment got delayed on the road, it never made it to the gig. Just so happened that Vanilla Fudge was on the gig with us— opening for us, okay? Vanilla Fudge, the opening act. And they let us use their equipment. The guitar player had a double-stack of Marshalls, and the bass player was using a triple-stack of S.V.T.s, amps, and the drummer had some set of great big oversized—I think those were the first fibes that we'd ever seen, fiberglass drums. That's how we found out we'd been using the wrong equipment all along for the sound we had and what we were trying to approach. We needed that Marshall, and I needed them S.V.T's. And within a few weeks, we had 'em. That's when we really changed from rhythm and blues, Motown wannabees into what we evolved into, the real Funkadelic. Those amps, and that big oversized set of drums Tiki had. (Marsh, *For the Record*, 33)

59. August Wilson, "Foreword," in *Speak My Name: Black Men on Masculinity and the American Dream*, edited by Don Belton (New York: Beacon Press, 1997), xi.

60. Marsh, *For the Record*, 41–42.

61. Ladd, "Hard Core Jollies in the Himalayas," 75–76.

62. David Mills, "The P-Funk Flashback: George Clinton Lands His Spaceship Here in D.C.," *Washington Post*, October 22, 1992, C1.

63. See "The Oppositional Gaze" in bell hooks, *Black Looks: Race and Representation* (Boston: South End Press, 1992), 115–31. Hooks might well add oppositional listening to her conceptualization of critical engagement here. She models oppositional listening in her critical work on hip-hop, including her essay "Sexism and Misogyny: Who Takes the Rap—Misogyny, Gangsta Rap, and *The Piano*," Z, February 1994, http://race.eserver.org/misogyny.html.

64. hooks, *Black Looks*, 116.

65. Ladd, "Hard Core Jollies in the Himalayas," 72.

66. Ibid.

67. Thomas Sayers Ellis, "From the Crib to the Coliseum: An Interview with Bootsy Collins," in *The Funk Era and Beyond: New Perspectives on Black Popular Culture*, edited by Tony Bolden (New York: Palgrave Macmillan, 2008), 91.

68. Alice Echols discusses James Brown's embrace of sophistication as a sartorial style in her essay "The Land of Somewhere Else: Refiguring James Brown in Seventies Disco," *Criticism* 50, no. 1 (Winter 2008): 19–41, especially 28–30. Despite his sometimes raw shouts and stripped-down beats, Brown saw smooth processed hair and expensive, well-cut suits as part of his performative stance of pride, and political and artistic cosmopolitanism and control.

69. Ellis, "From the Crib to the Coliseum," 92.

70. Indeed, in his queerly theatrical performance style, musical innovation, offbeat theories about the universe, often communal approach to bandleading, and longevity, George Clinton has much more in common with futuristic jazz great Sun Ra than with James Brown—a connection made by John Corbett in *Extended Play,* especially on pages 7–24. See also John Szwed's fantastic analysis of Sun Ra's life and performances in *Space Is the Place: The Lives and Times of Sun Ra* (New York: Da Capo Books, 1998).

71. Ellis, "From the Crib to the Coliseum," 95.

Chapter 4

1. Dale Peck, "Foreword." In *Queer 13: Lesbian and Gay Writers Recall the Seventh Grade,* edited by Clifford Chase (New York: William Morrow, 1998), xi.

2. Ibid., xii.

3. Audre Lorde, "The Uses of the Erotic: The Erotic as Power," in *Sister Outsider: Essays and Speeches* (Freedom, CA: Crossing Press, 1984), 53–54.

4. By the time Michael Jackson and his brothers signed with Motown, in 1968, his hometown of Gary, Indiana, had elected its first African American mayor, Richard G. Hatch, who would work on reversing Gary's institutionalized racism for the next twenty years. On the other hand, following the national pattern of Post-Soul deindustrialization happening nationally, over the arc of Jackson's career, Gary has seen a shaken economy, marked by white business flight and U.S. Steel's divestment of jobs. In 1987, the same year that Jackson recorded *Bad,* U.S. Steel jobs in Gary had shrunk from thirty thousand in the 1960s to six thousand. *Encyclopedia of Chicago,* http://en-cyclopedia.chicagohistory.org/pages/503.html. Since Jackson's death, tourism in Gary has increased, and a memorial and museum honoring him is in the works.

5. Nathaniel Mackey, "Cante Moro," in *Disembodied Poetics: Annals of the Jack Kerouac School,* edited by Anne Waldman and Andrew Schelling (Albuquerque: University of New Mexico Press, 1994), 79.

6. Francesca Royster, *Becoming Cleopatra: the Shifting Image of an Icon* (New York: Palgrave Macmillan, 2003), 5.

7. Roland Barthes, "The Grain of the Voice," in *Image, Music, Text,* translated by Stephen Heath (New York: Hill and Wang, 1978), 188.

8. Kobena Mercer, *Welcome to the Jungle: New Positions in Black Cultural Studies* (New York: Routledge, 1994), 310.

9. Riki Anne Wilchins, *Read My Lips: Sexual Subversion and the End of Gender* (Milford, CT: Firebrand Books, 1997), 133–34.

10. Leslie Feinberg, *Trans Liberation: Beyond Pink or Blue* (New York: Beacon Press, 1999), 9.

11. Kate Bornstein, *Gender Outlaw: On Men, Women, and the Rest of Us* (New York: Vintage, 1995), 13.

12. Ibid., 1.

13. Ibid., 4.

14. Philip M. Royster, personal Interview, September 10, 2004. For more on the spiritual roots of black popular musical performance, see also Philip M. Royster, "Hammer's 'You Can't Touch This': Rapper as Shaman for a Band of Dancers of the

Spirit," in *The Emergence of Black and the Emergence of Rap,* special issue of *Black Sacred Music: A Journal of Theomusicology* 5, no. 1 (Spring 1991): 60–67.

15. Michael Jackson, *Moonwalk* (New York: Doubleday, 1988), 161.

16. Ibid., 38–39.

17. See Ernest Hardy, "Michael Jackson: Bless His Soul," *Blood Beats,* June 26, 2009. http://earnesthardy.blogspot.com/2009/06/Michael-Jackson-bless-his-soul.html.

18. Fred Moten, "'Words Won't Go There': An Interview with Fred Moten by Charles Henry Rowell," *Callaloo* 27, no. 4 (2004): 957.

19. Margo Jefferson, *On Michael Jackson* (New York: Vintage Books, 2007), 69.

20. Ibid., 66–67.

21. Ibid., 70.

22. We might note the dominant themes of control, loss, and paranoia haunting several of the love songs sung by male vocalists that made *Billboard's* Top 25 Hot Hits of 1969, the year that the Jackson 5 recorded "Who's Lovin' You": the Temptations' "I Can't Get Next to You" (#3), the Rolling Stones' "Honky Tonk Women" (#4), Tom Jones's "I'll Never Fall in Love Again" (#8), the Foundation's "Build Me Up Buttercup (#9), Three Dog Night's "One" (#11), and Elvis Presley's "Suspicious Minds" (#18).

23. Certainly anyone fully alert and using the Internet for at least the last decade would be aware of the link between Michael Jackson and children, whether in terms of the 2003 accusations of child molestation and his trial and acquittal, or his own embrace of childlikeness and the culture of childhood at the Neverland Ranch, and the connection between the two, explored in Martin Bashir's documentary interview *Living with Michael Jackson: A Tonight Special* (2003). Still, Jackson's use of childhood as a space of freedom is a topic ripe for analysis. Certainly one could look at Jackson's fantastic construction of childlike home spaces, including Neverland Ranch; his official and unofficial participation in children's charities; his fierce (and sometimes odd) protection of his own children; and his use of children as images of innocence and integrity in songs/videos like "Black or White" and "The Earth Song." Margo Jefferson's *On Michael Jackson* has a highly suggestive final chapter on the child molestation trial and Jackson's own ghosts (106–38).

24. Jackson, *Moonwalk,* 81.

25. Indeed, as Robin D. G. Kelley points out, racial discrimination in the post-civil-rights period has continued, often taking blatant forms of violence: the Ku Klux Klan tripled its membership by the late 1970s; reported hate crimes, especially on college campuses, tripled between 1982 and 1989; and police killings and nonlethal violence continued around the country. But more subtle forms of racism also continued to grow, including the steady dismantling of legislative gains achieved by the civil rights movement. Cases like *Regents of the University of California v. Bakke* (1978) undermined the work of affirmative action decisions by claiming reverse discrimination. And the Reagan administration, beginning in 1980, saw to the slashing of expenditures of housing by 77 percent and education by 70 percent. Robin D. G. Kelley, "Looking Backward: African Americans in the Postindustrial Era," in *The Columbia Guide to African American History since 1939,* edited by Robert L. Harris Jr. and Rosalyn Terborg-Penn (New York: Columbia University Press, 2006), 101–19.

26. Jackson, *Moonwalk,* 96–97.

27. This experience is confirmed in Maureen Mahon's oral history of members

of the Black Rock Coalition, a Post-Soul generation of musicians who navigated the changing constraints of living spaces, social networks, and even radio musical formats in the 1970s and 1980s. Maureen Mahon, *Right to Rock: The Black Rock Coalition and the Cultural Politics of Race* (Durham, NC: Duke University Press, 2004). She interviews Angela, who grew up in the Midwest during the 1970s, who describes her family's response to her interest in rock.

> "I really got into rock just probably—honestly—by the old association breeds assimilation. I was surrounded by Caucasian teenagers who were listening to that and I dug it. . . . I had grown up on that kind of music. I was not into soul music or funk. The only time I really heard funk and soul was when I [visited] my father's side of the family, his brothers and sisters. . . . I would go to my aunts' houses and they would be listening to funk and they used to watch *Soul Train*—I used to watch *American Bandstand*. . . . One day I was just dancing—probably arrythmically—and my aunt looked at me and she went to my mother. She said, 'You know, we got to get some rhythm into Angela. She dances like a little white girl.'" (57)

28. Hilton Als, "Michael," *New York Review of Books,* August 13, 2009, 1.

29. José Esteban Muñoz, *Cruising Utopia: The Then and There of Queer Futurity* (New York: New York University Press, 2009), 1.

30. In his recent study of Michael Jackson's biography and the material culture that surrounds him, *Michael Jackson's Treasures,* Jason King includes multiple photos that capture Jackson's stunning ability to create shifting selves that nevertheless convey a sense of intimacy before the camera: cherubic and bubbly as a twelve year old; pensive and somewhat rebellious on the cover of *Ben;* as an outsider observer staring through an instamatic camera; GQ elegant and open-smiled at a photo shoot for *Off the Wall;* or fedora pulled down like Bogart, face masked in shadow. King also includes a telling anecdote, first told by biographer Dave Marsh, of Jackson strategically striking a pose in the face of the sometime violence of hysterical fans: on a San Francisco promotional tour in the Jackson 5's early days, young fans became so enthusiastic that they shattered a store window. Some of the fans were injured, blood and glass everywhere. Rather than panicking, Jackson froze, "much like the robot he portrayed in 'Dancing Machine,' in an attempt to convince the hysterical fans that he might be a store mannequin." Jason King, *Michael Jackson's Treasures: Celebrating the King of Pop in Memorabilia and Photos* (New York: Fall River Press, 2009), 46. While it might be tempting to see this gesture as a sign of Jackson's movement toward the bizarre and paranoid, as Marsh does, this moment might also demonstrate the seamlessness of Jackson's theatrical skills at this point, his ability to move to a new and more effective self when needed—in this case, to save his own life.

31. Perhaps even more than any of the other performers examined in this book, Michael Jackson inhabited the space of Post-Soul integrationist *communitas* awkwardly. On the one hand, in his songs, public performances, and charity work, as well as in his personal life and even his appearance, he was consistently interested in blurring racial lines. While he seemed to uphold the general idea of interconnectedness in his songs and in his public work—"We Are the World" and "Earth Song" being a visible examples—Jackson seemed notoriously uneasy in community and spent much of his time secluded, save for an inner circle of family and friends.

Chapter 5

1. Tony Kushner, *Angels in America: A Gay Fantasia on National Themes—Perestroika* (New York: Theater Communication Group, 1994), 19.

2. Joshua Gamson, *The Fabulous Sylvester: The Legend, the Music, the Seventies in San Francisco* (New York: Henry Holt, 2005), 139–40.

3. Kevin E. Quashie, *Black Women, Identity, and Cultural Theory* (New Brunswick, NJ: Rutgers University Press, 2003), 1.

4. Lyle Ashton Harris, personal Interview, April 23, 2005.

5. Bill Brewster and Frank Broughton, *Last Night a DJ Saved My Life: The History of the Disc Jockey* (New York: Grove Press, 2000), 421.

6. Miranda Sawyer, "State of Grace," *Guardian* (London), October 10, 2008.

7. See Mildred/Dréd Gerestant's performances of Jones in the film *Venus Boyz* (2002, dir. Gabrielle Baur). See also Jada Evans Braziel, "Dréd's Drag Kinging of Race, Sex, and the Queering of the American Racial Machine," *Women and Performance: A Journal of Feminist Theory*, vol. 15: 2, no. 30 (2005): 161–87.

8. Coco Fusco, *English Is Broken Here: Notes on Cultural Fusion in the Americas* (New York: New Press, 1995), 37.

9. Daphne A. Brooks, *Bodies in Dissent: Spectacular Performances of Race and Freedom, 1850–1910* (Durham, NC: Duke University Press, 2006), 5.

10. Maria J. Guzman, "Grace Jones's *One Man Show,* Music, and Culture," MA thesis, Ohio University, 2007, 7.

11. Brooks, *Bodies in Dissent,* 8.

12. Judith Butler, *Undoing Gender* (New York: Routledge, 2004), 3.

13. Toni Morrison, *Sula* (New York: Vintage Books, 2004), 54–55.

14. Darlene Clark Hine, "Rape and the Inner Lives of Black Women in the Middle West: Preliminary Thoughts on the Culture of Dissemblance," in *Words of Fire: An Anthology of African American Feminist Thought,* edited by Beverly Guy-Sheftall (New York: New Press, 1995), 380–87.

15. Julie Dash, with Toni Cade Bambara and bell hooks, *Daughters of the Dust: The Making of an African American Woman's Film* (New York: New Press, 1992), 5.

16. See bell hooks, "Writing the Subject: Reading *The Color Purple,*" in *Reading Black, Reading Feminist: A Critical Anthology,* edited by Henry Louis Gates Jr. (New York: Plume Books, 1995), 6,454–470; and Jacqueline Bobo, *Black Women and Cultural Readers* (New York: Columbia University Press, 1995).

17. See José Esteban Muñoz, *Disidentifications: Queers of Color and the Performance of Politics* (Minneapolis: University of Minnesota Press, 1999), 185.

18. Guzman, "Grace Jones's *One Man Show,* Music, and Culture," 38.

19. On the gendered Post-Soul strategies of satire in music, see Daphne A. Brooks's discussions of Mos Def's and Chris Rock's interventions in rock memory in "Burnt Sugar: Post-Soul Satire and Rock Memory," in *This Is Pop: In Search of the Elusive at the Experience Music Project,* edited by Eric Weisbard (Cambridge, MA: Harvard University Press, 2004), 103–17. Toward the end of this essay, Brooks looks to the confrontational but still undertheorized tactics of Grace Jones, along with performers Cassandra Wilson, Nina Simone, and others, as future ways of thinking about the satiric strain in women's Post-Soul music. Glenda R. Carpio's *Laughing Fit to Kill: Black Humor in the Fictions of Slavery* (Oxford: Oxford University Press, 2008) gives an excellent analysis

of the deep thread of antiracist resistance and incendiary tactics of Post-Soul black humor, including the works of Kara Walker and Dave Chappelle. In both Brooks's and Carpio's analyses we see ways that black performers use laughter as a means of unmasking histories of racism sometimes sublimated in the assimilated spaces of Post-Soul artistic success.

20. Gwendolyn DuBois Shaw uses the phrase "triple consciousness" to describe the art of Kara Walker and Adrian Piper, in *Seeing the Unspeakable: The Art of Kara Walker* (Durham, NC: Duke University Press, 2004), 157, n. 5.

21. Jan Nederveen Pieterse, *White on Black: Images of the Africa and Blacks in Western Popular Culture* (New Haven, CT: Yale University Press, 1995), 184. Janell Hobson offers a similar discussion of Jones as a stereotype of the animalistic black woman in her *Venus in the Dark: Blackness and Beauty in Popular Culture* (New York: Routledge, 2005).

22. Miriam Kershaw, "Grace Jones, Postcoloniality, and Androgyny: The Performance Art of Grace Jones," *Art Journal* 56, no. 4 (1997): 20.

23. Ibid.

24. Ibid., 22.

25. Ibid.

26. Homi K. Bhabha, "Sly Civility," in *The Location of Culture* (New York: Routledge, 1985), 93–101.

27. Here Jones brings to mind the work of African American visual artist Fred Wilson, which frequently uses racial kitsch collectables. Wilson's video installation *Me & It* (1995) uses two screens, one showing a racial kitsch figurine like a mammy doll, the other showing Wilson twisting his own body to imitate the inhuman gestures, postures, and facial expressions that the figurine depicts.

28. Carolyn Cooper *Noises in the Blood: Orality, Gender, and the "Vulgar" Body of Jamaican Popular Culture* (Durham, NC: Duke University Press, 1995), xi.

29. Ibid., 28.

30. Ibid., 29.

31. Jean-Paul Goude, *Jungle Fever,* edited by Harold Hayes (New York: Xavier Moreau, 1982), 103.

32. Ibid., 102.

33. See Francette Pacteau, *The Symptom of Beauty* (Cambridge, MA: Harvard University Press, 2004), especially 123–43. Pacteau sees Goude's relationship with Jones as grounded in the dynamic of fetishization of, anxiety about, and desire for African feminine beauty. She draws on Homi K. Bhabha's essay "The Other Question," which discusses the ways that the mask has been a product of colonial discourse, a campaign to "fix" the living body of the other into fetish. This, as Bhabha suggests, "is a defensive strategy of disavowal: the acknowledgement of 'otherness' and its reduction to open specific characteristic, culturally intelligible, familiar" (quoted in Pacteau, *The Symptom of Beauty,* 136). Many thanks to Jennifer Brody for calling Pacteau's work to my attention.

34. Goude, *Jungle Fever,* 103.

35. Ibid.

36. Ibid., 107.

37. Philip Auslander, *Liveness: Performance in a Mediatized Culture* (New York: Routledge, 1999), 3.

38. Dick Hebdige, *Subculture: The Meaning of Style* (London: Routledge, 1979), 25–26.

39. In its grotesque version of ballet, the video seems to be commenting on the construction of the black dancing body as the antithesis of the classical, and white, ballet body. See Brenda Dixon Gottschild, *The Black Dancing Body: A Geography from Coon to Cool* (New York: Palgrave Macmillan, 2005).

40. Jay Hedblade, "Grace Jones Falls Flat at House of Blues," *Chicago Tribune,* September 16, 1998, 2.

41. In Ramon Lobato's salute to Grace Jones, "Amazing Grace: Decadence, Deviance, Disco," he documents Jones's fascination for a new generation of musicians and consumers in the first decade of the twenty-first century, noting her recent appearance as special guest at London's avant-garde Triptych Festival in 2003, covers of her tracks by electro artists like Germany's DJ Hell, and her still steady schedule of appearances with DJ gigs at nightclubs and launchings around the world. Lobato suggests that Jones's most salient appeal for consumers right now might be a nostalgia for a "premillennial decadence"; her work "conjures up all the most heady excesses of a debouched decade, all the sartorial style that was the currency of 1980s mainstream club culture but is nowhere to be found of late, having gone back underground or decamped to the more fertile pastures of hip-hop and R&B. Ramon Lobato, "Amazing Grace: Decadence, Deviance, Disco," *Camera Obscura* 22, no. 65 (2007): 134–38, 135. We might consider what other narratives might be found beneath the surface of this image of decadence—perhaps here, the labor of keeping the image polished and in place?

42. Michel de Montaigne, "On the Cannibals," in *The Complete Essays,* edited and translated by M. A. Screech (London: Penguin, 2003). He writes:

> The courage with which they fight is amazing: their battles never end except through death of bloodshed, for they do not even understand what fear is. Each one carries back as a trophy the head of the enemy that he has skilled, and hangs it up at the entrance to his home. After having treated their prisoners well for a long time, giving them all the provisions that they could want, he who is the chief calls a great assembly of his acquaintances. He ties a rope to one of the arms of the prisoner and on the other end, several feet away, out of harm's way, and gives to his best friend the arm to hold; and the two of them, in the presence of the assembled group, slash him to death with their swords. That done, they roast him and eat him together, sending portions to their absent friends. They do this, not as is supposed, for nourishment as did the ancient Scythians; it represents instead an extreme form of vengeance. (238)

43. Tricia Rose, "Foreword," in *Black Cultural Traffic: Crossroads in Global Performance and Popular Culture,* edited by Harry J. Elam Jr. and Kennell Jackson (Ann Arbor: University of Michigan Press, 2005), vii.

44. Deborah Richards, "The Halle Berry One Two," *Callaloo* 27, no. 4 (2004): 1011.

Chapter 6

1. Mark Dery, "Black to the Future: Afro-futurism 1.0," in *Afro-Future Females: Black Writers Chart Science Fiction's Newest New-Wave Trajectory,* edited by Marleen S. Barr (Columbus: Ohio State University Press, 2008), 8.

2. Steven Shaviro, "Supa Dupa Fly: Black Women as Cyborgs in Hip Hop Videos," *Quarterly Review of Film and Video* 22 (2005): 169.

3. As Alondra Nelson suggests in her introduction to *Social Text's* special issue on Afrofuturism, "the 'myth of black disingenuity with technology,' to borrow a phrase from historian of science and medicine Evelynn Hammonds, does not account for the centrality of black people's labor in modernization and industrialization as well as the historical truths of black participation in technological development. Examples of such participation include the contributions of Garret Morgan, who invented the traffic light in 1923; the vernacular chemistry of Madame C. J. Walker, who created a multi-million-dollar black beauty business; the creation of the Lingo computer language by programmer John Henry Thompson; and pioneering music production techniques." Alondra Nelson, "Introduction: Future Texts," *Social Text* 20 (Summer 2002): 6.

4. Although John F. Szwed doesn't take up the issue of Sun Ra's sexual identity in a sustained way in his book-length study *Space Is the Place: The Life and Times of Sun Ra* (New York: Da Capo Press, 1998), he certainly presents him as queer in performance, bringing out his slanted view of the world. Slate writer Adam Schatz, in his review of Szwed's book, offers that Sun Ra's complex sexuality might help explain "his repudiation of physical reality as a 'prison,' his conviction that our bodies are mere vehicles, his obsession with secret layers of meaning" ("Brother from Another Planet: The Cult and Culture of Sun Ra," *Slate,* September 10, 1997, http://www.slate.com.id/3159).

5. John Gill, *Queer Noises: Male and Female Homosexuality in Twentieth-Century Music* (Minneapolis: University of Minnesota Press, 1995), 58–61.

6. Val Wilmer, "Obituary: Sun Ra," *Independent,* July 1, 1993, 14.

7. John F. Szwed, "Sun Ra, 1914–1993," in *Crossovers: Essays on Race, Music, and American Culture* (Philadelphia: University of Pennsylvania Press, 2005), 210.

8. Martha Mockus argues that while Ndegeocello might fittingly be called "queer," given her ability to cross boundaries, "To the best of my knowledge, Ndegeocello has never used that term about herself in public. Instead, she has emphatically criticized the white male connotations of 'gay.'" Martha Mockus, "Meshell Ndegeocello: Musical Articulations of Black Feminisms, in *Unmaking Race, Remaking Soul: Transformative Aesthetics and the Practice of Freedom,* edited by Christa Davis Acompora and Angela L. Cotton (Albany: State University of New York Press, 2007), 91. Ndegeocello has publicly complained that mainstream images of gay life are patterned on a white gay male aesthetic.

9. Andreana Clay, "Like an Old Soul Record: Black Feminism, Queer Sexuality, and the Hip-Hop Generation," *Meridians: Feminism, Race, Transnationalism* 8, no. 1 (2008): 64–65.

10. L. H. Stallings, *Mutha' Is Half a Word: Intersections of Folklore, Vernacular, Myth, and Queerness in Black Female Culture* (Columbus: Ohio State University Press, 2007), 253.

11. Ibid., 245.

12. Ndegeocello describes this ability to be the pulse of the music and the ability to move in a 2007 interview with Bill Murphy in *Bass Player* magazine: "My favorite bass player is Prince. . . . I love how he made 'Controversy.' It's a straight beat, but his bass is moving and shifting and feeling good, and it makes you dance. Gene Lake was always telling me, 'The moment you start counting bars, you'll lose the groove.' So I just find myself grating to the pulse, and I try to make the bass line—which is a separate thought—float along that grid. That's what works for me for now." Bill Murphy, "Mack Diva MeShell Ndegeocello," *Bass Player*, November 2007, 36. This issue of *Bass Player* featured Ndegeocello on the cover—the first woman to ever grace the cover of this magazine.

13. Steven Seidman, quoted in Eva Illouz, *Oprah Winfrey and the Glamour of Misery: An Essay on Popular Culture* (New York: Columbia University Press, 2003), 69.

14. On black music's relationship to the posthuman, see Alexander G. Weheliye's "'Feenin': Posthuman voices in Contemporary Black Popular Music," *Social Text* 20, no. 2 (Summer 2002): 21–47. Weheliye discusses the ways in which black popular music has negotiated the status of the posthuman with a difference. For black artists, the posthuman is always fraught with the ambivalent status of black as human. He suggests that we think of ways that technologically heightened and/or disembodied vocal expressions, in vocoders, for example, add new ways of thinking about this tarrying with the human and/or posthuman.

15. Mark Anthony Neal, "Afterbirth: An Interview with Me'shell Ndegeocello," SeeingBlack.com, November 21, 2003, http://seeingblack.com/2003/x112103/meshell.shtml.

16. Bertram Ashe, "Theorizing the Post-Soul Aesthetic: An Introduction," *African American Review* 41, no. 4 (Winter 2007): 614.

17. Lisa Suhair Majaj, "Arguments," in *Ordinary Lives*, edited by Rania Matar (New York: Quantuck Lane Press, 2009), 10.

18. Judith Butler, *Precarious Life: The Powers of Mourning and Violence* (London: Verso, 2004), xii–xiii.

19. For an insightful discussion of Ndegeocello's use of the Bible, see Farah Jasmine Griffin's "Adventures of a Black Child in Search of Her God: The Bible in the Works of Me'Shell N'Degeocello," in *African Americans and the Bible: Sacred Texts and Social Textures*, edited by Vincent L. Wimbush (New York: Continuum, 2000), 774–81. Griffin suggests that Ndegeocello uses the Bible to "tamper with the boundary between the sacred and the secular, body and soul, the erotic and the spiritual" (775).

20. Meshell Ndegeocello, quoted in Allison Powell, "Sybil of the Soul," *Interview*, July 1996.

21. In contrast, see Jason King's insightful analysis of Toni Braxton's use of gospel-inflected "heat" in "Toni Braxton, Disney, and Thermodynamics," *TDR: The Drama Review* 46, no. 3 (Fall 2002): 54–81. See also Daphne A. Brooks's smart analysis of the confessional mode in 1990s women's R&B, and its often undervalued importance to our understanding of changing material conditions shaping race, class ,and sexuality in the post-Soul era, in "'It's Not Right but It's Okay': Black Women's R&B and the House That Terry McMillan Built," in *The New Black Renaissance: The Souls Anthology of Critical African American Studies*, edited by Manning Marrable (New York: Paradigm Publishers, 2005), 168–82.

22. See, for example, Butler's dislocated black female narrator, Renee, in her final novel, *Fledgling*. Renee's very first words are "I awoke to darkness." Octavia E. Butler, *Fledgling: A Novel* (New York: Seven Stories Press, 2005), 1. Renee's identity and history have been wiped out through a systematic campaign of violence and erasure. Over the course of the novel, Renee recovers a partial history and identity as a black vampire through the lessons of her body's desires and her coalitions with others.

23. See Butler's discussion of post-9/11 censorship of dissent: "Because it would be heinous to identify as treasonous, as a collaborator, one fails to speak, or one speaks in throttled ways, in order to sidestep the terrorizing identification that threatens to take hold. This strategy for quelling dissent and limiting the reach of critical debate happens not only through a series of shaming tactics which have a certain psychological terrorization as their effect, but they work as well by producing what will and will not count as a viable speaking subject and a reasonable opinion within the public domain" (ibid., xix).

24. While here I consider the possibilities of music to explore desires and identity still in formation, Kara Keeling potently explores the productive impulse of the "not yet" in black and queer conceptions of the future in film. In her analysis of temporality in recent black queer films *Looking for Langston, Brother to Brother,* and especially the *Aggressives,* she explores the ways that such films anticipate the still unrecognizable and unintelligible of queer experiences and identities still in formation—the moments that she calls "poetry from the future." She writes that "Poetry from the future interrupts the habitual formation of bodies, and it is an index of a time to come in which what today exists potently—even if not (yet) effectively—but escapes us will find its time." Kara Keeling, "Looking for M__: Queer Temporality, Black Political Possibility, and Poetry from the Future," *GLQ: A Journal for Lesbian and Gay Studies* 15, no. 4 (2009): 567.

25. Moraga and Anzaldúa famously define "theory in the flesh" as "one where the physical realities of our lives—our skin color, the land or concrete that we grew up on, our sexual longings—all fuse to create a politic of necessity." Cherríe Moraga and Gloria Anzaldúa, eds., *This Bridge Called My Back: Writings by Radical Women of Color,* 3rd ed. (Berkeley, CA: Third Woman Press, 2002), 23.

26. On the erotic as a wellspring from which we might shape intentional engagement with the world, Lorde writes, "[O]nce we begin to feel deeply all the aspects of our lives, we begin to demand from ourselves and from our life-pursuits that they feel in accordance with that joy which we know ourselves to be capable of. Our erotic knowledge empowers us, becomes a lens through which we scrutinize all aspects of our existence, forcing us to evaluate those aspects honestly in terms of their relative meaning within our lives." Audre Lorde, "The Uses of the Erotic: The Erotic as Power," in *Sister Outsider: Essays and Speeches* (Freedom, CA: Crossing Press, 1984), 59.

27. Chela Sandoval's differential consciousness is very much grounded in the idea of eccentric negotiation of community through the space of the margins, and the performance of strangeness that is at the center of this book. She explains, "Differential consciousness is linked to whatever is not expressible through words. It is accessed through poetic modes of expression: gestures, music, images, sounds, words that plummet or rise through signification to find some void—some no-place—to claim their due. This mode of consciousness both inspires and depends on differential social

movement and methodology of the oppressed and its differential technologies, yet it functions outside speech, outside academic criticism, in spite of all attempts to pursue and identify its place of origin. In seeking to describe it, Barthes wrote toward the end of the end of his life that this mode of differential consciousness 'can only be reached' by human thought through an unconformable and 'intractable' passage—not through any 'synthesizing term'—but rather through another kind of 'eccentric' and 'extraordinary' term." Chela Sandoval, *Methodology of the Oppressed* (Minneapolis: University of Minnesota Press, 2000), 139.

Epilogue

1. Janelle Monáe, quoted in Hattie Collins, "The Guide," *Guardian* (London), July 10, 2010, 9.

2. See Tom Shone's Bowie-flavored review, "The Girl Who Fell to Earth," *Times* (London), July 4, 2010, 28.

3. Kitty Empire, "Janelle Monáe: 'Music Is the Weapon of the Future'—The Extraordinary Cyber Diva with a Mission to Unite People through Song," *Observer* (London), December 19, 2010, 12.

4. Collins, "The Guide," 9.

5. Empire, "Janelle Monáe," 30.

6. The manifesto can be found on the collective's website, Wondaland.blogspot .com.

7. Janelle Monáe, quoted in Empire, "Janelle Monáe," 12.

8. Janelle Monáe, quoted in Collins, "The Guide," 9.

9. See Angela Y. Davis, *Are Prisons Obsolete?* New York: Seven Stories Press, 2003.

10. See Michel Foucault's classic *Discipline and Punish: The Birth of the Prison* (New York: Vintage, 1995).

Bibliography

Acham, Christine. *Revolution Televised: Prime Time and the Struggle for Black Power.* Minneapolis: University of Minnesota Press, 2004.

Aldrige, Cathy. "The Ladies and Eartha: Pro-Con." *New York Amsterdam News,* January 27, 1968, 1.

Als, Hilton. "Michael." *New York Review of Books,* August 13, 2009.

Ashe, Bertram. "Theorizing the Post-Soul Aesthetic: An Introduction." *African American Review* 41, no. 4 (Winter 2007): 609–23.

Auslander, Philip. *Liveness: Performance in a Mediatized Culture.* New York: Routledge, 1999.

Auslander, Philip. *Performing Glam Rock: Gender and Theatricality in Popular Music.* Ann Arbor: University of Michigan Press, 2006.

Atkinson, Brooks. (untitled). *New York Times,* May 17, 1952, 23.

Awkward, Michael. *Soul Covers: Rhythm and Blues Remakes and the Struggle for Artist Identity (Aretha Franklin, Al Green, Phoebe Snow).* Durham, NC: Duke University Press, 2007.

Banes, Sally, and Andre Lepecki. "Introduction: The Performance of the Senses." In *The Senses in Performance, edited* by Sally Banes and Andre Lepecki. New York: Routledge, 2007. 1–8.

Barnett, LaShonda Katrice. *I've Got Thunder: Black Women Songwriters on Their Craft.* New York: Thunder's Mouth Press, 2007.

Baraka, Amiri and LeRoi Jones. *Black Magic: Poetry 1961–1967.* New York: Bobbs-Merrill, 1969.

Barthes, Roland. "The Grain of the Voice." In *Image, Music, Text,* translated by Stephen Heath. New York: Hill and Wang, 1978. 179–89.

Bartlett, Andrew. "Airshafts, Loudspeakers, and the Hip-Hop Sample: Context and African American Musical Aesthetics." In *That's the Joint! The Hip-Hop Studies Reader,* edited by Murray Forman and Mark Anthony Neal. New York: Routledge, 2004. 393–406.

Baynton, Douglas C. "Disability and the Justification of Inequality in American History." In *The New Disability History: American Perspectives.* New York: New York University Press, 2001. 33–57.

Beatty, Paul. *The White Boy Shuffle.* New York: Picador, 2001.

Bhabha, Homi K. *The Location of Culture.* New York: Routledge, 1985.

Bobo, Jacqueline. *Black Women and Cultural Readers.* New York: Columbia University Press, 1995.

Bolden, Tony. "Theorizing the Funk: An Introduction." In *The Funk Era and Beyond: New Perspectives on Black Popular Culture,* edited by Tony Bolden, 13–29. New York: Palgrave Macmillan, 2008.

Bornstein, Kate. *Gender Outlaw: On Men, Women, and the Rest of Us.* New York: Vintage Books, 1995.

Braziel, Jada Evans. "Dréd's Drag Kinging of Race, Sex, and the Queering of the American Racial Machine." *Women and Performance: A Journal of Feminist Theory* 15, no. 30 (2005): 161–87.

Brewster, Bill, and Frank Broughton. *Last Night a DJ Saved My Life: The History of the Disc Jockey.* New York: Grove Press, 2000.

Brooks, Daphne A. *Bodies in Dissent: Spectacular Performances of Race and Freedom, 1850–1910.* Durham, NC: Duke University Press, 2006.

Brooks, Daphne A. "Burnt Sugar: Post-Soul Satire and Rock Memory." In *This Is Pop: In Search of the Elusive at the Experience Music Project,* edited by Eric Weisbard, 103–17. Cambridge, MA: Harvard University Press, 2004.

Brooks, Daphne A. "'It's Not Right but It's Okay': Black Women's R&B and the House That Terry McMillan Built." In *The New Black Renaissance: The Souls Anthology of Critical African American Studies,* edited by Manning Marable, 168–82. New York: Paradigm Publishers, 2005.

Brooks, Daphne A. *Jeff Buckley's Grace.* New York: Continuum Books, 2005.

Brooks, Daphne A. "Journey: 'Lights.'" In "Critical Karaoke," by Joshua Cone, Ange Milinko, Greil Marcus, Ann Powers, and Daphne A. Brooks. *Popular Music* 24, no. 3 (2005): 423–27.

Brooks, Daphne A. "Nina Simone's Triple Play." *Callaloo* 34, no. 1 (Winter 2011): 176–97.

Brooks, Daphne A. "Planet Earth(a): Sonic Cosmopolitanism and Black Feminist Theory." In *"Cornbread and Cuchifritos," Ethnic Identity Politics, Transnationalization, and Transculturation in American Urban Popular Music,* edited by Wilfred Raussert and Michelle Habell-Pállan. Tempe, AZ: Bilingual Review Press, 2011.

Brown, Royal S. *Overtones and Undertones: Reading Film Music.* Berkeley: University of California Press, 1994.

Brown, Scot. "A Land of Funk: Dayton Ohio." In *The Funk Era and Beyond: New Perspectives on Black Popular Culture,* edited by Tony Bolden, 73–88. New York: Palgrave MacMillan, 2008.

Butler, Judith. *Bodies That Matter: On the Discursive Limits of "Sex."* New York: Routledge, 1993.

Butler, Judith. *Precarious Life: The Powers of Mourning and Violence.* New York: Verso, 2004.

Butler, Judith. *Undoing Gender.* New York: Routledge, 2004.

Butler, Octavia E. *Fledgling: A Novel.* New York: Seven Stories Press, 2005.

Byrd, Rudolph P., and Beverly Guy Sheftall. *Traps: African American Men on Gender and Sexuality.* Bloomington: Indiana University Press, 2001.

Carpio, Glenda R. *Laughing Fit to Kill: Black Humor in the Fictions of Slavery.* Oxford: Oxford University Press, 2008.

Carson, Mina, Tisa Lewis, and Susan M. Shaw. *Girls Rock! Fifty Years of Women Making Music.* Lexington: University Press of Kentucky, 2004.

Case, Sue-Ellen. "Toward a Butch-Femme Aesthetic." In *Making a Spectacle,* edited by Lynda Hart, 282–99. Ann Arbor: University of Michigan Press, 1989.

Charles, Ray, and David Ritz. *Brother Ray: Ray Charles' Own Story.* Cambridge, MA: Da Capo Press, [1978] 2004.

Cheng, Anne Anlin. *The Melancholy of Race: Psychoanalysis, Assimilation, and Hidden Grief.* New York: Oxford University Press, 2001.

Christian, Margena A. "Prince Continues His Purple Reign at 50." *Jet,* July 23, 2008, 58.

Clay, Andreana. "Like an Old Soul Record: Black Feminism, Queer Sexuality, and the Hip-Hop Generation." *Meridians: Feminism, Race, Transnationalism* 8, no. 1 (2008): 53–73.

Cohen, Cathy. "Punks, Bulldaggers, and Welfare Queens: The Radical Potential of Queer Politics?" In *Black Queer Studies: A Critical Anthology,* edited by E. Patrick Johnson and Mae G. Henderson. Durham, NC: Duke University Press, 2005. 21–51.

Collins, Hattie. "The Guide." *Guardian* (London), July 10, 2010, 9.

Cooper, Carolyn. *Noises in the Blood: Orality, Gender, and the "Vulgar" Body of Jamaican Popular Culture.* Durham, NC: Duke University Press, 1995.

Corbett, John. *Extended Play: Sounding Off from John Cate to Dr. Funkenstein.* Durham, NC: Duke University Press, 1994.

Cox, Aimee. "Thugs, Black Divas, and Gendered Aspirations." *Souls* 11, no. 2 (2009): 113–41.

Cox, Tom. "Funkenstein Lives: George Clinton Is 60, but He's as Barmy as Ever." *Guardian* (London), July 21, 2000. 14.

Crouch, Stanley. *Considering Genius: Writings on Jazz.* New York: Basic Civitas Books, 2006.

Cruse, Harold. *The Crisis of the Negro Intellectual: A Historical Analysis of the Failure of Black Leadership.* New York: Quill, [1967] 1984.

Cvetkovich, Ann. *An Archive of Feelings: Trauma, Sexuality, and Lesbian Public Cultures.* Durham, NC: Duke University Press, 2003.

Danielsen, Anne. *Presence and Pleasure: The Funk Grooves of James Brown and Parliament.* Middletown, CT: Wesleyan University Press, 2006.

Dash, Julie, with Toni Cade Bambara and bell hooks. *Daughters of the Dust: The Making of an African American Woman's Film.* New York: New Press, 1992.

Davis, Angela Y. *Are Prisons Obsolete?* New York: Seven Stories Press, 2003.

Davis, Sharon. *Stevie Wonder: Rhythms of Wonder.* London: Robson Books, 2003.

Davis, Tracy C., and Thomas Postlewait, eds. *Theatricality.* Cambridge: Cambridge University Press, 2004.

Decker, Jeffrey Louis. "The State of Rap: Time and Place in Hip-Hop Nationalism." *Social Text* 34 (1993): 53–84.

Derogatis, Jim. *Turn on Your Mind: Four Decades of Great Psychedelic Rock.* New York: Hal Leonard, 2003.

Dery, Mark. "Black to the Future: Afro-futurism 1.0." In *Afro-Future Females: Black Writers Chart Science Fiction's Newest New-Wave Trajectory,* edited by Marleen S. Barr, 6–13. Columbus: Ohio State University Press, 2008.

Devitt, Rachel. "Girl on Girl: Fat Femmes, Bio-queens, and Redefining Drag." In *Queering the Popular Pitch,* edited by Sheila Whiteley and Jennifer Rycenga, 27–40. New York: Routledge, 2006.

Díaz, Junot. *The Brief Wondrous Life of Oscar Wao.* New York: Riverhead Books, 2007.

Dick, Philip K. *Do Androids Dream of Electric Sheep?* New York: Del Rey, 1996.

Dickerson, James. *Women on Top: The Quiet Revolution That's Rocking the American Music Industry.* New York: Watson-Guptill Publications, 1998.

Doyle, Richard. "Finding Animals with Plant Intelligence: Attention, Doctores, Mysteries." Box.net, July 31, 2009. Web. April 12, 2010.

Dragonwagon, Crescent. *Stevie Wonder.* New York: Putnam Publishing Group, 1977.

Draper, Jason. *Prince: Chaos, Disorder, and Revolution.* New York: Hal Leonard, 2011.

Dreher, Kwakiutl. *Dancing on the White Page: Black Women Entertainers Writing Autobiography.* New York: State University of New York Press, 2008.

"Eartha Kitt Can Cook, Tells How She Learned in Latest 'Mag' Story." *Chicago Defender,* October 17, 1954, 19.

"Eartha Kitt's Outburst." *Chicago Defender,* January 23, 1968, 13.

"Eartha's 'Evil' Song Causes Row." *Chicago Defender,* November 28, 1953, 1.

Echols, Alice. "The Land of Somewhere Else: Refiguring James Brown in Seventies Disco." *Criticism* 50, no. 1 (Winter 2008): 19–41.

Ellis, Thomas Sayers. "From the Crib to the Coliseum: An Interview with Bootsy Collins." In *The Funk Era and Beyond: New Perspectives on Black Popular Culture,* edited by Tony Bolden, 89–106. New York: Palgrave MacMillan, 2008.

Ellis, Trey. "The New Black Aesthetic." *Callaloo* 12, no. 1 (1989): 233–43.

Empire, Kitty. "Janelle Monáe: 'Music Is the Weapon of the Future'—the Extraordinary Cyber Diva with a Mission to Unite People through Song." *Observer* (London), December 19, 2010, 12.

Eshun, Kodowo. "Further Considerations of Afrofuturism." *CR: The New Centennial Review* 3, no. 2 (2003): 287–402.

Eshun, Kodowo. "FUTURYTHMACHINE." In *The Popular Music Studies Reader,* edited by Andy Bennett, Barry Shank, and Jason Toynbee, 292–94. London: Routledge, 2006.

Eshun, Kodowo. *More Brilliant Than the Sun: Adventures in Sonic Fiction.* London: Quartet Books, 1998.

Feinberg, Leslie. *Trans Liberation: Beyond Pink or Blue.* New York: Beacon Press, 1999.

Foucault, Michel. *Discipline and Punish: The Birth of the Prison.* New York: Vintage Books, 1995.

Foucault, Michel. "Nietzsche, Geneaology, History." In *Language, Counter-memory, Practice,* edited by D. F. Boucherd. Ithaca, NY: Cornell University Press, 1977. 139–64.

Fraser, Carly. "Race, Post-Black Politics, and the Presidential Candidacy of Barack Obama." *Souls* 11, no. 1 (January 2009): 17–40.

Frith, Simon. *Performing Rites: On the Value of Popular Music.* Cambridge, MA: Harvard University Press, 1996.

Fuchs, Cynthia. "'I wanna be your fantasy': Sex, Death, and the Artist Formerly Known as Prince." *Women and Performance: A Journal of Feminist Theory* 8, no. 2 (1996): 137–51.

Fusco, Coco. *English Is Broken Here: Notes on Cultural Fusion in the Americas.* New York: New Press, 1995.

Gamson, Joshua. *The Fabulous Sylvester: The Legend, the Music, the Seventies in San Francisco.* New York: Henry Holt, 2005.

Garland-Thomson, Rosemarie. *Extraordinary Bodies: Figuring Physical Disability in American Culture and Literature.* New York: Columbia University Press, 1997.

Garland-Thomson, Rosemarie. "The Politics of Staring: Visual Rhetorics of Disability in Popular Photography." In *Disability Studies: Enabling the Humanities,* edited by Sharon L. Snyder, Brenda Jo Brueggemann, and Rosemarie Garland-Thomson, 56–75. New York: Modern Language Association of America, 2002.

George, Nelson. *Buppies, B-Boys, and Bohos: Notes on Post-Soul Black Culture.* New York: Harper Collins, 1992.

George, Nelson. *Post-Soul Nation: The Explosive, Contradictory, Triumphant, and Tragic 1980's as Experienced by African Americans (Previously Known as Blacks and Before That Negroes).* New York: Viking Press, 2003.

George, Nelson. *Where Did Our Love Go: The Rise and Fall of the Motown Sound.* London: Omnibus Press, 1986.

Gill, John. *Queer Noises: Male and Female Homosexuality in Twentieth-Century Music.* Minneapolis: University of Minnesota Press, 1995.

Gilroy, Paul. *The Black Atlantic: Modernity and Double-Consciousness.* Cambridge, MA: Harvard University Press, 1993.

Gilmore, Mikal. *Night Beat: A Shadow History of Rock & Roll.* New York: Doubleday, 1998.

Gilmore, Ruth Wilson. *Golden Gulag: Prisons, Surplus, Crisis, and Opposition in Globalizing California.* Berkeley: University of California Press, 2007.

Golden, Thelma. *Freestyle: The Studio Museum in Harlem.* New York: Studio Museum in Harlem, 2001.

Gonzalez, David. "Is There Life after Jimi?" *Newsweek,* April 30, 1990, 68.

Gottschild, Brenda Dixon. *The Black Dancing Body: A Geography from Coon to Cool.* New York: Palgrave Macmillan, 2005.

Gottschild, Brenda Dixon. *Digging the Africanist Presence in American Performance: Dance and Other Contexts.* New York: Praeger, 1998.

Goude, Jean-Paul. *Jungle Fever.* Edited by Harold Hayes. New York: Xavier Moreau, 1982.

Goude, Jean-Paul. *State of Grace: One Man Show.* Island Records, 1985.

Gramsci, Antonio. *Selections from the Prison Notebooks.* Translated by Geoffrey N. Smith and Quintin Hoare. New York: International Publishers Company, Incorporated, 1971.

Green, Tony. "Tracing Funk's Sources." *St. Petersburg Times,* November 27, 1994, 1F.

Grosz, Elizabeth. *Volatile Bodies: Toward a Corporeal Feminism.* Bloomington: Indiana University Press, 1994.

Griffin, Farah Jasmine. "Adventures of a Black Child in Search of Her God: The Bible in the Works of Me'Shell N'Degeocello." In *African Americans and the Bible: Sacred Texts and Social Textures,* edited by Vincent L. Wimbush, 774–81. New York: Continuum, 2000.

Griffin, Farah Jasmine. *In Search of Billie Holiday: If You Can't Be Free, Be a Mystery.* New York: Ballantine Books, 2001.

Griffin, Farah Jasmine. *"Who Set You Flowin'"? The African-American Migration Narrative.* New York: Oxford University Press, 1996.

Griffin, Farah Jasmine, and Salim Washington. *Clawing at the Limits of Cool.* New York: St. Martin's Press, 2008.

Guillory, Monique, and Richard C. Green. "By Way of Introduction." In *Soul: Black Power, Politics, and Pleasure,* edited by Monique Guillory and Richard C. Greene. New York: New York University Press, 1998. 1–4.

Guzman, Maria J. "Grace Jones's *One Man Show,* Music, and Culture." MA thesis, Ohio University, 2007.

Halberstam, Judith. *In a Queer Time and Space: Transgender Bodies, Subcultural Lives.* New York: New York University Press, 2005.

Hall, Carla. "In the Key of Green: Stevie Wonder Plants New Seed of Melody." *Washington Post,* December 5, 1979, B6.

Hall, Stuart. "What Is This 'Black' in Black Popular Culture?" In *Black Popular Culture,* edited by Gina Dent, 21–33. Seattle: Bay Press, 1992.

Hanchard, Michael. "Cultural Politics and Black Public Intellectuals." *Social Text* 14, no. 3 (Fall 1996): 95–108.

Hardy, Ernest. "Michael Jackson: Bless His Soul." *Bloodbeats,* Blogspot, June 26, 2009. http://ernesthardy.blogspot.com/2009/06/michael-jackson-bless-his-soul.html.

Harper, Phillip Brian. *Are We Not Men? Masculine Anxiety and the Problem of African American Identity.* New York: Oxford University Press, 1996.

Harper, Phillip Brian. "The Evidence of Felt Intuition: Minority Experience, Everyday Life, and Critical Speculative Knowledge." In *Black Queer Studies: A Critical Anthology,* edited by E. Patrick Johnson and Mae G. Henderson, 106–23. Durham, NC: Duke University Press, 2005.

Harris, Laura Alexandra. "Queer Black Feminism: The Pleasure Principle." *Feminist Review,* no. 54 (Autumn 1996): 3–30.

Harrison, Daphne Duval. *Black Pearls: Blues Queens of the 1920's.* New Brunswick, NJ: Rutgers University Press, 1990.

Hebdige, Dick. *Subculture: The Meaning of Style.* London: Routledge, 1979.

Hedblade, Jay. "Grace Jones Falls Flat at House of Blues." *Chicago Tribune,* September 16, 1998, 2.

Hemphill, Essex. *Ceremonies: Prose and Poetry.* San Francisco: Cleis Press, 1992.

Hine, Darlene Clark. "Rape and the Inner Lives of Black Women in the Middle West: Preliminary Thoughts on the Culture of Dissemblance." In *Words of Fire: An Anthology of African American Feminist Thought,* edited by Beverly Guy-Sheftall, 380–87. New York: New Press, 1995.

Hobson, Janell. *Venus in the Dark: Blackness and Beauty in Popular Culture.* New York: Routledge, 2005.

Holden, Stephen. "The Last Flower Child." *Village Voice,* December 3, 1979, 53.

Holland, Sharon Patricia. "Bill T. Jones, Tupac Shakur, and the (Queer) Art of Death." *Callaloo* 23, no. 1 (Winter 2001): 384–93.

Holland, Sharon Patricia. *Raising the Dead: Readings of Death and (Black) Subjectivity.* Durham, NC: Duke University Press, 2000.

hooks, bell. *Black Looks: Race and Representation.* New York: South End Press, 1992.

hooks, bell. "Feminism Inside: Toward a Black Body Politic." In *Black Male: Represen-*

tations of Masculinity in Contemporary American Art, edited by Thelma Golden, 127–40. New York: Whitney Museum of American Art, 1994.

hooks, bell. "Sexism and Misogyny: Who Takes the Rap—Misogyny, Gangsta Rap, and *The Piano." Z,* February 1994.

hooks, bell. "Writing the Subject: Reading *The Color Purple." In Reading Black, Reading Feminist: A Critical Anthology,* edited by Henry Louis Gates Jr. New York: Plume Books, 1995. 454–70.

Hughes, Langston. "Major Differences between Europe and America for Negro Theatrical Performers." *Chicago Defender,* May 23, 1953, 11.

Hunt, Dennis. "Kitt: The Tip of a Persona." *Los Angeles Times,* July 28, 1977, G13.

Illouz, Eva. *Oprah Winfrey and the Glamour of Misery: An Essay on Popular Culture.* New York: Columbia University Press, 2003.

Jackson, Buzzy. *A Bad Woman Feeling Good: Blues and the Women Who Sing Them.* New York: W. W. Norton, 2005.

Jackson, Michael. *Moonwalk.* New York: Doubleday, 1988.

Jefferson, Margo. *On Michael Jackson.* New York: Vintage Books, 2007.

Johnson, E. Patrick. *Appropriating Blackness: Performance and the Politics of Authenticity.* Durham, NC: Duke University Press, 2003.

Johnson, E. Patrick. "'Quare' Studies, or (Almost) Everything I Know about Queer Studies I Learned from My Grandmother." In *Black Queer Studies: A Critical Anthology,* edited by E. Patrick Johnson and Mae G. Henderson, 124–57. Durham, NC: Duke University Press, 2005.

Johnson, E. Patrick. "Strange Fruit: A Performance about Identity Politics." *TDR: The Drama Review* 47, no. 2 (Summer 2003): 88–116.

Johnson, Lydia. *Voyeurs de Venus.* Chicago, Chicago Dramatists, 2006. Unpublished play.

Jones, Ann Rosalind. "Writing the Body: Toward an Understanding of l'Ecriture Feminine." In *Feminisms: An Anthology of Literary Theory and Criticism,* edited by Robyn R. Warhol and Diane Price Herndl, 370–83. New Brunswick, NJ: Rutgers University Press, 1997.

Jones, Omi Osun Joni L. "Making Space: Producing the Austin Project." In *Experiments in the Jazz Aesthetic: Art, Activism, Academia, and the Austin Project,* edited by Omi Osun Joni L. Jones, Lisa L. Moore, and Sharon Bridgforth, 3–11. Austin: University of Texas Press, 2010.

Jourdain, Robert. *Music, the Brain, and Ecstasy: How Music Captures Our Imagination.* New York: Harper Collins Publishers, 1997.

Keeling, Kara. "Looking for M__: Queer Temporality, Black Political Possibility, and Poetry from the Future." *GLQ: A Journal for Gay and Lesbian Studies* 15, no. 4 (2009): 565–82.

Kelley, Robin D. G. "Confessions of a Nice Negro, or Why I Shaved My Head." In *Speak My Name: Black Men on Masculinity and the American Dream,* edited by Don Belton, 12–22. New York: Beacon Press, 1996.

Kelley, Robin D. G. "Into the Fire: 1970 to the Present." In *To Make Our World Anew: A History of African Americans,* edited by Robin D. G. Kelley and Earl Lewis, 265–341. Oxford: Oxford University Press, 2000.

Kelley, Robin D. G. "Kickin' Reality, Kickin' Ballistics: Gangsta Rap and Postindustrial

Los Angeles." In *Droppin' Science: Critical Essays on Rap Music and Hip-Hop Culture*, edited by William Eric Perkins. Philadelphia: Temple University Press, 1996, 117–58.

Kelley, Robin D. G. "Looking Backward: African Americans in the Postindustrial Era." In *The Columbia Guide to African American History since 1939*, edited by Robert L. Harris Jr. and Rosalyn Terborg-Penn, 101–19. New York: Columbia University Press, 2006.

Kelley, Robin D. G. *Yo' Mama's Disfunktional! Fighting the Culture Wars in Urban America*. Boston: Beacon Press, 1997.

Kempton, Arthur. *Boogaloo: The Quintessence of American Popular Music*. New York: Pantheon Books, 2003.

Kershaw, Miriam. "Grace Jones, Postcoloniality, and Androgyny: The Performance Art of Grace Jones." *Art Journal* 56, no. 4 (1997): 19–25.

Keyes, Cheryl. "Funkin' with Bach: The Impact of Professor Longhair on Rock 'n' Roll." In *The Funk Era and Beyond: New Perspectives on Black Popular Culture*, edited by Tony Bolden, 213–26. New York: Palgrave Macmillan, 2008.

King, Jason. "Michael Jackson: An Appreciation of His Talent." *Passed the Curve*, Blogspot, June 27, 2009. http://passedthecurve.blogspot.com/2009/06/michael-jackson-appreciation-of-his-html.

King, Jason. *Michael Jackson's Treasures: Celebrating the King of Pop in Memorabilia and Photos*. New York: Fall River Press, 2009.

King, Jason. "Toni Braxton, Disney, and Thermodynamics." *TDR: The Drama Review* 46, no. 3 (Fall 2002): 54–81.

Kitt, Eartha. *Alone with Me: A New Autobiography*. New York: H. Regnery, 1976.

Kitt, Eartha. *Rejuvenate! It's Never Too Late*. New York: Scribner, 2001.

Kitt, Eartha. *Still Here: Confessions of a Sex Kitten*. New York: Barricade Books, 1991.

Kitt, Eartha. *Thursday's Child*. London: Cassell, 1957.

Kushner, Tony. *Angels in America: A Gay Fantasia on National Themes—Perestroika*. New York: Theater Communication Group, 1994.

Ladd, Michael C. "Hard Core Jollies in the Himalayas, Staring at the Cosmic Slop: The Mothership Connection between Triple and Quadruple Consciousness." In *Rip It Up: The Black Experience in Rock 'n' Roll*, edited by Kandia Crazy Horse, 71–84. New York: Palgrave Macmillan, 2004.

Lehman, Christopher P. *A Critical History of Soul Train on Television*. Jefferson, NC: McFarland Publishers, 2008.

Levitin, Daniel J. *This Is Your Brain on Music: The Science of a Human Obsession*. New York: Dutton, 2006.

Linden, Amy. "The Last Maverick: Me'Shell NdegeOcello and the Burden of Vision." In *Rip It Up: The Black Experience in Rock 'n' Roll*, edited by Kandia Crazy Horse, 185–88. New York: Palgrave Macmillan, 2004.

Lipsitz, George. *Footsteps in the Dark: The Hidden Histories of Popular Music*. Minneapolis: University of Minnesota Press, 2007.

Lobato, Ramon. "Amazing Grace: Decadence, Deviance, Disco." *Camera Obscura* 22, no. 65 (2007): 134–38.

Lodder, Steve. *Stevie Wonder: A Musical Guide to the Classic Albums*. San Francisco: Backbeat Books, 2005.

Lorde, Audre. "The Uses of the Erotic: The Erotic as Power." In *Sister Outsider: Essays and Speeches,* 53–59. Freedom, CA: Crossing Press, 1984.

Lorde, Audre. *Zami: A New Spelling of My Name—a Biomythography.* Freedom, CA: Crossing Press, 1982.

Lott, Eric. *Love and Theft: Blackface Minstrelsy and the American Working Class.* New York: Oxford University Press, 1995.

Mackey, Nathaniel. "Cante Moro." In *Disembodied Poetics: Annals of the Jack Kerouac School,* edited by Anne Waldman and Andrew Schelling, 71–93. Albuquerque: University of New Mexico Press, 1994.

Mackey, Nathaniel. "Other: From Noun to Verb." *Representations* 39 (Summer 1992): 51–70.

Madhubuti, Haki. *Liberation Narrative: New and Collected Poems, 1966–2009.* Chicago: Third World Press, 2009.

Mahon, Maureen. *Right to Rock: The Black Rock Coalition and the Cultural Politics of Race.* Durham, NC: Duke University Press, 2004.

Majaj, Lisa Suhair. "Arguments." In *Ordinary Lives,* edited by Rania Matar, 10. New York: Quantuck Lane Press, 2009.

Marcus, Greil. "Speaker to Speaker." *Artforum,* March 1987, 11.

Marsh, Dave. *For the Record: George Clinton and P-Funk, an Oral History.* New York: Avon Books, 1998.

McRuer, Robert. *Crip Theory: Cultural Signs of Queerness and Disability.* New York: New York University Press, 2006.

Mercer, Kobena. "Monster Metaphors: Notes on Michael Jackson's *Thriller.*" In *Welcome to the Jungle: New Positions in Black Cultural Studies,* 33–52. New York: Routledge, 1994.

Mercer, Kobena. *Welcome to the Jungle: New Positions in Black Cultural Studies.* New York: Routledge, 1994.

Meriwether, Louise. "Blacks to South Africa: Progress or Sellout?" *New York Amsterdam News,* May 25, 1972, A5.

Michalko, Rod. *The Mystery of the Eye and the Shadow of Blindness.* Toronto: University of Toronto Press, 1998.

Miller, Lucy Key. "Front Views and Profiles." *Chicago Tribune,* August 17, 1953, B8.

Miller, Monica L. *Slaves to Fashion: Black Dandyism and the Styling of Black Diasporic Identity.* Durham, NC: Duke University Press, 2009.

Mills, David. "The P-Funk Flashback: George Clinton Lands His Spaceship Here in D.C." *Washington Post,* October 22, 1992, C1.

Mockus, Martha. "Meshell Ndegeocello: Musical Articulations of Black Feminisms." In *Unmaking Race, Remaking Soul: Transformative Aesthetics and the Practice of Freedom,* edited by Christa Davis Acompora and Angela L. Cotton, 81–102. Albany: State University of New York Press, 2007.

Montaigne, Michel de. "On the Cannibals." In *The Complete Essays,* edited and translated by M. A. Screech. London: Penguin Books, 2003. 228–41.

Moraga, Cherríe, and Gloria Anzaldúa, eds. *This Bridge Called My Back: Writings by Radical Women of Color,* 3rd ed. Berkeley, CA: Third Woman Press, 2002.

Morrison, Toni. *Beloved.* New York: Vintage Books, 2004.

Morrison, Toni. *Sula.* New York: Vintage Books, 2004.

Moten, Fred. *In the Break: The Aesthetics of the Black Radical Tradition.* Minneapolis: University of Minnesota Press, 2003.

Moten, Fred. "'Words Don't Go There': An Interview with Fred Moten by Charles Henry Rowell." *Callaloo* 27, no. 4 (2004): 953–66.

Muñoz, José Esteban. *Cruising Utopia: The Then and There of Queer Futurity.* New York: New York University Press, 2009.

Muñoz, José Esteban. *Disidentifications: Queers of Color and the Performance of Politics.* Minneapolis: University of Minnesota Press, 1999.

Murphy, Bill. "Mack Diva MeShell Ndegeocello." *Bass Player,* November 2007, 36–38.

Mutua, Athena. *Progressive Black Masculinities.* New York: Routledge, 2006.

Neal, Mark Anthony. "Afterbirth: An Interview with Me'shell Ndegeocello." Seeing-Black, November 21, 2003, http://seeingblack.com/2003/x112103/meshell.shtml.

Neal, Mark Anthony. "The Birth of New Blackness: The Family Stand's *Moon in Scorpio.*" In *Rip It Up: The Black Experience in Rock 'n' Roll,* edited by Kandia Crazy Horse, 121–27. New York: Palgrave Macmillan, 2004.

Neal, Mark Anthony. *New Black Man.* New York: Routledge, 2006.

Neal, Mark Anthony. *Songs in the Key of Black Life: A Rhythm and Blues Nation.* New York: Routledge, 2003.

Neal, Mark Anthony. *Soul Babies: Black Popular Culture and the Post-Soul Aesthetic.* New York: Routledge, 2002.

Neal, Mark Anthony. *What the Music Said: Black Popular Music and Black Public Culture.* New York: Routledge, 1999.

Nelson, Alondra. "Introduction: Future Texts." *Social Text* 20 (Summer 2002): 1–15.

Norment, Lynn. "Prince: What's the Secret of His Amazing Success?" *Ebony,* June 1985, 162.

Nugent, Benjamin. "Who's a Nerd Anyway?" *New York Times Magazine,* July 29, 2007, 15.

Ollison, Rashod. "Prince and His Evolution." *Jet,* July 5, 2010.

Omolade, Barbara. "Hearts of Darkness." In *Words of Fire: An Anthology of African American Feminist Thought,* edited by Beverly Guy-Sheftall, 362–78. New York: New Press, 1995.

Pacteau, Francette. *The Symptom of Beauty.* Cambridge, MA: Harvard University Press, 2004.

Palmer, Robert. "The Pop Life: Clinton's Satire Has a Bite." *New York Times,* May 7, 1986, C26.

Parks, Suzan-Lori. *Venus.* New York: Theatre Communications Group, 1997.

Patterson, Orlando. *Slavery and Social Death: A Comparative Study.* Cambridge, MA: Harvard University Press, 1992.

Peck, Dale. "Foreword." In *Queer 13: Lesbian and Gay Writers Recall the Seventh Grade,* edited by Clifford Chase. New York: William Morrow, 1998. xi–xii.

Peisch, Jeffrey. *Stevie Wonder.* New York: Ballantine Books, 1984.

Pernick, Martin S. *The Black Stork: Eugenics and the Death of "Defective" Babies in American Medicine and Motion Pictures since 1915.* New York: Oxford University Press, 1996.

Perone, James E. *The Sound of Stevie Wonder: His Words and Music.* Westport, CT: Praeger Publishers, 2006.

Peterson, Carla. "Foreword: Eccentric Bodies." In *Recovering the Black Female Body: Self-Representations by African American Women*, edited by Michael Bennett and Vanessa D. Dickerson, ix–xvi. New Brunswick, NJ: Rutgers University Press, 2001.

Phelps, Carmen. "Living the Funk: Lifestyle, Lyricism, and Lessons in Modern and Contemporary Art of Black Women." In *The Funk Era and Beyond: New Perspectives on Black Popular Culture*, edited by Tony Bolden, 183–92. New York: Palgrave Macmillan, 2008.

Pieterse, Jan Nederveen. *White on Black: Images of Africa and Blacks in Western Popular Culture*. New Haven, CT: Yale University Press, 1995.

Pinch, Trevor, and Frank Trocco. *Analog Days*. Cambridge, MA: Harvard University Press, 2002.

Poissant, Alvin. "An Analytical Look at the Prince Phenomenon." *Ebony*, June 1985, 170.

Powell, Allison. "Sybil of the Soul." *Interview*, July 1996.

Quashie, Kevin E. *Black Women, Identity, and Cultural Theory*. New Brunswick, NJ: Rutgers University Press, 2003.

"Readers, 'Fans' Join Pro and Con Predictions on Eartha Kitt Style." *Chicago Defender*, national ed., May 15, 1954, 19.

Reid-Pharr, Robert F. *Black Gay Man: Essays*. New York: New York University Press, 2001.

Richards, Deborah. "The Halle Berry One Two." *Callaloo* 27, no. 4 (2004): 1009–20.

Rose, Tricia. *Black Noise: Rap Music and Black Culture in Contemporary America*. Hanover, NH: Wesleyan University Press, 1994.

Rose, Tricia. "Foreword." In *Black Cultural Traffic: Crossroads in Global Performance and Popular Culture*, edited by Harry J. Elam Jr. and Kennell Jackson. Ann Arbor: University of Michigan Press, 2005. vi–viii.

Ross, Andrew. "The Gangsta and the Diva." In *Black Male: Representations of Masculinity in Contemporary American Art*, edited by Thelma Golden, 159–66. New York: Whitney Museum of American Art, 1994.

Rotberg, Robert. "Apartheid: Changes Are at the Surface." *Washington Post*, May 14, 1972, B5.

Rowden, Terry. *The Songs of Blind Folk: African American Musicians and the Cultures of Blindness*. Ann Arbor: University of Michigan Press, 2009.

Royster, Francesca. *Becoming Cleopatra: The Shifting Image of an Icon*. New York: Palgrave Macmillan, 2003.

Royster, Philip M. "Hammer's 'You Can't Touch This': Rapper as Shaman for a Band of Dancers of the Spirit." In *The Emergence of Black and the Emergence of Rap*. Special issue of *Black Sacred Music: A Journal of Theomusicology* 5, no. 1 (Spring 1991): 60–67.

Sandoval, Chela. *Methodology of the Oppressed: Theory Out of Bounds*. Minneapolis: University of Minnesota Press, 2000.

Sapphire. *Push: A Novel*. New York: Vintage Books, 1997.

Sawyer, Miranda. "State of Grace." *Guardian* (London), October 10, 2008.

Schatz, Adam. "Brother from Another Planet: The Cult and Culture of Sun Ra." *Slate*, September 10, 1997, http://www.slate.com.id/3159.

Schur, Richard. "Post-Soul Aesthetics in Contemporary African American Art." *African American Review* 41, no. 4 (Winter 2007): 641–54.

Scott, John L. "Eartha Kitt Opens Century City Stint." *Los Angeles Times,* December 11, 1969, H19.

Selvin, Joel. "Stevie Wonder: Mojo." In *Da Capo Best Music Writing, 2004,* edited by Mickey Hart and Paul Bresnick. Cambridge, MA: Da Capo Press, 2004. 292–302.

Senna, Danzy. *Caucasia: A Novel.* New York: Riverhead Trade, 1999.

Shaviro, Steven. "Supa Dupa Fly: Black Women as Cyborgs in Hip Hop Videos." *Quarterly Review of Film and Video* 22 (2005): 169–79.

Shaw, Gwendolyn DuBois. *Seeing the Unspeakable: The Art of Kara Walker.* Durham, NC: Duke University Press, 2004.

Shone, Tom. "The Girl Who Fell to Earth." *Times* (London), July 4, 2010, 28–29.

Smith, Barbara, ed. *Home Girls: A Black Feminist Anthology.* New York: Kitchen Table: A Women of Color Press, 1983.

Snyder, Susan L., and David T. Mitchell. *Cultural Locations of Disability.* Chicago: University of Chicago Press, 2006.

Stallings, L. H. *Mutha' Is Half a Word: Intersections of Folklore, Vernacular, Myth, and Queerness in Black Female Culture.* Columbus: Ohio State University Press, 2007.

Stockton, Kathryn Bond. *Beautiful Bottom, Beautiful Shame: Where "Black" Meets "Queer."* Durham, NC: Duke University Press, 2006.

Szwed, John F. *Space Is the Place: The Life and Times of Sun Ra.* New York: Da Capo Press, 1998.

Szwed, John F. "Sun Ra, 1914–1993." In *Crossovers: Essays on Race, Music, and American Culture,* 209–10. Philadelphia: University of Pennsylvania Press, 2005.

Tate, Greg. "Cult Nats Meets Freaky-Deke." In *Flyboy in the Buttermilk: Essays on Contemporary America,* 198–220. New York: Simon and Schuster, 1992.

Tate, Greg. "He Is Truly Free Who Is Free from the Need to Be Free: A Survey and Consideration of Black Male Genius." In *Black Male: Representations of Masculinity in American Art,* edited by Thelma Golden, 111–19. New York: Whitney Museum of Art, 1995.

Tompkins, Peter, and Christopher Bird. *The Secret Life of Plants.* New York: Harper & Row, 1973.

Touré. Review of *Sag Harbor* by Colson Whitehead. *New York Times Book Review,* May 3, 2009, 1.

Touré. *Who's Afraid of Post-Blackness? What It Means to Be Black Now.* New York: The Free Press, 2011.

Turner, Tina. *I, Tina.* As told to Kurt Loder. New York: Avon Books, 1987.

Vincent, Rickey. *Funk: The Music, the People, and the Rhythm of the One.* New York: St. Martin's Press, 1996.

Vogel, Shane. *The Scene of the Harlem Cabaret: Race, Sexuality, Performance.* Chicago: University of Chicago Press, 2009.

Vogel, Shane. "Where Are We Now? Queer World Making and Cabaret Performance." *GLQ: A Journal of Lesbian and Gay Studies* 6, no. 1 (2000): 29–60.

Waksman, Steve. "Black Sound, Black Body: Jimi Hendrix, the Electric Guitar, and the Meanings of Blackness." In *The Popular Music Studies Reader,* edited by Andy Bennett, Barry Shank, and Jason Toynbee, 64–70. London: Routledge, 2006.

Walcott, Rinaldo. "Reconstructing Manhood, or the Drag of Black Masculinity." *Small Ax* 13, no. 1 (2009): 75–89.

Walker, Kara. *Pictures from Another Time*. Edited by Annette Dixon. Ann Arbor: University of Michigan Museum of Art in association with D.A.P./Distributed Art Publishers, 2002.

Weheliye, Alexander G. "'Feenin': Posthuman Voices in Contemporary Black Popular Music." *Social Text* 20, no. 2 (Summer 2002): 21–47.

Weheliye, Alexander G. *Phonographies: Grooves in Sonic Afro-Modernity*. Durham, NC: Duke University Press, 2005.

Welton, Martin. "Seeing Nothing: Now Hear This . . ." In *The Senses in Performance*, edited by Sally Banes and Andrew Lepecki. New York: Routledge, 2007. 146–55.

Werner, Craig. *Higher Ground: Stevie Wonder, Aretha Franklin, Curtis Mayfield, and the Rise and Fall of American Soul*. New York: Crown Publishers, 2004.

White, Charles. *The Life and Times of Little Richard: The Authorised Biography*. London: Omnibus Press, 2003.

White, Shane, and Graham White. *Stylin': African American Expressive Culture from Its Beginnings to the Zoot Suit*. Ithaca, NY: Cornell University Press, 1998.

Whiteley, Sheila, and Jennifer Rycenga. "Introduction." In *Queering the Popular Pitch*, edited by Sheila Whiteley and Jennifer Rycenga, xiii–xix. New York Routledge, 2006.

Wilchins, Riki Anne. *Read My Lips: Sexual Subversion and the End of Gender*. Milford, CT: Firebrand Books, 1997.

Williams, Patricia. "Meditations on Masculinities." *Callaloo* 19, no. 4 (Fall 1996): 814–22.

Williams, Raymond. *Marxism and Literature*. London: Oxford University Press, 1978.

Wilmer, Val. "Obituary: Sun Ra." *Independent,* July 1, 1993, 14.

Wilson, August. "Foreword." In *Speak My Name: Black Men on Masculinity and the American Dream,* edited by Don Belton, xi–xiii. New York: Beacon Press, 1997.

Womack, Ytasha. *Post-Black: How a New Generation Is Changing African American Identity*. New York: Lawrence Books, 2010.

Wondaland Arts Society. *Wondaland*. http://wondaland.blogspot.com/.

Wright, Amy Nathan. "A Philosophy of Funk: The Politics and Pleasure of a Parliafunkadelicment Thang!" In *The Funk Era and Beyond: New Perspectives on Black Popular Culture,* edited by Tony Bolden, 33–50. New York: Palgrave Macmillan, 2008.

Young, Harvey. *Embodying Black Experience: Stillness, Critical Memory, and the Black Body*. Ann Arbor: University of Michigan Press, 2010.

Zibat, Eve. "A Summer Day of Chocolate Jam." *Washington Post,* July 3, 1978, B1.

Index